R. N Whybray

The Intellectual Tradition
in the Old Testament

R. N. Whybray

The Intellectual Tradition in the Old Testament

Walter de Gruyter · Berlin · New York
1974

Beiheft zur Zeitschrift für die alttestamentliche Wissenschaft

Herausgegeben von Georg Fohrer

135

ISBN 3 11 004424 2

Library of Congress Catalog Card Number: 73—78236

Printed in Germany

Satz und Druck: Walter de Gruyter & Co.

Bindearbeiten: Lüderitz & Bauer, 1 Berlin 61

To Hélène and Peter

Preface

I wish to thank those with whom I have discussed the subject of this study, especially members of the Faculty of Divinity at the University of Cambridge, the Faculty of Theology at the University of Durham, the Department of Theology at the University of Nottingham and the Department of Biblical Studies at the University of Sheffield, to whom some parts of it were read in their early stages, for their suggestions for its improvement. I am also indebted to my colleague, Dr. J. W. McKay of the University of Hull, for reading the typescript and for his constructive criticisms.

I should also like to express my thanks to Professor Dr. Georg Fohrer for his readiness to accept the work for inclusion among the Beihefte to ZAW.

R. N. Whybray

Table of Contents

Abbreviations

AB	The Anchor Bible
AK	Archiv für Kulturgeschichte
ANET	Ancient Near Eastern Texts Relating to the Old Testament, ed. by J. B. Pritchard, 1955²
ATD	Das Alte Testament Deutsch
BAT	Die Botschaft des Alten Testaments
BDB	A Hebrew and English Lexicon of the Old Testament, ed. by F. Brown, S. R. Driver and C. A. Briggs, 1907
BH	Biblia Hebraica, ed. by R. Kittel
BHS	Biblia Hebraica Stuttgartensia, ed. by K. Elliger and W. Rudolph
Bibl	Biblica
Bibl Or	Biblica et Orientalia
BK	Biblischer Kommentar
BSAW	Berichte über die Verhandlungen der Sächsischen Akademie der Wissenschaften zu Leipzig
BWANT	Beiträge zur Wissenschaft vom Alten und Neuen Testament
BZAW	Beihefte zur Zeitschrift für die Alttestamentliche Wissenschaft
CB	The Cambridge Bible for Schools and Colleges
CBQ	The Catholic Biblical Quarterly
EB	Etudes Bibliques
ET	English Translation
FRLANT	Forschungen zur Religion und Literatur des Alten und Neuen Testaments
G.-K.	Gesenius' Hebrew Grammar, ed. by E. Kautzsch, transl. by A. E. Cowley, 1910
HAT	Handbuch zum Alten Testament
HKAT	Handkommentar zum Alten Testament
HO	Handbuch der Orientalistik, ed. by B. Spuler
IB	The Interpreter's Bible
ICC	The International Critical Commentary
JB	The Jerusalem Bible
JBL	The Journal of Biblical Literature
JSS	The Journal of Semitic Studies
KA	Kunst und Altertum
KAT	Kommentar zum Alten Testament
KHC	Kurzer Hand-Commentar zum Alten Testament
Kö	Lexicon in Veteris Testamenti Libros, ed. by L. Koehler and W. Baumgartner, 1953
LXX	Septuagint
MT	Masoretic Text
NCB	The New Century Bible
NEB	The New English Bible
OS	Oudtestamentische Studiën

OTL	The Old Testament Library
Pesh	The Peshitta
RB	Revue Biblique
RGG	Die Religion in Geschichte und Gegenwart
RSV	The Revised Standard Version
Saec	Saeculum
SAT	Die Schriften des Alten Testaments
SB	Sources Bibliques
SBT	Studies in Biblical Theology
SNVAO	Skrifter utgitt av Det Norske Videnskaps-Akademi i Oslo
SOTS	The Society for Old Testament Study
SPAW	Sitzungsberichte der Preußischen Akademie der Wissenschaften zu Berlin
TC	Torch Bible Commentaries
ThLZ	Theologische Literaturzeitung
TR	Theologische Rundschau
TWNT	Theologisches Wörterbuch zum Neuen Testament, ed. by G. Kittel
Verb Sal	Verbum Salutis
VT	Vetus Testamentum
VT Suppl	Supplements to Vetus Testamentum
Vulg.	The Vulgate
WC	Westminster Commentaries
WMANT	Wissenschaftliche Monographien zum Alten und Neuen Testament
ZÄS	Zeitschrift für Ägyptische Sprache und Altertumskunde
ZAW	Zeitschrift für die Alttestamentliche Wissenschaft
ZB	Zürcher Bibelkommentare

Chapter I: The Problem

After several generations of intensive study in this field it is now generally accepted that the so-called "wisdom tradition", most notably exemplified in the books of Proverbs, Job and Ecclesiastes, was one of the main strands in the cultural life of ancient Israel. In recent years attempts have been made to demonstrate the importance and pervasiveness of this tradition, and numerous studies have been published which claim that its influence is to be found in a wide range of Old Testament books and passages[1].

---

[1] In Genesis it has been found in the Yahwistic narratives of the Creation and Fall by L. Alonso-Schökel, Motivos sapienciales y de alianza en Gen 2—3, Bibl 43 (1962), 295—316, and in the Joseph Story (Gen 37—50) by G. von Rad, Josephsgeschichte und ältere Chokma, VT Suppl I, 1953, 120—127 (= Gesammelte Studien zum Alten Testament, 1958, 272—280; ET in: The Problem of the Hexateuch, 1966, 292—300). E. Gerstenberger, Wesen und Herkunft des „apodiktischen Rechts", 1965, and W. Richter, Recht und Ethos, 1966 have attempted to show that Israel's legal traditions, especially in Exodus to Numbers, are closely related to her wisdom traditions. W. Weinfeld, The Origin of the Humanism in Deuteronomy, JBL 80 (1961), 241—247; Deuteronomy — the Present State of Knowledge, JBL 86 (1967), 249—262; Deuteronomy and the Deuteronomic School, 1972, 244ff., and others, including J. Malfroy, Sagesse et loi dans le Deutéronome, VT 15 (1965), 49—65; C. M. Carmichael, Deuteronomic Laws, Wisdom, and Historical Traditions, JSS 12 (1967), 198—206; J. W. McKay, Man's Love for God in Deuteronomy and the Father/Teacher—Son/Pupil Relationship, VT 22 (1972), 426—435, have found wisdom influence in Deuteronomy as a whole, while J. R. Boston, The Wisdom Influence Upon the Song of Moses, JBL 87 (1968), 198—202 has discovered it in Dtn 32. Von Rad, especially in: Der Anfang der Geschichtsschreibung im alten Israel, AK 32 (1944), 1—42 (= Gesammelte Studien, 148—168; ET The Problem of the Hexateuch, 166—204), has suggested that it is to be found in the so-called Succession Narrative (II Sam 9—20 I Reg 1f.); and this suggestion has been followed up in detail by R. N. Whybray, The Succession Narrative, SBT second series 9, 1968. J. Lindblom, Wisdom in the Old Testament Prophets, VT Suppl 3, 1955, 192—204, came to the same conclusion about a number of passages in the prophetical books, and other writers, including J. Fichtner, Jesaja unter den Weisen, ThLZ 74 (1949), 75—80 (= Gottes Weisheit, 1965, 18—26); S. Terrien, Amos and Wisdom in: Muilenburg-Festschrift, 1962, 108—115; H. W. Wolff, Amos' geistige Heimat, WMANT 18, 1964; E. Gerstenberger, The Woe-Oracles of the Prophets, JBL 81 (1962), 249—263; J. W. Whedbee, Isaiah and Wisdom, 1971, have written on particular aspects of this. The work of S. Mowinckel on "wisdom psalms", especially in Psalms and Wisdom, VT Suppl III, 1955, 205—224; The Psalms in Israel's Worship, II, 1962, ch. 16, is well known. S. Talmon has written on "Wisdom" in the Book of Esther, VT 13 (1963), 419—455. Von Rad,

Each of these studies is based on its author's own presuppositions about the nature of the "wisdom" whose influence he claims to have detected. By no means all of these authors, however, state these presuppositions clearly; and an analysis of their work would undoubtetly reveal very considerable differences.

This lack of unanimity is unfortunate since it is tending to create a state of scholarly confusion which may well make the word "wisdom" useless for the purposes of Old Testament study. Before any satisfactory investigation can be undertaken into the ramifications of "wisdom teaching" outside those books which are generally acknowledged to come under the heading of "wisdom literature", it is essential that some measure of agreement be reached about the fundamental character of this "wisdom" and the circles within which it was created and transmitted in Israel.

Until a few years ago some such measure of agreement did in fact exist. The view that Israelite wisdom was in the first place a *court* wisdom derived, in the form of a literary tradition, from the schools and courts of Egypt and other Near Eastern states about the time of Solomon[2] was widely accepted. But this view has recently been seriously challenged, and it is now regarded by a number of scholars[3] as a native Israelite phenomenon which developed, side by side with the legal traditions, from the principles of conduct formulated in the nomadic or semi-nomadic period for the regulation of life within the family or clan. This theory, if generally accepted, would give an entirely new direction to the search for "wisdom influence": if "wisdom" was one of the original and fundamental aspects of Israelite culture, it would be reasonable to suppose that it will have exercised a profound influence on the whole subsequent development of Israelite life and thought. Indeed, since it is generally agreed that one of its main characteristics is its intellectual or ratiocinative quality, it might well be supposed that wherever in the Old Testament an element of rational thought is found, this is due to the "wisdom" strand in the Israelite character. Such a view indeed appears to underlie some recent study of the subject[4].

Theologie des Alten Testaments, II 1960, 319ff. (ET Old Testament Theology, II 1965, 306ff.) has argued that wisdom is "the real matrix from which the apocalyptic literature originated". Other examples of this tendency to give "wisdom" an ever-increasing role in the formation of the Old Testament could easily be given.

[2] For this view see, among other works, H. Duesberg and I. Fransen, Les Scribes Inspirés, 1966[2].

[3] See especially the works of Gerstenberger, Richter and Wolff referred to on p. 1 n. 1.

[4] For example, it is commonly held that the form known as the "disputation" — that is, the method of argument which proceeds by question and answer — is a character-

Whatever may be the origins of the intellectual tradition represented by Proverbs, Job and Ecclesiastes and the historical relationship of this tradition to other traditions represented in the Old Testament, the interests of scholarly investigation are not served by the application of the word "wisdom" to every manifestation of the ability to use one's brains in ancient Israel.

In view of these developments, several writers have sought recently to restore a greater degree of precision to the use of such terms as "wisdom", "wisdom tradition", "wisdom influence" in Old Testament study[5]. In establishing criteria in this field it is clearly important to give consideration to such matters as vocabulary, style, range of interest and point of view. That which distinguishes "wisdom thought" from other definable types of thought must be distinguished from that which is common to Israelite thinking as a whole. This enterprise is an extremely difficult one for more than one reason. The historical development of "wisdom thought" has to be taken into account: "wisdom thought" is unlikely to have remained static during the eventful course of Israel's history, nor must it be forgotten that it is as likely to have been influenced by other traditions as to have influenced them. Especially in view of the paucity of present knowledge about the development of the "wisdom tradition" itself, precise evidence of these processes is, however, extremely difficult to obtain. A second difficulty is that, since it is precisely in types of literature *other* than those proper to "wisdom" that its influence is being sought, some criteria, especially those of form and style, lose a great deal of their force. It is hardly to be expected that, for example, narrative literature, when influenced by "wisdom" ideas, will also adopt the gnomic style of Proverbs or the poetical style of Job, both of which are entirely foreign to it.

---

istic "wisdom" form. Yet this is a very common method of argument which is found in many societies and requires no elaborate theory to account for its presence in the Old Testament. See R. N. Whybray, The Heavenly Counsellor, SOTS Monograph Series, 1971, 19ff.

[5] H. H. Schmid, Wesen und Geschichte der Weisheit, 1966; J. L. McKenzie, Reflections on Wisdom, JBL 86 (1967), 1—9; R. E. Murphy, Assumptions and Problems in Old Testament Wisdom Research, CBQ 29 (1967), 101—112; J. L. Crenshaw, Method in Determining Wisdom Influence upon "Historical" Literature, JBL 88 (1969), 129—142. Crenshaw's remark that the definition of wisdom must be "neither too broad nor too narrow" (130), and in particular his criticism (131) of von Rad's definition (Theology, I 418) of it as "practical knowledge of the laws of life and of the world, based upon experience" as falling into the former category is especially valuable, though his own definition of it (132) as "the quest for self-understanding in terms of relationships with things, people and the Creator" suffers from the opposite disadvantage.

These difficulties, which tempt the scholar to take short cuts and so to fall into subjectivism, raise doubts about the validity of the whole enterprise, and raise the question in what sense it is proper to use such terms as "wisdom", "wisdom tradition" at all. The English word "wisdom" is of course properly used in Old Testament contexts as a translation of the Hebrew *ḥokmā*, a word which occurs more frequently in the three "traditional" wisdom books, Proverbs, Job and Ecclesiastes, than in the whole of the remainder of the Old Testament. But in modern discussion it has come to be used in a much wider sense—or rather in a variety of wider senses. Since the discovery in other parts of the ancient Near East, especially in Egypt and Mesopotamia, of literature in some ways comparable to Proverbs, Job and Ecclesiastes it has been applied to these literatures also, even though they have no comparable key-word which may be regarded as the equivalent of *ḥokmā*.

This extension of the meaning of the term is applied in different ways by different writers. By some it is used loosely to indicate a general resemblance between various kinds of literature which in many ways — form, date, style, purpose, country of origin — differ widely from one another. Thus an Assyriologist, discussing Babylonian texts, can write: "'Wisdom' is strictly a misnomer as applied to Babylonian literature. As used for a literary genre the term belongs to Hebraic studies and is applied to Job, Proverbs and Ecclesiastes"[6], and yet to go on to suggest that it may nevertheless "be retained as a convenient short description", adding that "since Wisdom as a category in Babylonian literature is *nothing more than a group of texts which happen to cover roughly the same area*, there is no precise canon by which to recognize them"[7]. On the other hand, H. Brunner, writing on Egyptian literature, would prefer to avoid the term altogether. Although he retains the expressions "Weisheitsliteratur" and "Weisheitslehre" in his treatment of the Egyptian Instructions[8], and points out that these compositions had considerable influence on other types of Egyptian literature[9], he regards this terminology as "wenig glücklich"[10], and refuses it altogether to other works, such as the Protests of the Eloquent Peasant[11], which would certainly qualify for it in the kind of classification used by Lambert or by Old Testament scholars.

[6] W. G. Lambert, The Development of Thought and Literature in Ancient Mesopotamia, an essay which forms the introduction to his edition of Babylonian texts entitled Babylonian Wisdom Literature, 1960.

[7] Op. cit. 1f. The italics are mine.

[8] HO I/2, 90—110.

[9] P. 109f.

[10] P. 90 n. 1.

[11] Extracts in: ANET 407—410.

These two scholars, working in fields outside the Old Testament, have both, in spite of their apparently opposite attitudes to this question, grasped the nature of the problem more clearly than most Old Testament scholars. If the terms "wisdom" and "wisdom literature", as applied to the Old Testament, are to have any significance beyond that of a "convenient short description", it is necessary to determine with much greater precision than heretofore what meanings may legitimately be given to them. Towards this end it may be useful, as a preliminary step, to investigate afresh the use of the words *ḥokmā, ḥākām* and their cognates in the Old Testament. In other words, we may begin by attempting to discover what the Israelites themselves called "wisdom", and whom they regarded as "wise". It is true that terminological investigation alone is unlikely to suffice to determine the character of what is generally regarded as a cultural phenomenon: the mere occurrence or non-occurrence of these particular words, or indeed of other examples of so-called "wisdom vocabulary", in particular texts is no infallible guide to their right to be designated "wisdom literature"; nevertheless the meaning of *ḥokmā* and *ḥākām* lies at the heart of the matter. For it is upon the concept of the "wisdom of the sages", viewed as a distinct class within Israelite society, that the whole structure of Old Testament wisdom research has been built.

Chapter II: The "Wise" in Israel

I. "WISDOM" AS INTELLIGENCE

We may begin by considering the meaning of the adjective *ḥākām*, and in particular the widely held theory[1] that it is a technical term denoting a member of a distinct "professional" class[2].

The earliest occurrence of the word *ḥākām* in the Old Testament is almost certainly Jdc 5 29, where it refers to a woman or women[3] attending on Sisera's mother: "The wisest of her princesses answered her." Wisdom here is simply a natural endowment which some persons possess in greater measure than others. In the tenth century Succession Narrative also the two "wise women" (*'iššā ḥ*ᵃ*kāmā*, II Sam 14 2 20 16) of Tekoa and of Abel Beth-maacah are simply women who have acquired reputations in their own cities for quick-wittedness; they can hardly be called "professional", at least not in any sense comparable with the "professionalism" of the courtier[4]. Similarly in the same narrative work Jonadab, Amnon's friend, is described as *ḥākām m*ᵉ*'ōd*, "very clever" (II Sam 13 3).

This non-specific sense of *ḥākām* corresponds, as far as the evidence permits us to judge, to that which was current in Canaan at an even earlier period: in all the 6 occurrences of the root *ḥkm* in Ugaritic literature "wisdom" appears as an attribute, that is, a natural

---

1 Propounded by H. Gressmann, Israels Spruchweisheit im Zusammenhang der Weltliteratur, KA 6, 1925 and followed by, among others, W. O. E. Oesterley, The Book of Proverbs, WC, 1929, lxviii—lxxiii; W. Baumgartner, Die israelitische Weisheitsliteratur, TR 5 (1933), 259—288; J. Fichtner, Die altorientalische Weisheit in ihrer israelitisch-jüdischen Ausprägung, 1933; Jesaja unter den Weisen; J. Lindblom op. cit.; W. McKane, Prophets and Wise Men, SBT 44, 1965; R. N. Whybray, Wisdom in Proverbs, SBT 45, 1965; The Succession Narrative. The present study represents a considerable modification of my earlier views.

2 The terms "professional" and "professional class", which will be used frequently in the ensuing pages, are not strictly appropriate, since the structure of ancient societies differed considerably from our own. "Profession" is used here to denote a regular occupation sufficiently distinct to have warranted the use of a special appellation.

3 The subject (*ḥak*ᵉ*mōt*) is pl., the verb apparently sg. But see the commentaries.

4 See H. W. Hertzberg, Die Samuelbücher, ATD 10, 1956, 267 (ET I and II Samuel, OTL, 1964, 331); Duesberg and Fransen op. cit. 100; W. Richter op. cit. 184; H.-J. Hermisson, Studien zur israelitischen Spruchweisheit, 1968, 73.

endowment, of the god El[5]. It is generally recognized that the root is of north-west Semitic origin. In all these early examples the most natural interpretation is that it refers to innate intelligence of a quite general kind; and it is significant that in the overwhelming majority of its ocurrences in the Old Testament books of every period it is incontrovertibly used in this general sense. In Proverbs, for example, the "wise man" is most frequently contrasted with the fool; and it is significant that in two passages (Prov 6 6-8 30 24-28) "wisdom" is attributed to certain animals, clearly in the sense of innate intelligence. Similarly in Job 39 13-17 the ostrich is singled out as a particular case, God having mysteriously deprived it of "wisdom", so that it spends its days in a state of confusion, forgetting where it has laid its eggs. In Ecclesiastes, the latest of the Old Testament wisdom books, the same general sense is still the predominating one[6]. That this should be the case in these three books is particularly significant, since it is these which are most generally supposed to be the work of a special class of persons known technically as *ḥᵃkāmīm*. Yet it is only in a small number of passages, to which reference will be made later[7], that it is possible to argue that *ḥākām* in these books may have such a technical sense.

In fact these books employ the word in the sense which it possessed in the common speech of Israel. When Hosea asserts that Ephraim is a child born without intelligence (*hū'-bēn lō' ḥākām*) whose folly showed itself even before his birth (Hos 13 13) he is clearly referring to a contemporary understanding of "wisdom" as a natural endowment possessed by some persons but mysteriously withheld from others. Jdc 5 29 and II Sam 14 2 20 16 echo this view.

On the other hand, "wisdom" could also be acquired by those who did not originally possess it, provided that they did not belong to one of the categories of fool whose folly was incorrigible[8]. Such wisdom could be acquired through experience:

> When an insolent man is punished, the simple gains wisdom.
> (Prov 21 11)

It could also come from the observation of nature: so the sluggard is urged to "go to the ant" and learn from its ways (Prov 6 6-8).

[5] Keret II iv 2; Baal V v 30f.; II iv 41f.; II v 3f. (numeration following G. R. Driver, Canaanite Myths and Legends, 1956).

[6] E. g. "The heart of the wise is in the house of mourning; but the heart of fools is in the house of mirth" (7 4); "The words of the wise heard in quiet are better than the shouting of a ruler among fools" (9 17).

[7] See p. 43ff. below.

[8] On the different categories of fool see Oesterley op. cit. lxxxiv—lxxxvii; Duesberg and Fransen op. cit. 204—211.

Most frequently, however, it is the company and instruction of other "wise men" which make a man "wise". But this acquired wisdom was not distinguished in Israelite thought from innate wisdom: in both cases it is fundamentally the ability to get on in the world, to adapt oneself to circumstances, to deal with difficult situations. Even when it is acquired through instruction it is primarily shrewdness rather than a body of knowledge. The essential unity of the concept is apparent in those proverbs which assert that the — naturally — wise man can, through instruction, become *more wise*:

> The wise man may also hear and increase in learning,
> and the man of understanding acquire skill. (Prov 1 5)
>
> Give instruction to a wise man, and he will be still wiser;
> teach a righteous man and he will increase in learning. (Prov 9 9)

It is essentially this same non-specialized concept of wisdom which we find in those texts which relate wisdom in various ways to religious faith. The means by which it is acquired are different, but the end is the same: wisdom in the religious sense also is an intellectual quality which provides the key to happiness and success, to "life" in its widest sense. The stages by which the Israelites came to identify purely intellectual, human wisdom with God's gift of wisdom can be traced in Prov 1—9, especially in 2 1-9, where succeeding generations of writers have imposed their interpretations on an original statement that human guidance is the one thing needful:

> My son, if you receive my words and treasure up my
> commandments with you,
> making your ear attentive to wisdom
> and inclining your heart to understanding;
> yes, if you cry out for insight
> and raise your voice for understanding,
> if you seek it as silver
> and search for it as for hidden treasures;
> then you will understand the fear of Yahweh
> and find the knowledge of God.
> For Yahweh gives wisdom;
> from his mouth come knowledge and understanding;
> he stores up sound wisdom for the upright;
> he is a shield to those who walk in integrity,
> guarding the paths of justice
> and watching over the way of those who are loyal to him.
> Then you will understand righteousness and justice
> and equity, every good path[9].

---

[9] For a detailed explanation and further examples see Whybray, Wisdom in Proverbs, especially 72ff.

The process is also described in parabolic language in Sir 24, where Wisdom claims that although at first she was a divine gift to "every people and nation" she was later commanded by the "Creator of all things" to become the special possession of Israel, where she became specifically the mouthpiece of God in his communications with his chosen people:

> In the holy tabernacle I ministered before him,
> and so I was established in Zion. (Sir 24 10)

The Prologue to Deuteronomy also illuminates this point. According to Dtn 4 1-8 it is God's statutes and laws which confer "life"; but other nations, when they see Israel living happily under these laws which are so superior to their own, will marvel at the superior *wisdom* which the possession of those laws has conferred upon them. The observance of God's laws, therefore, *is* wisdom (Dtn 4 6), because it achieves the results which had traditionally been claimed for the practitioners of wisdom. Thus the well-known cliché of the later wisdom literature that the fear of Yahweh is the beginning, or essence, of wisdom (Prov 9 10 Ps 111 10 Sir 1 14; cf. Prov 1 7 15 33 Job 28 28) is a new definition of wisdom only in the sense that it points to a new way to obtain it. The means have changed; the essential nature of "wisdom" as a superior degree of intelligence, natural or acquired, which confers "life" remains unchanged.

The same is true of the passages in which Wisdom is personified. The purpose of the personification, at least in Prov 1 20ff. 8, is simply to bring out more vividly the urgent necessity of its acquisition and to add weight to the claim which is made for its effectiveness[10].

Similarly the attribution of wisdom to God himself does not change its essential character. We do not know how early the Israelites entertained this notion. In view of the widespread attribution of wisdom to various gods by the other nations of the ancient Near East, including the Canaanite god El[11], it was probably much earlier than the time of Isaiah, when it first appears in a datable passage in the Old Testament. The very notion of the creation of man implies that wisdom, like other human qualities, is conferred upon man by God, and thus that God himself possesses it *par excellence*. This is certainly implied by the theme of the tree of knowledge in the J narrative of Gen 2—3[12].

---

[10] See Whybray, Wisdom in Proverbs, 95ff. The further development of the personification of Wisdom in Ecclesiasticus and the Wisdom of Solomon does, however, introduce a new theological element.

[11] See n. 5 above.

[12] On this passage see also p. 105ff. below.

Why so little stress was placed on the notion by early Israel we cannot say. It is possible that the association of "wisdom" with particular deities in other religions created a difficulty which it took time to overcome[13], or that *ḥokmā* had early acquired a somewhat dubious, worldly connotation which made its direct attribution to Yahweh seem inappropriate[14]. But the earliest datable positive statement in the Old Testament that Yahweh is wise (Isa 31 2) stands in a context which makes it plain that the kind of wisdom which is attributed to him is essentially the same as human wisdom in its quite general sense. The statement that "he *also* is wise (*weḡam-hū' ḥākām*)" is clearly intended to assert that God possesses exactly the same kind of wisdom which those whom Isaiah is condemning claim to possess without divine assistance, but that he possesses it in infinitely greater measure[15].

Wisdom here is thus that superior intelligence which knows how to achieve success, in this case in war: that of the strategist whose business it is to win battles. The contrast between the mode of operation of those who "go down to Egypt for help and rely on horses" and that of Yahweh who, by virtue of *his* wisdom, "can bring about trouble" and who, "when (he) stretches out his hand . . . they will all vanish together" is not a contrast between two different kinds of wisdom but between the faulty intelligence of those who in their calculations fail to take account of "the Holy One of Israel or seek guidance from Yahweh", the source of all power, and the superior intelligence of Yahweh himself. In both cases it is implied that wisdom is the way to the successful achievement of one's aims. Wisdom is power, because it is the way to success.

The same concept of wisdom lies behind the other passages which attribute wisdom to God. Over half these passages (Isa 40 13f. Jer 10 12/51 15 Ps 104 24 Job 28 23-27 38 36f. Prov 3 19) refer to the creation of the world by God "in his wisdom". The use of the word "wisdom" here may owe something to its specialized use in connexion with craftsmanship and in particular with building[16]. It is a particular

---

[13] G. Fohrer, Die Weisheit im Alten Testament, in: Studien zur alttestamentlichen Theologie und Geschichte (1949—1966), 1969 (= TWNT VII, 476—496), 262f. Cf. J. Fichtner, Die altorientalische Weisheit, 117f.

[14] M. Noth, Die Bewährung von Salomos „Göttlicher Weisheit", VT Suppl III 1955, 232f.; H. Cazelles, Les débuts de la sagesse en Israël, in: Les Sagesses du Proche Orient, 1963, 34f. All those scholars who have discussed this subject have expressed their opinions with great caution.

[15] According to Fichtner, Jesaja unter den Weisen, 26 n. 22; M. Noth (op. cit.); G. Fohrer, Das Buch Jesaja II, ZB, 1962, 112, this word of Isaiah is ironical in intention. This does not affect the point.

[16] E.g. Prov 24 3: "By wisdom a house is built".

example of the use of a superior intelligence. In other cases (Job 9 4 15 8 Dan 2 20) God's wisdom is associated with his strength, and the point is the same as that of Isa 31 2. Job 15 8, irrespective of the question whether a mythological concept lies behind this verse[17], associates God's wisdom with knowledge: the point is the superiority of God's intelligence over that of man. In Esr 7 25 "wisdom" is used in a sense unique in the Old Testament: the phrase "the wisdom of your God which is in your hand" is clearly identical in meaning with "the law of your God which is in your hand" in 7 14. This identification of wisdom with the Torah later became a commonplace of Jewish literature. Its appearance in the Ezra rescript is intriguing; but the passage sheds no light on the meaning of "wisdom" considered as a human or divine attribute.

We may conclude from the above discussion that "wisdom" in the Old Testament is a general term denoting superior intellectual ability whether innate or acquired, in God, men or animals. It is therefore natural that the words "wise", "wisdom" should also have been used, in appropriate contexts, to refer to particular spheres in which human ability most clearly manifested itself.

Such special kinds of ability are indicated by a variety of grammatical constructions. The *ḥokmā* (sometimes *ḥokmat lēb*) of craftsmen was applied to the designing and making of various objects. In the case of Bezalel this is indicated by *lᵉ* with the inf. cstr. in its so-called "gerundial" function, in a clause which specifies the particular application: "And I have filled him with the spirit of God, in wisdom and understanding and knowledge and every kind of work, *in designing* (*laḥᵉšōb*) devices, *in making* (*laʿᵃśōt*) objects of gold and silver" (Ex 31 3f.). The infinitives indicate the direction taken by Bezalel's *ḥokmā*. Again in Ex 35 35 it is stated that God "filled them with *ḥokmat-lēb*, to make (or "in making") all kinds of work". Similar expressions are used of the "wisdom" of Hiram the Tyrian (I Reg 7 14). But exactly the same kind of phrase can be used of Solomon's "wisdom", which showed itself in quite a different way: "They saw that the wisdom of God was in him in the execution of (*laʿᵃśōt*) justice" (I Reg 3 28).

Similar indications of the direction taken by "wisdom" in a particular case can be given by means of the simple *waw* with the jussive: the final clause. In Gen 41 33 Joseph advises Pharaoh: "Let Pharaoh seek out an intelligent and wise man (*'īš nābōn wᵉḥākām*), that he may set him (*wīšītēhū*) over the land of Egypt." Pharaoh replies (v. 39): "There is no intelligent and wise man like you (*'ēn-*

[17] See my comment, and references to the relevant literature, in: The Heavenly Counsellor 54f.

nābōn wᵉḥākām kāmōkā)". Here also the wisdom is of a general kind; the function envisaged a particular one.

In Isa 19 12 the prophet addresses Pharaoh: "Where then are your wise men, that they may teach you (*wᵉyaggīdū nā' lāk*) . . . what Yahweh of Hosts has planned for Egypt?". This is one of the passages where it has been claimed that *ḥᵃkāmīm* is used in a technical sense to denote a class of "professional" wise men. This claim is not necessarily supported by the text. In the previous verse *ḥākām* is used attributively: "the wisest of Pharaoh's counsellors (*ḥakᵉmē yōʿᵃṣē parʿō*)". In view of this, "your wise men" may mean "your wisest (counsellors)", the general reference to superior intelligence among the counsellors being qualified by the final clause indicating the particular respect in which their wisdom is manifested.

In fact the two grammatical constructions under discussion are used elsewhere in connexion with wisdom in contexts where no such professional meaning is possible. In II Sam 14 20 king David is said to be "wise like the wisdom of God in knowing (*lādaʿat*) all that is on the earth". In this case "wisdom" takes the form of omniscience. In Jer 4 22 God complains about Israel that they are "clever in wrongdoing (*ḥᵃkāmīm hēmmā lᵉhāraʿ*) but do not know how to do good". Similarly with the final clause: in Jes 31 2 Yahweh is said to be "wise in bringing trouble (*ḥākām wᵉyābī' rāʿ*)"[18]. In Jer 9 11 (cf. Hos 14 10) the question is asked: "What man is wise enough to understand this (*mī-hā'īš heḥākām wᵉyābēn 'et-zō't*)?", referring to Israel's inability to grasp God's message. Cf. Ps 107 43: "Whosoever is wise, let him observe these things (*mī-ḥākām wᵉyišmor-'ēlle*)".

An examination of the contexts in which the words *ḥākām*, *ḥokmā* and their cognates occur shows that in every case what is meant is superior mental ability in a general sense, though this is often applied in a particular way. The fact that one is *ḥākām* does not mean that one can apply one's mind with equal success to every form of activity. In our own day we may use the word "intelligent" or the word "able" of a classical scholar or of a scientist; yet that classical scholar may be a fool when it comes to mathematics, and *vice versa*. There were specializations also in the ancient world: the man who could design candlesticks for the Tabernacle could not sail a ship or rule a kingdom. Yet in spite of the very different qualities of mind which were displayed by these different specialities, it was recognized that each form of intellectual excellence was governed by a man's mind (*lēb*)[19]; and it was the excellence of a man's *lēb* which gained for him the epithet

---

[18] Reading *wᵉyābī'* for MT *wayyābē'*.

[19] There seems to be no effective difference in meaning between *ḥᵃkam lēb* and *ḥākām*. Cf. the expression *lēb ḥākām*, "a wise mind" (e.g. I Reg 3 12).

ḥākām, as for us it would result in his being recognized as "intelligent" or "able".

It was therefore natural that "wisdom" should be ascribed to persons who performed special functions for which a degree of skill was required. On a humble level it was used of the sailors (Ps 107 27) who, in a tempest, "reeled and staggered like drunken men, and all their *ḥokmā* was in vain"; of professional wailing women (Jer 9 16); of snake charmers (*meḥukkām,* Ps 58 6); of builders (Prov 24 3); of craftsmen (Ex 31 3f. 35 35 I Reg 7 14 Isa 40 20 Jer 10 9). In Egypt (Gen 41 8 Ex 7 11) and Babylon (Dan 2 18 and frequently in Daniel) there was supposedly a class of "wise men" at court, taking their place together with magicians, sorcerers and persons employed to interpret dreams and to solve riddles[20].

Other passages use the words "wise", "wisdom" in referring to more exalted functions. In the Prologue to Deuteronomy "wisdom" is considered to be a necessary attribute of tribal leaders (Dtn 1 13. 15), and in one passage in Deuteronomy it is required of judges (Dtn 16 19; cf. I Reg 3 28). The idea that it is a prerequisite for successful government, whether by the king or his officers of state, is a commonplace (e.g. Gen 14 33 II Sam 14 20 I Reg 2 6 Isa 10 13), and it is attributed to the king's advisers who formulate state policy (e.g. Isa 19 11f.). It is also applied, in the later books of the Old Testament, to the scholar or philosopher: the "wisdom" which the author of Ecclesiastes sought is encyclopaedic knowledge: "I applied my mind to know and to search out and to seek wisdom and the sum of things" (Koh 7 25). A similar meaning is found in Dan 1 4, where the Jewish young men brought to the Babylonian court were *maśkīlīm bekol-ḥokmā,* "at home in all branches of knowledge"[21].

It is, however, important to observe that the use of the words *ḥākām, ḥokmā* and their cognates to denote superior ability in particular activities, whether professional or non-professional, does not prove the existence of any class of persons in Israel whose specific designation was "*the* wise men", or of any profession which was distinguished from others by the name *ḥokmā.* This can only be demonstrated if passages can be found in which a more general meaning is impossible or highly improbable.

Before an examination is undertaken of those passages where this has been held to be the case, one further general remark may be made. This concerns the fact that wisdom is, in the Old Testament, very frequently associated with *speech.* This connexion exists in all societies to some extent. The fool can usually be distinguished from the

---

[20] On this see 15f. below.

[21] NEB.

clever man by the things which he says, and by the things which he refrains from saying. This was, however, particularly the case in societies in which the spoken word was of greater importance than it is today. This connection which the Old Testament so frequently makes between wisdom and speech has helped to give credence to the view that *ḥākām* and *ḥokmā* were used in Israel to refer to those professions in which speech was of paramount importance, especially those of the politician with his "advice" (*'ēṣā*) and the teacher with his oral instruction (*tōrā*)[22]. Since this attachment of great importance to speech is remarkably similar to the emphasis placed on it in the education of the Egyptian scribe and in the instruction given by Egyptian schoolmasters, the identification of the word *ḥākām* with either the Israelite scribe or the Israelite wisdom teacher has seemed to some scholars to be a natural one, and it has been assumed that this is its meaning in a number of sayings in Proverbs where the *ḥākām* is represented as teaching or giving advice[23]. This is a most improbable hypothesis. It is generally agreed that in most occurrences of *ḥākām* in Proverbs, notably where the "wise man" is contrasted with the fool, or where a man is said to be "wise in his own eyes", the word is used in a non-technical sense; and there is no evidence to support a theory of two strata within a single section of Proverbs distinguishable by two quite different meanings of the word, which would be the only way of explaining an otherwise confusing, and therefore improbable, phenomenon. Moreover there are other passages in the Old Testament (e. g. Gen 41 39 II Sam 13 3) where *ḥākām* is used of cleverness of speech but with no professional connotation[24].

The passages where a professional meaning of *ḥākām* and its cognates may appear to have more substance must now be examined. This claim has been made with regard to three professions, though these overlap to some extent: the counsellor or political adviser of the king, the teacher or schoolmaster, and the author of "wisdom literature"[25].

---

[22] So, e.g., von Rad, Theologie, I 428ff. (ET 430ff.). Speech was also characteristic of the prophet, but in his case the "word" was not his own but God's.

[23] E.g. 13 14 15 12 16 23.

[24] On this question see further p. 43ff. below.

[25] The further use of the term *ḥākām* in the inter-testamental and later periods lies outside the scope of this study.

II. A PROFESSIONAL CLASS?

A. The "Wise Man" as Counsellor

There is no doubt that the Israelite kings maintained in their service a body of men who both advised them and administered their policies[26]. There are abundant references to these officials in the books of Kings and also in Isaiah and Jeremiah. They appear to have been known by a number of different titles: they were the "servants" (*ʿᵃbādîm*) of the king, but also the "princes" (*śārîm*) of the kingdom. Most of them probably belonged to the class of "scribes" (*sōpᵉrîm*). The term "counsellor" (*yōʿēṣ*) is also used. There were also specific offices of state, each with its proper title. The question to be investigated is whether these persons, or some section of them, were also known collectively by the title "the wise men" (*haḥᵃkāmîm*).

1. "Wise Men" at Foreign Courts

The only passages where this phrase appears unequivocally to refer to a class of persons attendant on a king are passages which refer not to Israel but to foreign countries. Even here, however, it is not certain that these were counsellors or political advisers. In Gen 41 8 the king of Egypt summons *ʾet-kol-ḥarṭummē miṣraim wᵉʾet-kol-ḥᵃkāmêhā* to interpret his dream. This phrase is usually taken to refer to two classes of person: "Egypt's wise men and her magicians." But in the narrative which follows no distinction is made between these two groups, and it is possible that this is a case of hendiadys, meaning "all Egypt's cleverest magicians"[27]. Similarly in Ex 7 11 it is said of Pharaoh, *wayyiqrāʾ . . . laḥᵃkāmîm wᵉlamᵉkaššᵉpîm*. Here again the usual translation is "he called . . . the wise men and the magicians"; but again no distinction is made in the ensuing narrative between the two groups, and the only activity attributed to them is magical: they reply to Moses' turning of his rod into a serpent by doing the same with theirs "by their secret arts". No mention is made of any other kind of "wisdom", and the translation "cleverest magicians" is a possible one. However this may be, these two passages

---

[26] For further details see R. de Vaux, Les institutions de l'Ancien Testament, I 1958, 195—203 (ET Ancient Israel: Its Life and Institutions, 1961, 127—132) and the literature there cited in the bibliography; Duesberg and Fransen op. cit. 147—176; and also the discussions in McKane op. cit. 15—47; Whybray, The Heavenly Counsellor, 31—33.

[27] See H. A. Brongers, Merismus, Synekdoche und Hendiadys in der Bibel-Hebräischen Sprache, OS 14, 1965, 100—114.

offer no evidence that the "wise men" of Egypt were counsellors or political advisers.

It has already been pointed out[28] that in Isa 19 12 the reference to Pharaoh's "wise men" equally does not necessarily refer to a professional class.

In the case of Babylon the evidence points somewhat more definitely to a class of *ḥ^a^kāmīm*. In Jer 51 57, "I will make her princes and her wise men drunk, her viceroys and governors and warriors", they are included in what appears to be a list of the leading "professional" classes, although it would be unwise to press precision too far in a passionate and poetical oracle of doom. The same applies to Jer 50 35: "A sword hangs over the Chaldaeans ..., over the people of Babylon, her princes and wise men." These passages, however, give no indication of the function of these *ḥ^a^kāmīm:* they may be magicians or diviners rather than counsellors. This is certainly true of the frequently mentioned "wise men of Babylon" (*ḥakkīmē bābēl*) in the Aramaic portions of Daniel (ch. 2. 4. 5), whose function is not political advice but the interpretation of signs and dreams.

In the case of Edom, Ob 8 states that Yahweh "will destroy (the)[29] wise men from Edom, and understanding (*t^e^būnā*) from the mount of Esau; and your warriors, O Teman, will be disheartened." Here the reference is probably to "wisdom" in the sense of superior intelligence: there is no indication that *ḥākām* is used in a technical sense to designate a professional class.

In Est 1 13, where the Persian king asks the advice of "the wise men who were experts in times" (*laḥ^a^kāmīm yōd^e^ʿē hāʿittīm*), it is probable that the reference is to groups of learned men at court, of which one consisted of astrologers[30]. Here *ḥākām* appears to have a professional sense.

The evidence for the use of *haḥ^a^kāmīm* as a technical term denoting a professional class at the courts of foreign monarchs is by no means consistently positive. Moreover, in almost every case where this interpretation is a possible or probable one, it is not certain that these men were counsellors or political advisers; in some cases this is improbable. But even if this was so in some instances, the fact that some Israelite writers believed that there was such a professional class in the service of foreign kings provides no proof that such a class existed in Israel or Judah.

[28] p. 12 above.

[29] There is no article in the Hebrew.

[30] Or possibly of lawyers. Cf. the NEB translation of *yōd^e^ʿē hāʿittīm* as "versed in misdemeanours".

2. "Wise Men" at Israelite Courts

Our information concerning Israelite court life and the political administration of the kingdoms of Israel and Judah, especially the latter, is relatively abundant, although the incidental nature of most of the references to these does not permit a full reconstruction[31].

a) Historical narratives

In the three lists of the great officers of state of David and Solomon (II Sam 8 16-18 20 23-26 I Reg 4 2-6), collectively referred to in I Reg 4 2 as the *śārīm,* we find the *mazkīr,* possibly "herald", the *sōpēr,* "scribe" or "secretary" (two of these are named in I Reg 4 3), the *ʿal-hammas* or officer in charge of forced labour, the *ʿal-hanniṣā-bīm* or officer in charge of the provincial governors, the *rēʿe hammelek* or "friend of the king", and the *ʿal-habbayit* or "comptroller of the household". Most of these titles recur in the historical narratives. There is no reference to an office of "wise man".

In the historical narratives a variety of persons and groups of persons are represented as having dealings with kings of Israel or of Judah. Some of these evidently belong to the king's immediate entourage; others appear to be more representative of the nation as a whole. In a large number of these narratives the king either asks for and receives advice or has it offered to him. The advice is sometimes given by a prophet or a priest, and sometimes (for example, II Sam 19 5ff.) by a named individual. Besides these we find groups such as "the elders of Israel" (II Sam 17 4. 15); "the elders of the household" (II Sam 12 17); "the elders of the land" (I Reg 20 7-9); "the servants of the king" (II Sam 12 21 I Reg 1 2 II Reg 6 11f. 7 12f.); "the old men (*zeqēnīm*)" and "the young men (*yelādīm*)" (I Reg 12 6-14). One individual, Ahithophel, is referred to by his title "David's counsellor" (*yōʿēṣ dāwīd,* II Sam 15 12). There is also some evidence for the use of the expression *ʾīš ʿēṣā*[32]. On no occasion in any of these narratives is the word *ḥākām* used[33].

ḥākām is in fact never used as the title of any person or as the designation of any group of persons in any narrative in the historical books or in Isaiah or Jeremiah which refers to the court or the administrative establishment. Here a few examples may be given of

---

[31] See de Vaux op. cit. I 195ff. (ET 127ff.).

[32] See Whybray, The Heavenly Counsellor, especially 27—29. 31—33.

[33] This is also true of the narratives concerning Saul and concerning the early years of David, before the monarchical institutions were fully established. It is also true of the narratives in Chronicles, which are either dependent on material from Kings or date from a much later time.

passages where, if the word had been in use in this connection, it might be expected to occur.

In II Reg 18 18 Hezekiah sends his officers to meet the Assyrian officials and to reason or negotiate with them. The composition of the embassy is specified in detail. It consists of the master of the household (*'al-habbayit*), the Secretary (*sōpēr*) and the "herald" (*mazkīr*); there is no *ḥākām*. In II Reg 24 14 a list is given of the classes of people deported with Jehoiachin: the *śārīm*, the army officers (*gibbōrē haḥayil*), the craftsmen (*ḥārāš*) and the smiths (*masgēr*).

In Jer 26, when Jeremiah is brought to trial, we are told of the parts played by the people, princes and elders. In none of these passages, nor in similar ones, do we find mention of the *ḥᵃkāmīm*. Moreover, in no narrative in the historical books, nor in any other prose narrative, does any Israelite king consult *the*, or *his*, wise men; and, as has been said, in no administrative list does the title *ḥākām* appear. These are remarkable facts. It is difficult to avoid the conclusion that this is because there was no such class, at any rate in the sense of a royal counsellor or political adviser[34].

b) Isaiah

There remain a number of non-narrative texts, all from the books of Isaiah and Jeremiah, in which the occurrence of the words *ḥākām* (usually in the pl.) and *ḥokmā* in political, or supposedly political, contexts has frequently been regarded as proof of the existence of this class. It should be noted from the outset that these are all poetical texts with one exception (Jer 18 18); and that even there, as will be shown, there is reason to suppose that the style is not fully prosaic. The character and exigences of poetical composition considerably lessen the value of these passages as witnesses to the precise terminology of political institutions in comparison with administrative and narrative texts.

---

[34] It should also be noted that no such class is mentioned in any of the administrative or other types of texts from Ras Shamra, or in any extant Canaanite or Phoenician inscription. This is significant in view of the probability that the administrative system instituted in Israel by David and Solomon was at least to some extent modelled on those of Jerusalem and other Canaanite cities before their incorporation into Israel. Similarly in the Aramaic Words of Ahiqar the adjective *ḥkym* occurs several times (lines 1. 12. 28. 35. 42) qualifying the noun *spr*, „scribe", and once (line 178) in the sense of "wise man" in a wisdom saying, but never in the sense under discussion. It is clear from Ahiqar (line 12, where Ahiqar is called *spr' ḥkym' y'ṭ 'twr klh*, "wise scribe and counsellor of all Assyria"), that for the author (or translator) of this work the proper titles of a royal official of this kind were "scribe" and "counsellor" (*y'ṭ* = Heb. *yō'ēṣ*). Cf. McKane op. cit. 28ff.

In Isa 29 14 Yahweh announces that, as a punishment for the people's failure to offer him more than a superficial and mechanical worship, "the wisdom of its wise men shall perish, and the understanding (*bînā*) of its men of understanding (*n^ebōnāw*) shall be hidden". The threat is clearly one of a failure of sound political judgment which will inevitably lead to political or military disaster and to the downfall of the nation. *ḥākām* and *nābōn* in this case, therefore, refer to political sagacity; but the poetical parallelisms *ḥokmā/bînā* and *ḥākām/nābōn* are an indication that it would be foolish to attempt to deduce the existence of a class of professional *ḥ^akāmîm* from a text of this kind. If, indeed, such misuse of poetical language were to be permitted, it would be necessary to conclude that Isaiah is referring not to *one* professional class existing in the Judah of his day, but to *two*: the *ḥ^akāmîm* and the *n^ebōnîm*. But such a line of reasoning would be absurd.

The use of these two words as poetical parallels is in fact probably derived from the phrase *ḥākām w^enābōn* which, together with the variant *nābōn w^eḥākām*, occurs in prose texts in the sense of "able (man)"[35]. The parallelism itself occurs elsewhere in poetical texts in which there is no political reference, and no reason to suppose a professional meaning[36]. Consequently in spite of the fact that the context of Isa 29 14 is a political one, it is highly improbable that *ḥākām* is here used in a technical professional sense[37].

In Isa 31 2, where it is asserted by the prophet that "he (Yahweh) also is wise", the context is again political[38]: the wisdom of Yahweh, by which he is able to control events and "bring disaster", is sharply contrasted, by implication (the words *ḥākām* and *ḥokmā* are not actually used of them in this passage) with the ineffectiveness of the "wisdom" of those who so confidently "go down to Egypt and

---

[35] *ḥākām w^enābōn*, Dtn 1 13 4 6 I Reg 3 12; *nābōn w^eḥākām*, Gen 41 33. 39.

[36] Isa 5 21 Hos 14 10 Prov 1 5 17 28 18 15 Koh 9 11. On *nābōn* see further p. 147f. below.

[37] Baumgartner op. cit. 279 and Fichtner, Jesaja unter den Weisen, 21, cite this and other passages from Isaiah and Jeremiah in support of such a technical meaning for *ḥākām*, but without giving supporting arguments. For McKane op. cit. 70f. this conclusion follows from his assumption that "the *ḥ^akāmîm* who are attacked by Isaiah and Jeremiah ... are to be equated with a class of officials who existed from the time of David onwards", for which he claims that there is "abundant evidence" which is "generally accepted" (42). In spite of his admirable discussion of the meaning of *sōpēr* in the Old Testament, however, he really offers no proof that the word *ḥākām* was used in a similar way. Lindblom op. cit. 194 argues on the basis of other prophetic texts that this was so, but does not think that Isa 29 14 is to be taken in this way.

[38] See Fichtner, Jesaja unter den Weisen, 21. 25; Lindblom art. cit. 197; McKane op. cit. 72f.

rely on horses" (v. 1); but it would be rash to argue from this indirect reference that the (supposed) "wisdom" of these politicians means more than that they claimed to possess superior intelligence.

In Isa 5 21 there occurs the sentence "Woe to those who are wise (*ḥᵃkāmīm*) in their own eyes and understanding (*nᵉbōnīm*) in their own esteem"[39]. Here the parallel between *ḥākām* and *nābōn* suggests, as in 29 14, a non-technical sense for the former. But an even stronger reason for believing this to be so is the use of the phrase *ḥᵃkāmīm bᵉʿēnēhem*, "wise in their own eyes". In the singular the phrase "wise in (one's) own eyes" occurs 5 times in Proverbs (3 7 26 5. 12. 16 28 11), where it is used in a quite general sense of the conceited man, the wicked man, or the fool. Fichtner, followed by McKane, takes its use in Isaiah as an indication that this prophet was a former member of the class of *ḥᵃkāmīm* to whose specialized vocabulary it belonged, and concludes that now, as a prophet, he used it to turn the tables on his former colleagues. Their boasted "wisdom" was really folly, and Isaiah uses a phrase from their own textbook to drive home his point[40].

This argument, however, presupposes rather than proves the existence of the technical meaning of *ḥākām*, since it takes for granted that the word has two meanings upon which Isaiah is able to play. Moreover the fact that the phrase "wise in (one's) own eyes" occurs, apart from this passage, only in Proverbs does not constitute proof that it was exclusively used by the authors of wisdom books and their circle. It may well have been in common use.

McKane assumes that the whole of 5 19-24 are to be regarded as directed towards the same group of people, and concludes from the use of *ʿēṣā*, "policy", and its correlative *maʿᵃśe*, "action", in v. 19 that v. 21 refers exclusively to politicians. This might appear to lend some support to the theory of a technical meaning for *ḥᵃkāmīm* here; but in fact this passage is part of a larger context (v. 8-24) consisting of a series of "woe-oracles". The woe-formula recurs in v. 20. 21. 22. It cannot be assumed that the groups of persons addressed in these oracles are identical in each case, even though they were all presumably members of the ruling classes whose functions and activities to some extent overlapped[41]. McKane's reference to v. 19 in order to explain v. 21 is therefore not valid.

---

[39] Cf. Fichtner 21. 23. 25; Lindblom 194; McKane 65—67.

[40] Lindblom does not accept this view, but regards *ḥākām* as having a general reference here, as in 29 14. H. Wildberger, Jesaja, BK 10/1, 1968, 194, thinks a reference to politicians possible but not certain.

[41] Wildberger op. cit. 180 considers that each of the oracles was originally independent and addressed to a specific circle of hearers in a particular situation; and that the arrangement in a series is secondary. This is shown above all by the similarity

The origin and original purpose of "woe-oracles" remain a subject of controversy[42]; but catalogues of ethical norms, whether positive or negative and whether in the form of prohibitions (e. g. the Decalogue) or curses (e. g. Dtn 27 15-26) are not necessarily intended individually to point the finger of condemnation at the same persons. In this case the woes condemn a wide variety of deplorable practices and states of mind: expropriation of smallholders, drunkenness, falsehood, blasphemy, reversal of ethical norms and corruption in the lawcourts. In none of these is a professional class condemned as such. It is therefore probable that in v. 21 "wise in their own eyes" also has a non-technical reference, and refers simply, as in Proverbs, to the unpleasant and ultimately irreligious trait of conceit[43].

c) Jeremiah

In Jer 9 22 *ḥākām* (without the article) occurs in a list together with "the mighty man" (*haggibbōr*) and "rich man" (*ʿāšīr*): "Let not a wise man boast of his wisdom, nor the mighty man of his strength; let not a rich man boast of his riches[44]." Here the word *gibbōr* is perhaps used in the professional sense of "warrior": this may be the reason why it is the only one of the series which has the article[45],

---

of v. 11 with v. 22: such repetition would be impossible to explain if the whole series had been spoken on the same occasion.

[42] For a recent discussion of this form of speech see E. Gerstenberger, The Woe-Oracles of the Prophets. Gerstenberger's attempt to show that woe-oracles and wisdom literature had a common origin in "the popular ethos", whatever its merits, does not, however, point to a borrowing of this form by Isaiah from the wisdom circles of his day, since the formula, and even the word *hōy*, "woe", are never used by the authors of Proverbs, nor do they occur in the other two Old Testament wisdom books, Job and Ecclesiastes. H. W. Wolff op. cit. agrees with Gerstenberger's conclusions, but C. Westermann, Grundformen prophetischer Rede, 1964², 138—142 (ET Basic Forms of Prophetic Speech, 1967, 190—198), connects the woe-oracle not with wisdom speech but with the curse. See also p. 125f. below.

[43] Fichtner, Jesaja unter den Weisen, 21, finds a reference to professional *ḥᵃkāmīm* in one other Isaian passage: 3 3. Here the phrase *ḥᵃkam ḥᵃrāšīm*, probably "the man skilful in magical arts", appears between *yōʿēṣ*, "counsellor", and *nᵉbōn lāḥaš*, "skilful enchanter". Fichtner proposes the omission of *ḥᵃrāšīm* as a gloss and the repointing of *ḥᵃkam* as *ḥākām*, "wise man". The emendation was first made many years ago and has been widely accepted (e.g. BDB, Kö, BH), but is rejected by D. Winton Thomas in BHS. It is also implicitly rejected by both Lindblom 194 and McKane 96. In any case a theory based solely on an emendation without the support of other evidence from Isaiah would hardly be worth consideration.

[44] Cf. Fichtner 20; Lindblom 195; McKane 89f.

[45] F. Giesebrecht, Das Buch Jeremia, HKAT 3/2, 1894, 60, explains the article here as an indication of membership of a class, referring to G.-K. § 126, 3 (126, 1. m in modern editions).

although a general meaning "strong, courageous" is equally possible[46]. However this may be, "rich" is certainly not the designation of a professional class, and the view of Fichtner, Lindblom and McKane that this is so in the case of *ḥākām* is at best unproven.

Jer 8 8 is a much disputed passage: "How can you say, 'We are wise, and the law of Yahweh is with us'? Yet behold, the false pen of (the) scribes has made it into a lie. Wise men will be put to shame, they will be dismayed and taken; they have spurned the word of Yahweh; and what use will their wisdom be to them?" (*ḥakāmīm* — twice — and *sōpᵉrīm* have no article). A number of scholars[47] identify these "wise men" with the scribes who are mentioned in the same passage, though they do not all agree about the identity of these two groups. This identification is improbable. In v. 8 the change from the second to the third person implies that the prophet is making a distinction between two groups of people; otherwise we should expect him to say, "*Your* false pen has made it into a lie". The fact that "wise men" subsequently appears in the following verse with a third person verb does not invalidate this point. V. 9 has the character of a general statement in which the prophet now refers ironically to these self-styled "wise men"[48] and announces their discomfiture[49].

The further identification of these *ḥakāmīm* by some scholars[50] with the politicians and royal counsellors is even more improbable: all that we are told about them is that they claim to possess the law of Yahweh, a claim which does not in any way correspond with what is known of the attitudes and characteristics of this class[51].

---

46 So, e.g., NEB, where no indication is given of the variation in the use of the article.

47 B. Duhm, Das Buch Jeremia, KHC, 1901; P. Volz, Das Buch Jeremia, KAT, 1928²; H. Ranston, The Old Testament Wisdom Books and their Teaching, 1930, 13; H. Cazelles, A propos d'une phrase de H. H. Rowley, VT Suppl III, 1955, 29; W. Rudolph, Jeremia, HAT 1/12, 1958²; McKane op. cit. 102—112; Weinfeld, Deuteronomy and the Deuteronomic School, 151. 158.

48 It is unlikely that *ḥakāmīm* in these verses refers to two different groups of people, since this would introduce an intolerable confusion and render Jeremiah's words unintelligible to his audience.

49 Lindblom 196 n. 2 also takes the view that the *sōpᵉrīm* and *ḥakāmīm* in this passage are two distinct groups.

50 E.g. Cazelles op. cit. 29.

51 The view of Mowinckel, Psalms and Wisdom, 206 (followed by R. B. Y. Scott, Priesthood, Prophecy, Wisdom and the Knowledge of God, JBL 80, 1961, 1—15) that "the classes of intellegentzia" in ancient Israel were not sharply defined and that "the borders between them . . . were fluctuating" may have some truth in it, but the fact remains that there is no evidence elsewhere in the Old Testament to support the idea, which would follow from Cazelles' interpretation, that possession of the Torah of Yahweh was ever the basis of the politician's claim to authority,

The other problems connected with this extremely obscure passage need only be briefly alluded to here. Controversy has centred upon two points especially: the question what, in the time of Jeremiah, the phrase "the law of Yahweh" meant; and, related to this, the question of the relationship between the scribes whose "pen ... has made it into a lie" and the "wise" who boast that they possess it. The relationship between the "scribes" of v. 8 and "those who handle the law" in Jer 2 8 has also been discussed[52]. The difficulties of these problems have given rise to a number of theories about the identity of the "wise men" here. Evidently although, as has been seen, they are not to be identified with the scribes, there was some connection between the two groups: the falsifying activity of the scribes had in some way undermined the validity of the claim to be wise which Jeremiah is concerned to show to be false.

These "wise men" have been identified by various scholars as priests, Deuteronomists, forerunners of the later scribes who were students of the Law of Moses, and expounders of the Law of which the scribes were the editors. The passage has also been interpreted as marking a turning-point in the development of the functions of the *ḥakāmīm* as wisdom teachers who now for the first time began to include the written Torah in their curriculum[53].

The very variety of the views which have been put forward is an indication that no interpretation of the word *ḥakāmīm* in this passage as a distinct class is able to do full justice to the complexity of the problems involved. One possibility has, however, been neglected: whatever may be the true solution of the other problems raised by the passage, the word *ḥakāmīm* makes excellent sense here if it is understood in a quite general sense. The prophet is addressing an unspecified audience of his fellow-citizens, whose mood is one of confidence. The fact that they base this confidence on their possession of the law of Yahweh suggests that the reforms of Josiah are already in operation; and they believe, like the author of Dtn 4 6, that the possession of the Law gives them a wisdom, that is, a superior understanding, which sets them above other nations. Towards this confident claim Jeremiah adopts an attitude similar to that which he adopted in his Temple Speech towards those who placed excessive trust in their possession of Yahweh's Temple (7 4), and one which is in fact in line with the warning of Deuteronomy itself (Dtn 4 9ff.): reliance on God's special gifts to his people as if they were not conditional

---

and without the existence of such a claim an attack of this kind by Jeremiah would be meaningless.

[52] See among other works the literature referred to in the foregoing footnotes.

[53] See the discussion in G. Östborn, Tora in the Old Testament, 1945, 112—126.

upon their proper use is a form of pride which leads to disaster: then, "what use will their wisdom be to them?"[54].

We now come to the passage on which the greatest stress has been laid by those who argue[55] for the existence of the *ḥᵃkāmīm* as a distinct class: Jer 18 18. "Then they said, 'Come, let us make plots against Jeremiah, for (*kī*) law (*tōrā*) shall not perish from priest, nor counsel (*ʿēṣā*) from wise man (*ḥākām*), nor word (*dābār*) from prophet. Come, let us smite him with the tongue, and let us not heed any of his words[56].' "

The identity of the speakers is not stated; but it is generally taken for granted that the passage refers to three "professional" classes who together formed the mainstay of the state[57]. As the "word" was the peculiar function of the prophet and the law of the priest, so was counsel (*ʿēṣā*) of the politician; and, since priest and prophet are distinct "professional" classes, *ḥākām* here must similarly have a precise "professional" meaning.

That "counsel" was a characteristic function of the politician is a fact which needs no further demonstration[58], but the word *ʿēṣā* is by no means confined to this meaning. It can be used of any kind of advice, and also has the meaning "plan, scheme", in which sense it may be as much an activity of the wicked (Ps 1 1 Job 10 3 21 16 22 18)

---

[54] A. Weiser, Das Buch Jeremia, ATD 20, 1966[5], 72, also understands "wise" here as having a general reference to the people's false confidence in their possession of God's law, although he unduly restricts the meaning of "law" here to sacrificial regulations. Giesebrecht op. cit. 53f. and J. Bright, Jeremiah, AB 21, 1965, 65, also take it in a general sense.

[55] With regard to this passage this is the view of the majority, although not all who hold it identify this class with the politicians. It is assumed, or propounded, by, among others, Giesebrecht, Baumgartner, Fichtner, Cazelles, Lindblom, McKane, Rudolph, Weiser. See also B. Gemser, Sprüche Salomos, HAT 1/16, 1963[2], 3, on this and other passages from Jeremiah.

[56] Many commentators, following LXX, omit *'al* and render "and let us pay attention to his words", on the grounds that an agreement to take no notice of Jeremiah's words would be a weak sequel to an agreement to take the more positive course of plotting against him, whereas an agreement to listen carefully to his words in the hope of finding evidence which could be used against him would make good sense as a specific proposal of a means whereby the plot could be put into effect. This may have been the reasoning which led LXX to omit the negative particle; but it ignores the fact that the prophetic word was normally regarded as something possessing great destructive force, which men disregarded at their peril. The decision to ignore it was no insignificant one but one which required great determination. On the reason why the decision was taken in this case see p. 29f. below.

[57] Scott, however (Priesthood, Prophecy, Wisdom 3), regards this as doubtful.

[58] On this word see especially P. A. H. de Boer, The Counsellor, VT Suppl III 1955, 42—71.

or of the poor (Ps 14 6) or of any other individual or group as an activity of men especially trained to give political advice or to form national policy. Since the formulation of plans and the giving of good advice both require the use of the mind, it is natural that *ʿēṣā* and *ḥākām* should occur together in close association; but it does not follow that whenever they are found together they have technical or specialized meanings. For example, when in Prov 12 15 it is stated that

> The way of a fool is right in his own eyes,
> but a wise man (*ḥākām*) listens to advice (*ʿēṣā*)

it is clear that both words are being used in a quite general sense: it is simply superior intelligence, and not any special status or training, which impels a man to listen to advice rather than to be confident that he is always right; and the giving of such advice similarly requires no special training: it is simply the kind of friendly advice given in ordinary social intercourse.

The precise meaning of these two words in the triple statement in Jer 18 18 can therefore be ascertained only by a consideration of the context in which the statement stands. Unfortunately, owing to the contextual isolation of the passage in which it occurs[59], the commentaries are by no means in agreement about its meaning. The difficulty is that in this speech by Jeremiah's enemies the relevance of the triple statement to their intention to plot against him is not at all clear. Rudolph, summing up earlier theories, suggests that there are three main ways in which it may be explained: the enemies of Jeremiah may be saying that they do not need Jeremiah, because the authority of these three groups of men is sufficient for their purposes (or for the stability of the state); or that they will have no difficulty in dealing with him and putting him out of the way because they have these three authorities on their side; or that it is necessary that he should be removed and silenced because he has undermined the confidence of the nation by prophesying that the *tōrā* of the priests will cease, the wisdom of the professional *ḥᵃkāmīm* will be confounded, and the divine revelation mediated through the prophets will fail (cf. 4 9 8 9)[60].

Rudolph is correct in saying that of these solutions the third is the most probable. No explanation can be regarded as satisfactory which does not adequately explain the force of the word *kī*, "for,

---

[59] It is generally, though not universally, agreed by the commentators that this verse, although in its present position it has a general appropriateness to its context because of its reference to plots against Jeremiah, was originally an independent unit.

[60] Op. cit. 114. Other interpretations have been proposed, but none of them merits detailed study here.

because", which is the only material clue to the relationship between the triple statement and its context. It signifies that the triple statement provides some sort of motive, reason or justification for the decision to plot against Jeremiah. Judged by this criterion, the first solution referred to by Rudolph is unsatisfactory because Jeremiah's insignificance or irrelevance would hardly be a sufficient reason to plot against him. The second solution founders on the use of the words *lō'-tō'bad*, "shall not perish".

The verb *'ābad* (qal), when applied to abstract human qualities or characteristics, denotes cessation or extinction[61]; when followed by *min-*, "from", it specifies the person(s) affected[62]. It is in this sense that Jeremiah asks ironically about the Edomites, "Has counsel perished (*'ābᵉdā*) from the men of understanding?" (49 7)[63], and that Ezekiel, in terms similar to those of the passage under consideration, asserts that "law will perish (*tō'bad*) from priest and counsel from elders" (7 26). The use of the impf. in Jer 18 18 (as also in Ez 7 26) may be regarded as indicating futurity, or, more probably, an action which is regarded as possible or desirable[64]. The use of the negative *lō'* brings the phrase under the heading of negative sentences which "express actions, etc., which cannot or should not happen"[65]. The triple statement is therefore either an assertion that these three groups of person will continue their characteristic activities in the future, or, more probably (the difference is a small one), that the cessation of their activities in the future is undesirable or unthinkable. It is not a statement about the power of these groups in the present situation, or about their reliability as allies against Jeremiah, and therefore cannot be taken to be a motive clause encouraging the proposed action against him on such grounds.

The third type of solution, commended by Rudolph as the most probable, supposes that the triple statement is a specific condemnation of Jeremiah's own teaching: he had prophesied that these three activities would shortly cease; his opponents express their confidence that they will not, or their determination that they shall not, and it is this determination which provides the motive for their action against him. They take the prophetic word of Jeremiah, or at least

[61] E.g. of vigour (Job 30 2), counsel (Dtn 32 28), vision (Ez 12 22), courage (Jer 4 9), hope (Ps 9 19 Prov 10 28 11 7 Ez 19 5 37 11 Job 8 13 Thr 3 18), desire (Ps 112 10).

[62] E.g. Jer 49 7 Ez 7 26.

[63] There is general agreement among the commentators that this is the meaning. Whether *bānīm* is to be understood as the ptc. (elsewhere unattested) of *bīn* rather than as the pl. of *bēn*, "son", or whether it should be emended to *mᵉbīnīm*, *nᵉbōnīm* or the like is a problem which is immaterial for the present purpose.

[64] S. R. Driver, A Treatise on the Uses of the Tenses in Hebrew, 1892, § 37.

[65] G.-K. § 107w.

his influence as a prophet, seriously, and resolve to put him out of the way to prevent what he had prophesied from coming to pass.

It is true that Jeremiah had on other occasions announced that these three types of person, priests, prophets and "wise men", would suffer frustration or disaster, although nowhere else in his recorded prophecies are all three mentioned together. In 4 9 priests and prophets are associated with the king and the "princes" (*haśśārīm*): "on that day, says Yahweh, courage shall fail (*yōʾbad lēb*) the king and the princes; the priests shall be appalled (*nāšammū*) and the prophets dumbfounded (*yitmāhū*)." The picture is one of a breakdown of the nerve and efficacity of these persons in the face of disaster "in that day"; and it is reasonable to suppose that these persons and groups are mentioned because it is they who are the leaders and authorities on whom the nation depends. If they fail, the nation is lost. Here we observe that prophets and priests are mentioned together with other classes, but that there is no mention of "wise men".

In 8 9, where "wise men have been (or "will be")[66] put to shame (*hōbīšū*), dismayed (*ḥattū*) and taken (*wayyillākēdū*)", it has already been argued that these "wise men", who are not here directly associated in their condemnation with any other group, are not to be regarded as a distinct professional class[67].

A passage from Ezekiel has also been cited in this connection[68]: "And you shall seek a vision from a prophet and teaching (*tōrā*) from a priest and counsel (*ʿēṣā*) from elders (*zeqēnīm*)" (Ez 7 26). The passage goes on to refer (v. 27) to other persons and groups: "The king shall mourn and (the) prince (*nāśīʾ*) shall be clothed in horror, and the hands of the people of the land will tremble with terror[69]." Although here it is elders rather than wise men who are associated with counsel, this passage has been held to be relevant to the discussion on the supposition that between the time of Jeremiah and that of Ezekiel the class of wise men as political advisers had given way to that of the elders[70]. There is, however, no other evidence to

---

[66] The pf. verbs could have a past reference, or they could be so-called "prophetic perfects" with a future reference. The context, in which these men *are saying* (*tōʾmerū*, v. 8), that they are wise, implies that their evil fate lies in the future.

[67] See p. 22—24 above. Weiser also cites 14 13ff. 23 9ff., in which the prophets are attacked (with a single reference to priests in 23 11) in this connection. In neither of these passages is there a reference to all three groups.

[68] By Fichtner art. cit. 20f. and Rudolph 114, among others.

[69] On the textual problems see W. Zimmerli, Ezechiel I, BK 13/1, 1969, 165. There may have been some expansion.

[70] Fichtner, Jesaja unter den Weisen, 21. Zimmerli op. cit. 184 admits this possibility, but he regards the triple statement here as a later addition to Ezekiel's prophecy adapted from Jer 18 18.

confirm this theory, and this passage, far from supporting the view that there was a distinct professional class of wise men, is capable of being used in precisely the opposite sense: as suggesting either that the terminology was fluid and imprecise, or that there was no commonly accepted belief that any three classes in particular constituted the pillars of the state.

The third interpretation referred to by Rudolph is more satisfactory than the others in that Jeremiah had on various occasions attacked and prophesied the collapse of priests, prophets and "wise men", and this might well have been the motive for making plots against him. Nevertheless a number of considerations suggest that this interpretation also does not do full justice to the evidence. The chief of these concerns the *form* of the statement.

Its style contrasts sharply with the ordinary prose style of its context. The fact that the article is not attached to any of the six singular nouns which appear in it suggests that it is poetical in character; and this impression is confirmed by its balanced, rhythmical form. If this is so, it is probable that it is a quotation, introduced by the particle *kī*, a quotation which serves the purpose of supporting in some way the resolve of the speakers to plot against Jeremiah[71]. Viewed apart from its present context it strongly resembles the literary type of the "numerical proverb" represented in the Old Testament by a number of examples in Prov 30[72]. It lacks, however, the title-line, which states the number of things to be compared. It is possible that the speakers, in order to introduce it neatly into their speech, have abbreviated a numerical saying of which the full form began with a phrase such as "Three things shall never perish ..." or "Two things shall never perish, and three shall not be overthrown ..."[73]. But such an hypothesis is unnecessary. There are examples outside the Old Testament of numerical sayings[74] which

[71] It might be argued that it is a quotation from a poetical oracle of Jeremiah himself, negated by the addition of *lō'*, "not". But, as has already been pointed out, there is no evidence that Jeremiah had in fact spoken these words or that he associated these groups in a single condemnation.

[72] 30 7f. 11-14. 15b-16. 18-19. 21-23. 24-28. 29-31.

[73] On the numerical saying see W. M. W. Roth, Numerical Sayings in the Old Testament, VT Suppl XIII, 1965; G. Sauer, Die Sprüche Agurs, 1963. Roth's comment on such sayings that "when they occur in poetry, they tend to be more evenly built than their counterparts in prose" (7) is perhaps significant here.

[74] E.g. Ahiqar, line 83: "A blow for a slave, rebuke for a maid; and for all thy servants discipline"; line 104: "Why should wood strive with fire, flesh with a knife, a man with a king?" (A. Cowley, Aramaic Papyri of the Fifth Century B.C., 1923, 214f. 222f.). That this form is not peculiar to Ahiqar but that both forms were generally current is strongly suggested by the fact that Ahiqar also knew the longer form: "Two things ... and of three ..." (line 92; op. cit. 215. 223).

have no title-line and do not specifically refer to the number of things to be compared[75].

It would seem probable, therefore, that the threefold statement in Jer 18 18 was a saying sufficiently well-known to be quoted in support of an argument. Now it is a characteristic of such sayings that they bring together a number of objects, persons, situations or the like which have common characteristics: for example, things which are insatiable (Prov 30 15f.), incomprehensible (Prov 30 18f.), intolerable (Prov 30 21-23), small yet wise (Prov 30 24-28), stately in their stride (Prov 30 29-31). In most cases, though not invariably, the common characteristic is specifically referred to. This is so in Jer 18 18, where the common characteristic is stated in the phrase *lō'-tō'bad*: "will never cease". The activities concerned are all activities which, to all appearances, are likely to go on for ever, and their cessation is unthinkable. With the negative, we have a list of "unthinkable things" comparable with the lists of incomprehensible, intolerable and insatiable things in Prov 30.

In what sense these things are unthinkable can only be understood on the basis of the application which is given to the saying in the context[76]. The clue is to be found in the words which follow it, words to which insufficient attention has hitherto been given: "Come, let us smite him with the tongue, and let us not heed any of his words[77]." The conspirators are here encouraging one another to take the dangerous step of attacking one who claims to be a prophet whose words are the words of Yahweh, charged with power to "destroy and to overthrow" as well as to "build and to plant"[78]. To plot against Jeremiah was dangerous, since it was probable that, when the conspiracy became known to him, he would turn against them with words which might destroy them. This contemporary belief is illustrated by the account of Jeremiah's word spoken against his adversary Hananiah, with its fatal consequences[79]. Against such retaliation their own words (*lāšōn*) with which they propose to secure his elimination would be useless.

The meaning of the passage turns, then, on the question of words and their power. No less than five different kinds of "word" are

---

[75] Prov 30 11-14 has been regarded by some scholars as an example of this type of saying, but it is not certain whether it is an originally numerical saying, or whether its elements have been combined at a later stage. See, among other treatments of this passage, W. McKane, Proverbs, OTL, 1970, 650f.

[76] It is possible that, like many other sayings in the "wisdom" literature, it is, perhaps deliberately, open to more than one interpretation. But our only concern here is with the interpretation given to it by Jeremiah's opponents.

[77] On the text see p. 24 n. 56 above.

[78] 1 10. [79] 28 16f.

referred to in this verse: the "law" of the priest, the "word" of the prophet, the "counsel" of the "wise man", the specific words of Jeremiah and the accusing words of his opponents. If Jeremiah was a true prophet, these last were embarking on a dangerous course. But they comfort themselves by quoting a saying which expresses contempt for the words of "prophets". The link between the three kinds of person referred to in the saying is that they never stop talking. Priests are constantly uttering "torah"; it would be unthinkable that they should ever cease to do so. Similarly "clever men" are always giving advice; and prophets likewise pour out a continuous spate of words.

It may be significant that in this saying the characteristic activity of the prophet is referred to simply by the word *dābār,* without any qualification. The prophetic word was no ordinary word, since it was in fact not the prophet's own word but the word of Yahweh spoken through him. Consequently it is not normally referred to simply as "word" in the Old Testament except in contexts which make it plain that this is understood to be so. In a "wisdom saying", which has no literary context, "word" by itself, without the qualification "of Yahweh", suggests that the prophet's word is a mere human word, of no more consequence than the word of any other man. It is contemptuous, having somewhat the same implication as the phrase *'īš śᵉpātayim,* the "mere talker", in Job 11 2. The same note of contempt is echoed in the phrase with which the conspirators end their speech: "let us not heed any of his words (*kol-dᵉbārāw*)".

It is not possible to be sure at what period this saying originated; but its contemptuous attitude suggests that it may have been coined not long before it was quoted in this passage. As the book of Jeremiah abundantly testifies[80], this was a period when a mass of prophets, Jeremiah included, constantly presented to the people the unedifying spectacle of bitter and ruthless strife among themselves, taking the form of denunciations of one another as false prophets who claimed to speak in the name of Yahweh but were really liars and deceivers. It is not surprising that in consequence the people were left not merely confused about the identity of the true prophets, but also sceptical and disillusioned about the prophetic office itself. The conspirators in Jer 18 18 reflect this attitude of contempt, and quote the saying to persuade themselves that they have nothing to fear from Jeremiah's words.

This interpretation also fits the references to the priests and the "wise men". While it is not possible to give a precise date to this verse, nor to the saying which is incorporated into it, it is probable that the

---

[80] Especially 6 13-15 8 10-12 14 13-16 23 9-40 26 27 8-17 28 29 8f. 24-32.

plot against Jeremiah took place during the reign of Jehoiakim[81]. This turbulent and disastrous period was one in which there was confusion in Judah in matters both religious and political. There was evidently no shortage of *tōrā* from the priests: some of them, like some of the prophets, encouraged false hopes, and so, when disaster followed disaster, brought their office into disrepute[82]. It is equally probable that there was no shortage of self-styled "wise men" to offer their advice about what should be done. The saying expresses a general sense of disillusionment with all those who, whether in the name of Yahweh or out of their self-professed "wisdom", had offered, and continued to offer, their confident "solutions" to the critical problems of the day.

If this is the true interpretation of Jer 18 18, the triple saying is not, as is generally believed, a reference to three professional classes who form the mainstay of the Judaean state. It is simply a contemptuous reference to three kinds of people whose common characteristic is that they are for ever talking, but whose talk is valueless. They are *'anᵉšē śᵉpātayim*.

3. Conclusions

All those passages which might seem to offer proof of the use of *ḥākām* as the designation of a professional class of royal counsellors and politicians have now been reviewed. In each case it has been shown that this sense is improbable, if not impossible. The frequent use of this adjective as an *attribute* of such men seems to be confined to Isaiah; it testifies to the fact that in his day the politicians thought of themselves as possessing superior intelligence, a claim which Isaiah rebuked in emphatic terms as bordering on blasphemy. The relative frequency with which the word occurs in political contexts in Isaiah has misled earlier scholars into concluding that it had a technical meaning; but this theory would be tenable only if it occurred with this meaning in at least one administrative text or historical narrative. Such is not the case. The prose texts show clearly that the proper term for the class in question was *śārīm*[83].

B. The "Wise Man" as Teacher

In order to assess the validity of the hypothesis that the word *ḥākām* is used in the Old Testament as the technical appellation of

[81] This is the consensus of the commentaries.

[82] See Jer 5 31 6 13-15 8 10-12.

[83] See p. 17 and n. 31 above.

a professional class of teachers, it is first necessary to discuss the character and methods of ancient Israelite education[84].

1. General Considerations

It is agreed by all authorities that education in the most general sense was the responsibility of the father, who inculcated in his own children not only the basic knowledge required for daily living and the pursuit of the hereditary occupation of the family, but also social, moral and religious principles[85]. The mother also had her part in the education of her children, sons as well as daughters[86].

In addition, two classes of men are frequently represented as teaching the people: the prophets and the priests. Whether these gave instruction specifically to children is uncertain[87].

General education of this kind must in certain cases have been supplemented by a more specialized instruction. This applies particularly, though not solely, to the arts of reading and writing. While the comparative simplicity of the alphabetic script in use in Palestine, in contrast with the systems of writing employed in Egypt and Mesopotamia, may have enabled a relatively large proportion of the population to read and write a few simple words, it is unlikely that more than a few were fully literate in the sense of an ability to derive information and enjoyment from reading books[88]. That there was a distinction between the "educated" and "uneducated" classes in Israel at this time can hardly be disputed. The areas of dispute are the extent and identity of the educated classes and the educational methods employed.

---

[84] On this see especially A. Klostermann, Schulwesen im Alten Israel, in: Th. Zahn-Festschrift, 1908, 193—232; L. Dürr, Das Erziehungswesen im Alten Testament und im Alten Orient, 1932; Hermisson op. cit. 113—136; de Vaux op. cit. I 82—85.

[85] For religious instruction given by the father see Gen 18 19 Ex 12 24ff. 13 8ff. Dtn 4 9ff. 6 7ff. 20ff. 32 7. 46.

[86] Prov 1 8 6 20 31 1. 26.

[87] The child Samuel was left in charge of the priests at Shiloh not simply to be educated but to become a professional resident member of the temple staff: he was "given to Yahweh all the days of his life" (I Sam 1 11). The priest Jehoiada "instructed" (*hōrāhū*) king Jehoash (II Reg 12 3), but this instruction may not have been confined to his childhood; moreover this is a special case, sufficiently remarkable to be singled out for mention.

[88] The Old Testament evidence on the diffusion of literacy is complex and difficult to assess. For different views see Klostermann op. cit. 201; Dürr op. cit. 107; G. R. Driver, Semitic Writing, 1954², 88f.; de Vaux op. cit. 82; Hermisson op. cit. 98—103.

2. Schools in Israel?

There is, as is generally agreed, no direct, unequivocal evidence in the Old Testament of the existence of a regularly organized system of education[89]. The word "school" (*bēt-midrāš*) occurs for the first time in the literature of the second century B. C. (Sir 51 23).

This silence has suggested to some writers[90] that education was of a private character, provided, for a fee, by a class of teachers known as *ḥᵃkāmīm*, either as private tutors in the houses of the rich, or as itinerant teachers who taught in the open air. The texts cited in defence of this theory are, however, hardly sufficient to constitute proof.

There is some slight evidence that in some cases tutors were appointed for the sons of kings[91]; but the reference in I Reg 12 8 to the young men who had "grown up" with Rehoboam is hardly sufficient to demonstrate that this education was also available to others[92]. Moreover, none of these supposed tutors is referred to as a *ḥākām*.

With regard to the theory of itinerant open-air teachers, the two passages which have been cited as proof are Prov 1 20ff. 8 1ff., where a personified Wisdom takes her stand in the streets and squares and other prominent parts of the city and offers instruction to the passers-by. The style and contents of her message, particularly in the second of these passages, closely parallel those of the teacher who in other parts of Prov 1—9 addresses his "son"[93], and to this extent the activities of Wisdom here are modelled on those of the human teacher; but it does not follow that the references to the places where the instruction is given are to be taken literally and accepted as evidence that there were wisdom teachers who taught or advertised their services in the streets.

The imagery of Wisdom's public offer of her wares can be explained in other ways. It may be the intention of the author to

---

89 E.g. Dürr 110; de Vaux 84f.; Hermisson 113.

90 Klostermann 204—206; P. Humbert, Weisheit, RGG V, 1931², 1802; de Vaux 84.

91 The priest Jehoiada instructed Jehoash (II Reg 12 3). The other passages cited are by no means as clear. The emendation of II Sam 12 25 to yield the meaning that the prophet Nathan was Solomon's tutor is not, despite the authority of Wellhausen, Budde and Nowack, necessarily correct (see W. Hertzberg, Die Samuelbücher, ATD 10, 1956, 255 [ET I and II Samuel, OTL, 1964, 317]). The function of the "guardians" (*'ōmᵉnīm*) of Ahab's sons (II Reg 10 1. 6) is not clear; it is certainly possible that they were, or included, tutors. The same may be said of the statement in I Chr 27 32 that David's uncle Jonathan, described as a *yōʿēṣ 'īš-mēbīn*, and other notables were "with the king's sons".

92 So Hermisson 118.

93 1 8. 10. 15 2 1 3 1. 11. 21 4 1 (pl.). 10. 20 5 1. 7 (pl.). 20 6 1. 3. 20 7 1. 24 (pl.).

suggest the easy attainability of wisdom, and its superiority over other commodities, by "lining her up" beside the other "merchants" with their stalls[94]; and there is also clearly an intentional contrast with the other "woman", the prostitute or adulteress, who offers her wares in the street[95]. The same intention is observable in Prov 9 1-6, where Wisdom invites the "simple" to her house, in a fashion similar to that of the "foolish woman" of v. 13-18. In all these cases the allusiveness of the imagery makes it hazardous to assume that "wisdom" here is a cipher for "wise man", and to draw specific conclusions about the activities of the latter[96].

Prov 17 16, "Why should a fool have a price in his hand to buy wisdom[97], though he has no sense?", has been similarly over-interpreted. It has been supposed by a number of commentators[98] that this refers to a custom of paying fees to *ḥᵃkāmīm*, that is, to professional wisdom teachers. The point of the saying is that the fee does not compensate for the pupil's lack of ability. While this is a possible interpretation, the compressed form of the saying makes it almost impossible, as with many of the sayings in Proverbs, to be certain of the exact nuance which the author has tried to convey. It would be possible to take the second half of the saying as a separate sentence: "Is it to buy wisdom, although he has no sense?". It is also possible that there is a play on two of the meanings of *qānā:* "acquire", and "buy". The second meaning is suggested by the word *mᵉḥīr*, "price", in the first half of the saying; but elsewhere in Proverbs the verb *qānā* is used with *ḥokmā* as its object in contexts where "buy" is clearly not the meaning[99]. Here the fool is ridiculed for thinking that wisdom, which he has been recommended to acquire, is a commodity to be bought in the market like anything else, and so for coming with money in his hand to purchase it. In view of the

---

94 Note the comparisons with commercial activity in 8 8. 10. 11. 19.

95 7 6-12 9 13-16.

96 Cf. Hermisson 122.

97 Cf. also the phrase *qᵉnē ḥokmā*, "buy wisdom", or "acquire wisdom", in 4 5.

98 Klostermann 206; R. B. Y. Scott, Proverbs and Ecclesiastes, AB 18, 1965, 111. C. H. Toy, Proverbs, ICC, 1899, 346, and B. Gemser, Sprüche Salomos, 73, consider that the meaning is metaphorical. McKane, Proverbs, 504f., appears to incline towards the literal interpretation.

99 4 5. 7 are addressed to those who are already "sons" sitting at the feet of their teacher. Even if he is a professional schoolmaster, it is unlikely that he is at this point appealing to them to pay their fees! Also in 16 16, where the acquisition of wisdom is said to be preferable to (the acquisition of) gold, "buy" would be an inappropriate translation. The saying does not suggest that gold should be used to pay for wisdom, but rather that while wealth is good, wisdom is even better. In 18 15, where it is *daʿat*, virtually synonymous with *ḥokmā*, which is the object of *qānā*, the verb is parallel with *biqqēš*, "seek". In 15 32 23 23 the text is uncertain.

uncertainty about the interpretation of this verse it cannot be regarded as offering proof of the existence of a class of professional "wise men" who gave lessons for a fee.

It should also be observed that in none of the passages considered above does the word *ḥākām* occur. In each case the argument for a class of *ḥ^akāmīm* is purely inferential.

Nevertheless, although the case for a class of freelance teachers in business for themselves is as fragile as that for a class of professional private teachers, there is a wide measure of support for the view that for certain specialized and restricted groups in Israel there were institutions for which the only possible English equivalent is "schools"[100]. That is to say, there existed for the purpose of giving specialized training regularly organized classes comprising a number of pupils, whose teachers were "professional" in the sense that they were not the parents, or relations, or even tribal heads, of the pupils, and that their teaching was given on a regular basis and occupied a substantial part, though not necessarily the whole, of their time.

Four main types of argument have been adduced to support this theory.

a) *Arguments from the existence of Hebrew literature.* The Old Testament for the most part provides little direct evidence concerning the circles in which its various types of literature originated, or the identity of the readership for which they were intended. Nevertheless it is clear that already in the pre-exilic period at least four bodies of literature (including "oral literature") were already beginning to take shape: the priestly (especially laws and psalms), the prophetic, the historical, and the "wisdom" literatures. It is argued that, whatever may have been the degree of literacy existing in Israel at that time, the skill and culture needed for the composition of such literature presupposed a degree of education such as parental instruction could not have provided. It has therefore been proposed that at one or more of the following centres of intellectual activity "schools" must have existed: the court, the temple, and the prophetical group of disciples[101].

[100] E.g. R. Kittel, Geschichte des Volkes Israel II—III, 1929, 717—720; P. Humbert, Recherches sur les sources égyptiennes de la littérature sapientiale d'Israël, 1929, 181ff.; Dürr op. cit. 107ff.; Baumgartner op. cit. 269f.; Östborn op. cit. 113; A. Bentzen, Introduction to the Old Testament, I 1948, 171f.; K. Galling, Die Krise der Aufklärung in Israel, 1952, 5—10; Fohrer, Weisheit, 250; Mowinckel, Psalms and Wisdom, 206f.; Gemser op. cit. 2f.; W. Richter, Recht und Ethos, 1966, 189. 191f.; Hermisson op. cit. 113. 122. 129.

[101] With regard to the court as an intellectual centre, this argument has assumed its classical expression in the theory of a "Solomonic enlightenment": see, for example, Galling op. cit.

b) *Arguments from foreign analogies.* The existence of schools and of a scholastic system in the surrounding states of Egypt, Babylonia, and the Hittite Empire from a period anterior to the emergence of Israel is well documented[102], and there may well have been scribal schools in some of the cities of Canaan, although the evidence here is indirect[103]. It is argued that these schools were an indispensible feature of government organization in the comity of nations to which Israel belonged from the time of David and Solomon onwards, and that it can be presumed that these kings, who to a large extent modelled their administration and court style on those of their imperial neighbours, will not have failed to establish at least one, in Jerusalem[104].

c) *Arguments from the complexity of royal administration.* Although the alphabetic script which was exclusively used within Palestine in Israelite times was much simpler to learn than the scripts of Egypt and Babylonia, it has been argued[105] that among the officials and administrators at the Judaean court there must have been men capable of carrying on an international diplomatic correspondence requiring competence in Egyptian, Accadian and other languages; and that in other ways also the complexity of the tasks imposed upon these officials by the relative sophistication of the government machine necessitated a specialized training such as was given to scribes in the neighbouring countries.

d) *Arguments from the similarities between Old Testament and foreign wisdom literature.* Since the pioneering work of Erman and Humbert[106] on the literary affinities of Egyptian and Israelite wisdom literature, a generation of research has proved beyond doubt that the

---

[102] On Egyptian education see E. Otto, Bildung und Ausbildung im Alten Ägypten, ZÄS 81 (1956), 41—48; H. Brunner, Altägyptische Erziehung, 1957; on education in Mesopotamia, G. R. Driver, Semitic Writing, 62—73; J. J. A. van Dijk, La sagesse suméro-accadienne, 1953, 21—27; A. Falkenstein, Die babylonische Schule, Saec 4 (1953), 125—137.

[103] The city-name Kiriath-sepher or Kiriath-sopher (Jos 15 15) may point to the existence of a scribal class in Canaan (Gemser op. cit. 2), but not necessarily to the existence of a school (see Hermisson 116 n. 2). It seems clear from the discovery of practice-tablets found in the library attached to the temple of Baal at Ugarit that there was a scribal school there (C. F. A. Schaeffer, The Cuneiform Texts of Ras Shamra-Ugarit, 1939, 35ff.; cf. Bentzen op. cit. 171; Hermisson), but this does not prove that such was the case in the Canaanite cities with which Israel came into contact.

[104] On the evidence for such imitation, and for the employment of foreign scribes at the Judaean court, see R. de Vaux, Titres et fonctionnaires égyptiens à la cour de David et de Salomon, RB 48 (1939), 394—405; J. Begrich, Sōfēr und Mazkīr, ZAW 58 (1940), 1—29.

[105] E.g. by S. Morenz in: HO I/2, 194—206.

[106] A. Erman, Eine ägyptische Quelle der Sprüche Salomos, SPAW, 1924; Humbert, Recherches.

latter is an integral part of a widespread international tradition, and that the Israelite authors were at least in part familiar with foreign, especially Egyptian, wisdom books[107]. Since many of these books were evidently composed for use as textbooks in schools, it has been argued that this is also true of their Israelite counterparts, especially of Prov 1—9, where the form as well as the contents appear to portray the same scholastic situation[108].

These arguments are almost entirely inferential. There is no clear direct reference to a school in the Old Testament. Isa 28 9f. has frequently been taken to refer to the teaching of the alphabet to small children[109], but this interpretation is open to doubt[110]. In Isa 50 4 the prophet compares his attitude of attention to Yahweh's teaching to that of pupils (*limmūdīm*) daily paying attention to their master. *limmūdīm* is usually taken to refer to pupils in a school; but in view of the fact that on the only other occasion in the Old Testament (Isa 8 16) where the word is clearly used as a noun, it refers to the disciples of a prophet rather than to pupils in a school, it would be unwise to restrict its meaning in this way. The disciples of a prophet were certainly not schoolboys; and it is more probable that in Isa 50 4 Deutero-Isaiah was thinking of a disciple's relationship to his master than to an educational institution in the usual sense of the word[110a].

The reference to the *mēbīn* and *talmīd*, "master" and "pupil", in the description of David's arrangements for the music in the temple which Solomon was to build (I Chr 25 8) has been held[111] to imply the existence of a school there; but here again the evidence is hardly convincing. It implies no more than the obvious fact that there must have been musical instruction in order to preserve a continuity of skilled musicians; but such instruction may well have been private and comparable to the normal instruction in the hereditary craft of the family given by fathers to their sons. There is no suggestion here of any more general education; and it is also to be observed that any

---

107 Among the recent literature on this subject see G. von Rad, Hiob xxxviii und die altägyptische Weisheit, VT Suppl III, 293—301 = Gesammelte Studien, 1958, 262—271 (ET The Problem of the Hexateuch, 1966, 281—291); S. Morenz, Ägyptische Beiträge zur Erforschung der Weisheitsliteratur Israels in: Les Sagesses du Proche-Orient Ancien, 1963, 63—71; R. N. Whybray, Wisdom in Proverbs; C. Kayatz, Studien zu Proverbien 1—9, 1966.

108 See especially Whybray, Wisdom in Proverbs.

109 E.g. by Klostermann 214ff.; Driver, Semitic Writing, 89f.

110 Hermisson 119; G. R. Driver, Another Little Drink — Isaiah 28:1—22 in: D. W. Thomas-Festschrift, 1968, 53f. — reversing his earlier opinion.

110a NEB translates *limmūdīm* by "teaching".

111 E.g. by H. L. Jansen, Die spätjüdische Psalmendichtung, SNVAO 3, 1937, 38.

historical information which may have been preserved here probably refers, in view of the Chronicler's general performance as an "historian", not to the state of affairs in the pre-exilic Temple but to that of the second Temple in the author's own time towards the end of the Old Testament period.

The first three of the above arguments for the existence of schools in Israel would certainly not, by themselves, be sufficient to prove the case. The most that they prove is that during the period of the monarchy Israel had a scribal class like other nations, and that, as in Egypt and Mesopotamia, there were enough people of relatively high cultural attainment in Israel to produce and appreciate literary works of high artistic merit. Both these facts are sufficiently obvious.

It is, however, questionable to what extent it is legitimate to compare the state of affairs in Israel, even during the comparatively short period of the united monarchy, when the fortunes of the nation were at their height, with that of the Egyptian and Mesopotamian empires, or even of those individual city-states of the latter about which we have information. The population of Jerusalem was never large[112], and the amount of business to be done smaller than some recent writers appear to imagine. A relatively small number of families of scribes exercising a hereditary profession would probably have sufficed to transact the business, both public and private, of the entire nation. There is evidence that in Israel, as elsewhere, the scribal profession was hereditary[113]; and it is possible that the scribal techniques, together with other branches of knowledge familiar to educated men, may have been handed down from father to son[114]

---

[112] It is difficult to assess the population of ancient cities, even when thorough archaeological investigation has been possible, which is not the case with Jerusalem. However, Kathleen M. Kenyon, the most recent excavator, states that the Jebusite city covered only some 10.87 acres and that David did not extend it, and opines that during Solomon's reign "only the official parts of Jerusalem were changed, and that the rest continued much as before" (K. M. Kenyon, Jerusalem: Excavating 3000 Years of History, 1967, 30. 50. 62).

[113] That the Shisha who was the father of the scribes Elihoreph and Ahijah, who served under Solomon (I Reg 4 3) is to be identified with the Sheva or Sheya (II Sam 20 25; Shavsha in I Chr 18 16) who filled the same office under David is generally accepted: see the commentaries. The references to Shaphan, who was scribe during the lifetime of Jeremiah, and his family (II Reg 22 2-14 Jer 26 24 29 3 36 11-15) show that this was a family of hereditary scribes. These are examples of men who were at the head of their profession and occupied important positions in the government; but the "families of scribes who lived in Japez" of I Chr 2 55 were presumably examples of more humble hereditary scribal families.

[114] Or possibly by senior officials to new recruits in the profession. H. L. Jansen op. cit. 56 points out that even in Egypt after the introduction of a school system much of the instruction of officials was done under an apprentice system.

without recourse to schools or other professional teachers, as is recorded of the scribe Ahiqar, who himself taught his nephew Nadin, whom he had adopted as his son, "wisdom" and "counsel" to enable him to succeed him as "counsellor of all Assyria" in the service of Esarhaddon[115].

Apart from the theory of "schools for officials" or "scribal schools" attached directly to the court[116], it has been suggested by some writers, in view of the fact that both in Egypt and Mesopotamia at various times schools appear to have been connected with temples, that there was a school attached to the Temple at Jerusalem. This has been envisaged by some as having been not simply a school for priests or for specialized temple scribes, but the central seat of learning which provided scribes for the use of the state as well as for the Temple and other purposes, and the source of various types of Old Testament literature[117]; by others, on the other hand, as only one type of school among others[118]. Some scholars have gone further and postulated a wide variety of types of school: Hermisson[119] speaks of schools for court officials, for the Temple and for scribes of lesser importance; von Rad[120] adds the possibility of Levitical schools distinct from those for priests and temple scribes, and even of specialized schools for the children of various types of craftsman.

The arguments for the existence of a variety of schools in pre-exilic Israel are based mainly on the variety of kinds of literature in the Old Testament, while those for a single school are based on the view that too sharp a distinction should not be drawn between these. The latter argument is drawn once again from the analogy of non-Israelite schools, in which more than one type of literature appears to have been produced[121]. In other words, in the virtually total absence of tangible evidence, each writer has drawn inferences from his own view of the character of Old Testament literature and literary tradition, together with certain assumptions about the structure of Isra-

---

115 Ahiqar, lines 17—21 (Cowley op. cit. 212. 220). Cf. Driver, Semitic Writing, 89.

116 As proposed by, among others, Baumgartner 269f.; H. Cazelles, A propos d'une phrase de H. H. Rowley, 29f.

117 Östborn 113. 123; Jansen op. cit. 57—63. 100; Mowinckel, Psalms and Wisdom, 207; A. H. J. Gunneweg, Mündliche und schriftliche Tradition der vorexilischen Prophetenbücher, 1959, 78—80. 119—121; McKane, Prophets and Wise Men, 36—38; J. Muilenburg, Baruch the Scribe, in: G. Henton Davies-Festschrift, 1970, 227—230.

118 E.g. Bentzen op. cit. 171f.

119 Op. cit. 98—103. 113—122. 129—131.

120 Weisheit in Israel 31f.

121 So, e.g., Östborn, Muilenburg.

elite society and the degree of foreign influence on Israelite institutions.

The fourth of the arguments outlined above, namely that based on the similarity of some parts of Proverbs both in contents and form to texts from Egypt and elsewhere which are known to have been written as school textbooks, is by far the strongest. That Prov 22 17ff. is directly influenced by the Egyptian Instruction of Amen-em-opet is universally admitted[122], and there is reason to believe that the earliest strand in Prov 1—9 consisted of short Instructions whose form, and to some extent whose content, are based on Egyptian models[123]. The fact that many resemblances exist between sayings in other parts of Proverbs and Egyptian and Mesopotamian wisdom literature in style, subject and basic point of view[124] greatly strengthens the argument for a direct knowledge of such works on the part of Israelite authors, though in some cases there may have been some mediation through the now almost totally lost Canaanite wisdom literature[125]. In the case of Job and Ecclesiastes direct literary influence is less certain[126].

The question is therefore whether the direct knowledge of non-Israelite "school-literature" which some Israelite scribes certainly possessed necessarily implies the existence of similar schools, with professional teachers, in Israel, or whether the more prominent families of scribes, who certainly had international contacts, could have acquired such knowledge, adapted it for domestic use, and handed it on in the form of characteristically Israelite Instructions and collections of proverbs within a purely family system of education[127]. It

---

[122] The theory was first proposed by Erman. Occasional attempts to prove that the Egyptian work is dependent on a Hebrew source (e.g. E. Drioton, Sur la sagesse d'Aménémopé, in: A. Robert-Festschrift, 1957, 254—280) have not been generally accepted. [123] See especially Whybray, Wisdom in Proverbs.

[124] On Egyptian parallels see especially Humbert, Recherches; on connections with Mesopotamian literature see, inter alia, Cazelles, Débuts.

[125] See W. F. Albright, Some Canaanite-Phoenician Sources of Hebrew Wisdom, VT Suppl III, 1955, 1—15; Cazelles, Débuts.

[126] See, e.g., J. Gray, The Book of Job in the Context of Near Eastern Literature, ZAW 82 (1970), 251—269; O. Loretz, Qohelet und der Alte Orient, 1964.

[127] The question whether the themes treated in Proverbs as a whole point to school education has been very widely discussed. Hermisson 122—125 and G. von Rad, Weisheit in Israel, 1970, 35, consider that the collections in Proverbs were used in schools but not necessarily written for this purpose: their interest is wider than that of the classroom. The views of Gerstenberger, Wesen und Herkunft des apodiktischen Rechts, and others on the origin of much of the "wisdom" material in a "Sippenethos" does not really affect the question, though Gerstenberger's theory (130. 141) that the schools were late institutions which merely gathered together material which had already been largely formed in the non-professional

is improbable that this question will ever be answered with certainty, in view of the absence of direct references to schools in Israel.

One feature of the instruction given in Proverbs, however, makes it unwise to assume that such literature was written for or used in schools. This is the number of references which are made to teaching given by the *mother*. Although it is generally agreed by the commentators that these references cannot be interpreted otherwise than in a literal sense, their significance for our understanding of education in Israel has not been fully appreciated.

The references are four: Prov 1 8 6 20 31 1. 26. In 1 8 and again in 6 20, verses which form part of introductory sections to formal Instructions, the pupil is urged, in sentences which stand in poetical parallelism, to pay attention to his father's instruction (*mūsār*) or command (*miṣwā*) and not to reject or forsake his mother's teaching (*tōrā*). 31 1 is the superscription to the Instruction which follows (31 2-9) and describes it as "the words of Lemuel king of Massa, which his mother taught him". In 31 26, which is part of the poem (31 10-31) praising the virtues of the "capable wife" (*'ēšet-ḥayil*), it is said of her that "she opens her mouth with wisdom (*b^eḥokmā*), and the teaching of kindness[128] (*tōrat-ḥesed*) is on her lips".

These references to the mother as the teacher of her children are unique in ancient Near Eastern literature[129]. It is clear that what is referred to here is not simply the early training of small children, for which of course the mother was mainly responsible, at least in the early stages. While the teaching of the "capable woman" in 31 26 is not specifically stated to be teaching given to the children, and might be interpreted as referring to the instruction given to servants, 31 1-9, which in other respects resembles the "royal instructions" of Egypt and Mesopotamia[130], is the only work of its kind attributed to a woman. The fact that it is of non-Israelite origin and yet neither Egyptian nor Mesopotamian, but from one of the smaller states of the ancient Near East[131], may in itself be significant, as showing that

context of the clan assigns to the school such a secondary role in the formation of Proverbs that, if correct, it greatly weakens the argument that the very existence of such collections presupposed a school system. The same may be said of Richter's Recht und Ethos.

[128] Or "loyalty" (so NEB).

[129] So Duesberg and Fransen 231f. and a number of commentaries.

[130] The Egyptian Instruction for King Meri-ka-re (A. Erman, The Literature of the Ancient Egyptians, 1927, 75—84; ANET 414—418) and the Instruction of King Amen-em-het (Erman 72—74; ANET 418f.); the Babylonian or Assyrian Advice to a Prince (Lambert, Babylonian Wisdom Literature, 110—115).

[131] Massa was probably, though not certainly, a kingdom in N. Arabia: see the commentaries. That the Israelites were aware of the "wisdom" of other and smaller

Israel was familiar with the cultures of peoples whose way of life was simpler than that of the peoples of the great empires, and that it may be misleading to regard the latter as providing the best parallels in the sphere of education. The fact that they provide virtually the only parallels available, since the literature of the smaller nations has almost entirely disappeared, does not make these more valid.

But the most significant of these passages are 1 8 and 6 20. Here the father and mother are placed on exactly the same footing as teachers of their children[132], and in passages which are quite clearly not isolated sayings like the other references in Proverbs to the obligation of obedience and respect for parents[133], but introductions to formal Instructions[134] of the very type which most closely resembles those of Egypt. The phraseology of these sentences corresponds almost exactly to that of their Egyptian counterparts[135], even in such a detail as the combination of a positive command ("hear") with a negative warning ("do not reject/forsake")[136]; and this throws into greater relief the one feature which is entirely unique in them: the mention of the mother. It is difficult to avoid the conclusion that this feature is an example of the adaptation of the Egyptian tradition to the peculiar situation in which the Israelite instructions were composed: a domestic situation in which the father and mother together shared the responsibility for the education of the child.

It does not, of course, follow from this that the mother shared with the father in the strictly technical and professional instruction of her son: the Instructions in Prov 1—9 are of a mainly moral character, and may have originally been taught orally. The significance of the reference to the mother lies rather in the fact that it shows that at least in these instances the words "father" and "son" must, like "mother", be understood literally as expressing family relationships, and not, as usually in Egypt, the relationship between a professional teacher and his pupil[137]. This in turn suggests that the other Instructions in Prov 1—9, which have the same general form, but in which the mother is not mentioned, may also be genuine parental

---

nations than Egypt and Mesopotamia is also attested in such passages as I Reg 5 10f. 10 1-10 Jer 49 7.

132 See Oesterley op. cit. 7.

133 10 1 15 20 19 26 20 20 23 22. 25 28 24 29 15 30 11. 17. In 4 3 the reference to the mother is probably not original: see Whybray, Wisdom in Proverbs, 44 n. 2.

134 1 8-19 6 20-32. See Whybray, Wisdom in Proverbs, 39—41. 48f.

135 See Whybray 33—37.

136 Humbert, Recherches, 70.

137 This is admitted by most commentators. Gemser op. cit. 21 admits that the phrase "my son" in these chapters is not necessarily a literary borrowing from Egyptian wisdom literature. But in general the implications of this have not been perceived.

instructions, and that the use of the phrase "my son" in other passages in Proverbs[138] ought also to be interpreted in this way.

The evidence for the existence of schools with professional teachers in Israel, at any rate until late times, is, then, not conclusive. It remains no more than a possibility, upon which it would be hazardous to construct further hypotheses. The present uncertainty on the question is reflected in the wide differences of scholarly opinion concerning the character, number and variety of these supposed schools.

3. *The ḥākām in Proverbs*

It is in the light of this uncertainty that we must consider the hypothesis, frequently put forward[139], that in some passages in Proverbs the word *ḥākām* can only refer to a professional teacher[140]. The proponents of this theory admit that in the overwhelming majority of cases *ḥākām* in Proverbs is to be interpreted in a general and non-professional sense, but insist that in these few cases such an interpretation is unsatisfactory.

Three passages in particular might appear to provide plausible evidence for this hypothesis: 13 14 15 12. 31.

> a) The teaching of a wise man (*tōrat ḥākām*) is a fountain of life
> for the avoidance of the snares of death (13 14).

The word *tōrā* in Proverbs does not, however, have a professional connotation. Of the other 6 passages which refer to teaching given by a specific person, 2 refer to instruction given by a mother to her son (1 8 6 20) and one to that given by the "capable wife" (31 26). In the other three cases (3 1 4 2 7 2) the author of the Instructions of chapters 1—9 uses it to refer to his own teaching (*tōrātī*); but, as has already been suggested[141], there is reason to suppose that he was the pupil's own father rather than a professional teacher. To assume a professional connotation here would be to beg the question.

Similarly, the phrase "fountain of life" (*meqōr ḥayyīm*) is not restricted to references to professional teaching. It occurs in 4 other passages of the Old Testament. In Ps 36 10 it is associated with Yah-

---

138 In the section dependent on Amen-em-opet, 23 15. 19. 26 24 13. 21; also 19 27 27 11. The use of the pl. *bānīm* in 4 1 5 7 7 24 and (in a speech by Wisdom) 8 32 does not affect the point.

139 Most recently by Hermisson 133ff.; von Rad, Weisheit in Israel, 35.

140 Other passages cited by von Rad in this connection relate to the argument that the *ḥakāmīm* were authors (rather than teachers); these are considered on p. 48ff. below.

141 P. 38ff. above.

weh; in Prov 10 11 it is identified with the mouth of the righteous (*ṣaddīq*), which is contrasted with that of the wicked; in Prov 14 27, where the second line is identical with that of 13 14, it is identified with the fear of Yahweh; and in 16 22 with wisdom, contrasted with folly.

> b) An arrogant man (*lēṣ*) does not like to be reproved;
> he will not go to wise men (*'el-ḥ^a^kāmīm lō' yēlēk*) (15 12).

The phrase "go to wise men" can hardly be interpreted as referring to the frequentation of a professional educational establishment. The phrase *hālak 'el* does not occur elsewhere in the Old Testament in any sense comparable to its use here, and the saying can hardly mean more than that the arrogant man[142] does not frequent the company of those who are known to be wise, because he knows that they will express disapproval of his way of life.

> c) The ear which listens to wholesome admonition (*tōkaḥat ḥayyīm*)
> will abide among wise men (*b^e^qereb ḥ^a^kāmīm tālīn*) (15 31).

The normal meaning of the verb *līn/lūn* is "stay the night"; but it is also used frequently in a metaphorical sense of a moral quality or condition of life which "abides" with a man or a community for a considerable time, or permanently: righteousness (Isa 1 21); evil thoughts (Jer 4 14); a curse (Zech 5 4); weeping (Ps 30 6); error (Job 19 4) can "abide" in or with a man. Similarly a man can "abide" in good (Ps 25 13) or in honour (Ps 49 13). Again, strength can "abide" in the back of Leviathan (Job 41 14). There is no exact parallel to the usage in Prov 15 31, but the natural interpretation of this verse is that the man who values good advice will spend much of his time in the company of men known to be wise, or, alternatively, that such a man will himself gain acceptance as one of them. There is nothing in this verse to suggest that the "wise men" in question are professional teachers.

A few other verses in Proverbs might be added to the list, but these also provide no positive evidence in favour of the theory that *ḥākām* in Proverbs sometimes means a professional teacher.

12 18 and 15 2 refer to the beneficial effects of the "tongue of wise men" (*l^e^šōn ḥ^a^kāmīm*) as healing and knowledge respectively, in contrast to the disastrous effects of unconsidered speech. A similar contrast is made in 15 7. The contrast made in these verses between wisdom and folly indicates a general meaning for *ḥākām*. In 16 23 it is the mind of a wise man (*lēb ḥākām*) which ensures that his speech will be prudent and persuasive: again a general meaning is indicated.

---

[142] On the meaning of *lēṣ* see F. Buhl, Die Bedeutung des Stammes *lūṣ* oder *līṣ* im Hebräischen, in: Wellhausen-Festschrift, 1914, 81—86.

Finally in 25 12 a "wise reprover" (*mōkīaḥ ḥākām*) is said to be "to a listening ear like a gold ring or an ornament of gold". This verse is perhaps significant in that, while the general meaning is similar to that of some sayings considered above — in particular, the phrase "listening ear" (*'ōzen šōma'at*) occurs also in 15 31 —, *ḥākām* is here clearly used adjectivally, and the noun which it qualifies — "reprover" — has a quite general sense. This verse suggests strongly, if further proof were needed, that in Proverbs a man is called "wise" not in view of his profession but of his natural and recognized ability to give good advice.

4. "*Teacher*" *in Biblical Hebrew*

This conclusion is further supported by a comparison between the way in which the word *ḥākām* is used in educational contexts and the usage of other words meaning "teacher". Since these words all have the participial form it is often difficult to distinguish between verbal and nominal senses; however, in the following examples the meaning "teacher" is probable.

a) *mōre* and *m^elammēd* together

In Prov 5 13 the foolish young man laments,

> I did not listen to the voice of my teachers (*mōrāy*),
> and I did not incline my ear to my instructors
> (*m^elamm^eday*).

b) *mōre* alone

II Chr 15 3 refers to a "priest who is a teacher" (*kōhēn mōre*). Here a participial sense ("teaching priest") is also possible.

In Job 36 22 Elihu exclaims, referring to God, "Who is a teacher (*mōre*) like him?".

In Isa 9 14 Hab 2 18 there is a reference to a "teacher of lies" (*mōre-šeqer*).

In Isa 30 20 the prophet speaks of "your teacher" (*mōrékā*), probably referring to God[143].

c) *m^elammēd* alone

In Ps 119 99 the psalmist, addressing God, exclaims: "I have more understanding than all my teachers (*m^elamm^eday*), for thy testimonies are my meditation."

---

[143] In this verse MT twice has the pl. form "teachers"; but the verb is sg., and the 6 MSS which have the singular form are probably correct. On Joel 2 23 see the commentaries.

d) *mēbīn*

As already noted[144], *mēbīn ʿim-talmīd* in Chr 25 8 probably refers to a musician and his pupil[145].

There are thus in biblical Hebrew several words meaning "teacher", though none of these necessarily designates a professional schoolmaster. Two of them, as the parallelism in Prov 5 13 shows, were interchangeable. None of them is ever associated, in poetical parallelism or otherwise, with *ḥākām*. It is also to be noted that, whereas in the case of *mōre* and *melammēd* forms with pronominal suffixes (e.g. "my/your teachers") are regularly found, the word *ḥākām* never occurs in didactic or educational contexts with a suffix. Since *ḥākām* occurs far more frequently than either *mōre* or *melammēd* as a noun and in similar contexts, it is remarkable that, if "teacher" is one of its meanings, no author should ever have chosen to write [*ḥakāmī*] or [*ḥakāmay*] in the sense of "my teacher(s)".

5. *The ḥākām in Job, Ecclesiastes and the Psalms*

The passages from Proverbs discussed above are the only passages in the Old Testament where there is any possibility of interpreting *ḥākām* as "teacher"[146]. In this connection it should be pointed out that even in the other "wisdom books" of the Old Testament the word is almost always used in a very general sense. Of the 8 ocurrences in Job, in one it refers to God (9 4), in one it is used adjectivally (*geber ḥākām*, 34 34), and in 5 other cases (5 13 15 2 17 10 34 2 37 24) it refers, sometimes contemptuously, to a natural or acquired human "wisdom" of a general kind. The only case where *ḥakāmīm* might be interpreted as referring to a distinct class of men is 15 18: "What wise men have told, and their fathers have not hidden". Whoever these "wise men" were, there is no indication here that the information which they imparted was given in the context of a school[147].

In Ecclesiastes the word occurs 21 times. Kohelet's use of the word is remarkably similar to that of Proverbs. In 12 cases[148] the "wise man" is contrasted, as frequently in Proverbs, with the fool.

---

144 P. 37f. above.

145 The meaning of *mebīnīm* in Esr 8 16 is uncertain; it may mean "men of understanding". In II Chr 26 5 *mēbīn* as applied to Uzziah's tutor is participial.

146 On those passages where it has been variously interpreted as "teacher" and "author" see p. 48ff. below.

147 See further p. 53f. below.

148 2 14. 16 (twice). 19 4 13 6 8 7 4. 5. 7 9 17 10 2. 12.

In 6 cases[149] the reference is to a general human wisdom of the kind which the author himself set out to acquire (1 13). Sometimes this is praised for its usefulness (e.g. 7 19); elsewhere (e.g. 8 17) its limitations are stressed. In 9 15 there is no reason to suppose that the "poor wise man" (*'iš miskēn ḥākām*) who by his wisdom delivered the city belonged to a special class of "wise men".

In 12 9a (*weyōtēr šehāyā qōhelet ḥākām 'ōd limmad-da'at 'et-hā'ām*) the relationship between the two statements that Kohelet was *ḥākām* and that he taught knowledge to the people is uncertain since the meaning of *yōtēr še* is disputed. If, with most of the older translations and commentaries and some more recent writers[150] it is taken to mean "in addition to, besides the fact that", Kohelet's wisdom is differentiated from his teaching activity, and the context offers no help in determining the meaning of *ḥākām*, except to show that it does *not* refer to his teaching activity[151]. If, on the other hand, as most commentators believe[152], *yōtēr še* means "moreover, in addition to this", the clauses are simply co-ordinate: "And, moreover, Kohelet was *ḥākām*; he repeatedly (*'ōd*)[153] taught knowledge to the people." If this is correct, it is possible that the clauses are intended to be synonymous: to be a *ḥākām* was to be a teacher of the people. But this does not, even if correct, necessarily refer to a professional function.

The second half of the verse, which describes Kohelet's activity more precisely, is unfortunately even more difficult to interpret than the first; but it certainly refers to the composition or collection

---

149 7 19 8 1. 5. 17 9 1. 11.

150 E.g. G. Wildeboer, Der Prediger (KHC 17), 1898, 166; G. A. Barton, The Book of Ecclesiastes (ICC), 1908, 197; P. Volz, Hiob und Weisheit (SAT 3/2), 1921, 256; R. Gordis, Kohelet: The Man and His World, 1951, 342; R. B. Y. Scott, Proverbs and Ecclesiastes (AB 18), 1965, 256; W. Zimmerli, Das Buch des Predigers Salomo (ATD 16), 1967, 248f.; also RSV and JB.

151 Those who understand *yōtēr še* in this way interpret the statement as meaning either that Kohelet was not only a scholar but also a teacher (Wildeboer, Volz, Scott, Zimmerli), or that he was not only a wisdom teacher with a restricted group of pupils, but also that he reached a wider public (*hā'ām*) through his writings (so O. S. Rankin, The Book of Ecclesiastes, IB V, 1956, 86f.).

152 E.g. H. Lamparter, Das Buch der Weisheit: Prediger und Sprüche, BAT 16, 1959², 145f.; H. W. Hertzberg, Der Prediger, KAT 17/4, 1963, 216—218; A. Baruch, Ecclésiaste, Verb Sal AT 3, 1968, 193f.; K. Galling, Der Prediger, HAT 1/18, 1969, 123f.; also apparently NEB ("So the Speaker in his wisdom . . . ").

153 The meaning of *'ōd* here is also disputed. There is no clear evidence elsewhere of its use as an adversative connecting particle or of its in any way marking a new beginning. It is therefore probably best to take it as an adverb meaning "continually, regularly". The theory of Gordis that *yōtēr še . . . 'ōd* means "not only . . . but also" is hardly justified by the Mishnaic evidence which he adduces. On this see Hertzberg 217.

by Kohelet of "many proverbs" (*mᵉšālīm harbē*). This most probably refers to his literary work: it was through his writings that he "taught the people". This literary activity intended for a wide circle of readers does not by any means necessarily suggest a professional teacher, and there is no reason to suppose that his designation as *ḥākām* is anything more than a tribute to his superior skill as a writer. To draw any more definite conclusions from such a disputed text would in any case be hazardous.

Finally in 12 11 there is a reference to the "words of (the) wise" (*dibᵉrē ḥᵃkāmīm*). This phrase, which occurs also in Prov 22 17, will be considered in the next section. Once more there is no specific indication here of instruction given in a school by a professional schoolmaster.

ḥākām occurs only twice in the Psalms. In Ps 49 11 a contrast is made between the wise man and the fool. In Ps 107 43 ("Whoever is wise, let him give heed") there is equally no professional meaning intended[154].

In view of the above evidence we are justified in concluding that, while as an adjective *ḥākām* is a most appropriate word to apply as a description to a man whose great knowledge qualifies him to instruct and guide others, it never, in the Old Testament, has the meaning of "teacher", nor does the plural *ḥᵃkāmīm* denote a class of professional teachers.

C. *The "Wise Man" as Author*

It is a commonplace of modern wisdom research that the "wisdom literature" of the Old Testament was composed by members of a specific class of men who are referred to as "the wise" or "the sages". This opinion is closely related to that discussed in the previous section that there was a class of teachers, also known as "the wise". On the precise identification of this class there is some difference of opinion; but it is a common view that the "wisdom books" were composed in the context of the school, whether as textbooks or as the literary products of an intellectual activity associated with the school. Clearly not all schoolmasters would be authors, but the authors would be leading and influential members of the schoolmaster class. The doubts which have been thrown in the preceding pages upon the existence

---

[154] It is not the intention of this study to pursue the further development of the use of the term in the Apocryphal and Rabbinic literatures. By the Rabbinic period it had acquired a professional or semi-professional meaning, but this was a later development.

of schools and schoolmasters in Israel does not dispense us from examining the view that *ḥᵃkāmīm* was used in the Old Testament as a technical term denoting a class of authors.

It should be pointed out before the relevant passages are examined that the use of the definite article ("*the* wise men") is hardly justified by the evidence of the Old Testament itself, and makes an assumption which begs the question. The definite form *haḥᵃkāmīm* occurs only 3 times in the Old Testament, and never with reference to such a specific class. In Ex 36 4 II Chr 2 6 it refers to skilled craftsmen, and in Koh 9 1 it is linked with "the righteous", and clearly has a quite general reference[155]. Of the 9 cases where the plural form occurs with the suffix, which has, equally with the article, the effect of conferring definiteness on a noun or adjective, 7 refer to non-Israelite "wise men" of various kinds[156]; one refers to Israelite craftsmen (II Chr 2 13), and the remaining example (Isa 29 14), which has already been discussed[157], clearly does not refer to men of letters. In 4 passages the form *laḥᵃkāmīm* occurs. Here the grammatical form does not indicate whether the noun or adjective is definite or not. In 3 of these cases the context shows that it is definite; but 2 of these (Ex 7 11 Est 1 13) refer to non-Israelite "wise men", while in the third (Koh 9 11) the word occurs as a member of a list of a very general kind, including the swift and the strong; here it is quite clear that no special professional class is meant. The fourth case (Prov 24 23) is one which requires special consideration and will be examined below[158].

There remains the possibility that in some poetical passages, where a noun may be definite even though the article is lacking, *ḥᵃkāmīm* should be translated by "*the* wise men"[159]. Only the context can decide. The fact remains that textual proof of the existence of

[155] The Old Testament is also very sparing in its use of the article with the sg. *ḥākām*. Of the 6 occurrences, one is adjectival (*hā'îš heḥākām*, Jer 9 11); in 2 cases (Koh 2 14. 16) *heḥākām* is contrasted with the fool (*hakkᵉsîl*), and in the remaining 3 (Job 15 2 Koh 8 1. 17) there is nothing to suggest any but a general sense. The f. pl. *ḥᵃkāmōt* occurs once (Jer 9 16) in the sense of "women skilled in lamentation".

[156] Gen 41 8 Est 6 13 Isa 19 12 Jer 50 35 51 57 Ez 27 8. 9.

[157] P. 19 above.

[158] The sg. form *leḥākām*, which is clearly definite, occurs 3 times. In Koh 2 16 6 8 its general meaning is shown by the fact that the wise man is contrasted with the fool; in 7 19, as has already been indicated (p. 47 above), the sense is also a general one.

[159] There are thirty occurrences of *ḥᵃkāmīm* in poetical books and passages: Job 5 13 15 18 34 2 Ps 49 11 Prov 1 6 3 55 10 14 12 18 13 20 14 3. 24 15 2. 7. 12. 31 18 15 22 17 29 8 30 24 Koh 7 4 9 17 12 11 Isa 5 21 19 11 44 25 Jer 4 22 8 8. 9 10 9 Ob 8. Only a few of these passages offer any support for the theory in question, and these — together with the question of their poetical character, where relevant — will be discussed below (p. 55 ff.).

a distinct group of writers known as "*the* wise men" is nowhere to be found in the Old Testament.

The case for the existence in Israel of such a class rests almost entirely on 6 verses: Prov 1 6 22 17 24 23 25 1 Job 15 18 Koh 12 11.

Three of these verses are of crucial importance because they constitute the titles of 3 sections of Proverbs, and make statements about their authorship.

In Prov 22 17 the words *dib^{e}rē ḥ^{a}kāmīm* ostensibly form part of the first half of a poetical line:

> Incline your ear, and hear the words of (the)[160] wise men;
> and apply your heart to my knowledge[161].

However, the virtually universal opinion that these two words do not belong to the original poetical line, but originally preceded it and formed the title or heading of the entire section which follows is certainly correct.

V. 17-21, which form the general introduction to the section, are written in the first person singular[162]; and a reference to a plural *ḥ^{a}kāmīm* as being their authors is out of place. Moreover the two words overload the metre. On the other hand it is not improbable that an editor should have added the title "words of wise men" to the whole section, either ignoring the first person singular style or understanding it as not to be taken literally.

But if *dib^{e}rē ḥ^{a}kāmīm* are a title and not part of the initial poetical line of the section, they must be regarded as prose, not poetry; and in that case the absence of the article before *ḥ^{a}kāmīm* is most significant. The phrase is almost universally rendered, "*The* words of *the* wise"; but this cannot be correct. Without the article and in prose, both nouns must be indefinite; and something like "words of wise men" is the only rendering possible. The title is, then, simply an indication that the section which follows is to be regarded as an important piece of instruction, being the work of men of intelligence and skill. No other interpretation is possible.

unless it follows the pattern of older Hebrew which often neglects the definite article

In view of this, it becomes clear that 24 23 must be given a similar interpretation. The first three words of this verse (*gam-'ēlle laḥ^{a}kāmīm*) constitute the title of the next section of Proverbs, that which immediately follows 22 17ff. The word *gam*, "also", is best to be explained in this connection: this title was added by the same editor who supplied the title in 22 17. But if this is so, the conventional translation "These also are (the) sayings of *the* wise" is incorrect. The form *laḥ^{a}kāmīm*

[160] No article.

[161] There is no reason to correct *l^{e}da'tī* to *lādā'at* here.

[162] *l^{e}da'tī*, v. 17; *hōda'tīkā*, v. 19; *kātabtī*, v. 20.

itself gives no indication whether the word is definite or indefinite; but it is extremely probable that the latter is the case. The intention of the title is to recommend this section as yet another work distinguished by its superior quality.

25 1 consists of a sentence in prose which forms the title of the section embracing ch. 25—29: "These also are proverbs of Solomon which the men of Hezekiah king of Judah edited[163]." The reference is presumably to the earlier collection of "Solomonic" proverbs beginning in 10 1 and furnished with the title "Proverbs of Solomon".

The phrase "men of Hezekiah" is an unusual one. Elsewhere in the Old Testament *'anᵉšē*, "men of", preceding a proper name, always refers to a body of men of war serving under the personal leadership of one man. Moreover, it occurs only in the narratives concerning the life of David. The only names to which it is attached are those of David himself[164], Saul[165], Joab[166], Abner[167] and Ittai the Gittite[168], and it is used solely in military contexts[169].

Clearly the phrase "men of Hezekiah" in Prov 25 1 denotes a body of men in the service of the king; equally clearly these were not men of war, but scribes whose duties consisted, no doubt among other activities, of maintaining and transmitting the literary "wisdom" tradition. Why they are referred to by a title otherwise known to us only in military contexts and in the narratives of an earlier age it is impossible to say. We can only presume that this title was in regular

---

163 The meaning of *he'tīqū* remains uncertain despite much discussion. See, in addition to the commentaries, R. B. Y. Scott, Solomon and the Beginnings of Wisdom in Israel, VT Suppl III, 1955, 273 n. 2; Cazelles, Débuts, 31 n. 4. In post-biblical Hebrew the hi. of *'tq* is regularly used in the sense of "copy, transcribe"; but this sense is not otherwise attested in the Old Testament. The transmission, as part of the biblical text, of a colophon merely noting the recopying of an old scroll would be extremely unusual, and it is probable that some kind of editorial work is meant.

164 *'anᵉšē dāwīd*, I Sam 23 3 24 5 II Sam 19 42 21 17; *'ᵃnāšāw*, "his men", referring to David, I Sam 18 27 23 5. 13. 24. 26 24 3. 4. 7. 8. 23 25 13. 20 27 8 29 2. 11 30 1. 3. 31 II Sam 2 3 5 6. 21 16 13 17 8; *'ᵃnāšay*, "my men", spoken by David, I Sam 23 12; *'ᵃnāšékā*, "your men", spoken by Achish king of Gath to David, I Sam 28 1.

165 *'ᵃnāšāw*, referring to Saul, I Sam 23 25. 26 31 6.

166 *'anᵉšē yō'āb*, II Sam 20 7; *'ᵃnāšāw*, referring to Joab, II Sam 2 32.

167 *'anᵉšē 'abnēr*, II Sam 2 31; *'ᵃnāsāw*, referring to Abner, II Sam 2 29.

168 *'ᵃnāšāw*, referring to Ittai, II Sam 15 22.

169 *'ᵃnāšékā* in the Queen of Sheba's words to Solomon (I Reg 10 8 II Chr 9 7) is probably to be emended, with LXX and Pesh, to *nāšékā*, "your wives". The phrase "the men of Hamor" in Jdc 9 28 is not in the same category since Hamor was not a contemporary leader but an ancestor. The only possible non-military use of the expression (apart from Prov 25 1), and the only one which does not refer to the time of David, is the reference to the "men" of Abraham or his servant in Gen 24 59. Here it probably means "servants": cf. *'anᵉšē habbayit*, Gen 39 11.

use in the time of the editor who inserted this note, and in a sense somewhat different from that in which it had been used in the earlier period. However this may be, the point which is of significance for the present discussion is that in this passage, the only one which specifically refers to the activity of royal scribes in the field of "wisdom" literature, the word *ḥᵃkāmīm* is not used. If there were in fact a body of professional literary men known as *ḥᵃkāmīm*, it is precisely here that we might expect it to occur. At the very least Prov 25 1 cannot be said to offer evidence for the existence of such a class.

There remains one more passage in Proverbs which is relevant to the discussion: Prov 1 6. Here the phrase *dibᵉrē ḥᵃkāmīm*, identical with the title of 22 17, occurs again, but this time as part of a poetical line:

> to understand a proverb (*māšāl*) and a figure (*mᵉlīṣā*),
> words of wise men (*dibᵉre ḥᵃkāmīm*) and their riddles (*ḥīdōtām*).

This verse may well be an addition to the original passage, v. 1-5[170]; but if so it is an interpretation of that passage, and to be understood in the context which the passage provides. V. 1-5 were originally composed as an introduction to the series of short Instructions which formed the original stratum of Prov 1—9[171], and their purpose is to commend these to the reader. V. 6, it may be presumed, has the same purpose, although it may refer to the whole book of Proverbs rather than simply to the original Instructions in ch. 1—9[172].

In this context the four types of saying mentioned in v. 6 may be presumed to refer to the contents of all or part of the book which follows, although the poetical form warns us against regarding the verse as a prosaic list. If this is so, the natural interpretation of *dibᵉrē ḥᵃkāmīm* here is that the phrase refers to the kind of material so designated in 22 17, where, as has been shown[173], there is no proof of a professional meaning for *ḥᵃkāmīm*.

The phrase *dibᵉrē ḥᵃkāmīm* also occurs in Koh 12 11. The interpretation of this verse is very uncertain[174], but it is generally agreed that it is the work of an editor, and that its intention is to commend these "words of wise men". There is some uncertainty whether

---

[170] See Whybray, Wisdom in Proverbs, 38 n. 1.

[171] Whybray 33—52.

[172] It could be argued, for example, that only the numerical proverbs, of which there is only one example in ch. 1—9 (6 16-19) can rightly be called "riddles" (*ḥīdōt*); but this argument should not be pressed, as the meaning of *ḥīdā* is not entirely clear.

[173] P. 50 above. It should be noted that *ḥākām* occurs in the previous verse (1 5) in a clearly non-professional sense.

[174] See the commentaries.

it is to be regarded as prose or poetry[175], and consequently no conclusion can be drawn from the absence of the article. But here also there is nothing to indicate that a professional sense is intended: nowhere in Ecclesiastes is *ḥākām* so used, and it is probable that the phrase has the same meaning as in the other two passages where it occurs.

The final passage relevant to the discussion is Job 15 17-19, where Eliphaz states his intention of declaring to Job "what he has seen", which he further qualifies as

> what wise men have told (*yaggīdū*),
> and their fathers have not hidden[176];
> to them alone was the land given,
> and no stranger passed among them.

The imperfect form *yaggīdū* in the first line of v. 18 does not indicate whether the appropriate translation is "tell" or "told, have told". The message which Eliphaz then proceeds to relate (v. 20-35) about fate of the wicked man is nothing new, but rather commonplace "wisdom" teaching.

Eliphaz' purpose in these two verses is clearly to give additional weight to what he has to say by claiming that it is based not only on his personal experience but also on a long tradition of wisdom going back to the time of the first settlement of the Israelites in Canaan[177]. This does not suggest that the "wise men" in question are

---

[175] See the commentaries.

[176] Or, "hidden from them". MT has *w^e^lōʾ kih^a^dū mēʾ^a^bōtām*, "and they did not hide from their fathers". Houbigant's proposal, inspired by LXX, to read *w^e^lōʾ kih^a^dūm ʾ^a^bōtām* and to translate this by "and their fathers did not hide from them" has been widely accepted, though the grammatical difficulty involved in translating *kih^a^dūm* by "they hid *from* them" has led to alternative emendations and explanations of the text. F. Horst, Hiob 1—19, BK 16/1, 1968, 227, accepts the suggestion that the original text had *w^e^lōʾ kih^a^dū mēhem ʾ^a^bōtām*, "and their fathers did not hide from them". M. H. Pope, Job, AB 15, 1965, 110, followed by A. C. M. Blommerde, Northwest Semitic Grammar and Job, Bibl Or 23 (1969), 74f., suggests that the initial letter of MT's *mēʾ^a^bōtām* was originally an enclitic *mem* at the end of the previous word simply adding emphasis to the verb. Blommerde, however, does not follow Pope in also regarding the *final* letter of *ʾ^a^bōtām* as an enclitic, leaving the form *ʾābōt*, "the fathers". In spite of these different explanations there is a consensus among modern commentators that "(their) fathers" is to be taken as the subject of "did not hide".

[177] Although Eliphaz is represented in the Book of Job (2 11) as a Temanite, it is most improbable that the author of the poem, which is addressed to Jewish readers, is referring to a local Temanite tradition. The giving of the land is a clear reference to Israelite traditions. The precise allusion intended by the assertion that at that time "no stranger passed among them" is not entirely clear, but its purpose is

professional authors or teachers claiming to possess a specialized technique confined to their own class, but rather that "wisdom" of this kind has always been the property of the nation of Israel as a whole, or at least available to all, thanks to the activity of men of superior intelligence who passed on their insights both to their contemporaries and their descendants[178].

D. Conclusion

The above discussion shows that there is no evidence in the Old Testament for the existence of a class of writers known as "the wise men", or indeed of *any* class of men so designated. The phrase "the wise men" in connection with the Old Testament is a modern phrase which does not correspond to the facts. This conclusion is of more than merely philological interest. For the very currency of the phrase in modern research has tended to confine the discussion within very narrow limits. The discovery that the application of the term "wise" to the authors of certain books does not imply that they were members of a specific professional class makes it possible to re-examine those books which have been labelled "wisdom literature" in a new way. Freed from the necessity of enquiring "Who were the wise men?" we may now ask to what extent the authors of Proverbs, Job and Ecclesiastes may be said to have stood in a common "tradition", and what was the character of that tradition. Only if these questions can be answered satisfactorily will it be possible to go further and to enquire whether some of the other books of the Old Testament belong to, or bear the marks of, that tradition.

---

evidently to assert the purity of the tradition which Eliphaz has received, and it may be polemical in intention.

178 Similarly in 8 8 there is no reason to suppose, as is usually done, that "their fathers" (*'ᵃbōtām*; LXX and Vulg. have simply "fathers", which some commentators consider to be the original reading, while Pope believes that the final letter may once again be the enclitic *mem*) refers specifically to a professional tradition of wisdom teachers or authors. In Sir 8 9, with which this passage is frequently compared, the case is quite different: there *'btm*, "their fathers", clearly refers, as the context shows, to the "fathers" (parents or teachers) of contemporary *śbym*, "elders" or "scholars" (cf. *sāb* in Mishnaic Aramaic), not to "the fathers" in the sense of the patriarchs.

Chapter III: Proverbs, Job and Ecclesiastes and their Authors

The fact that Proverbs, Job and Ecclesiastes together contain more occurrences of the root *ḥkm* than the whole of the rest of the Old Testament is itself an indication that their authors had a special regard for the intellectual qualities denoted by this root which sets their work apart from the great majority of the other books, and suggests that they exemplify in a peculiar degree a distinct intellectual tradition in ancient Israel[1]. Yet at the same time the little information ~~white~~ which? can be gleaned concerning these men suggests that they belonged to a variety of circles within Israel rather than that they consciously followed and promoted the continuance of a narrow tradition within a small circle.

I. PROVERBS

Seven of the sections of Proverbs are provided with titles. Two of these (1 1 10 1) attribute the sections which follow to Solomon; one (25 1) to court scribes working on an older "Solomonic" text; two (30 1 31 1) to non-Israelite writers; and two (22 17 24 23) simply to unnamed men of superior intelligence or skill.

It has frequently been assumed that the tradition of Solomonic authorship is a court tradition. This, indeed, is not impossible; but it is equally possible, and indeed probable, that there were traditions and legends about Solomon which were not confined to the court, and which may even have originated in quite different circles.

The main collection of stories about Solomon (I Reg 3—11) is composed of material of many different kinds. Besides that which is annalistic or based on contemporary historical records composed at court there is, for example, a large block of material of particular interest to the priests of Jerusalem, and which has later been elaborated in the interests of that priesthood; this interest is also amply attested in II Chronicles. Again, the tradition of Solomon's apostasy,

[1] In the pages which follow the phrases "wisdom", "wisdom tradition" and the like will be avoided as far as possible except when reference is made to the opinions of other scholars. Reference will be made instead to the "intellectual tradition" of Israel. The use of this phrase is not, of course, intended to imply that there were no intellectual activities outside this particular tradition; it is used merely as a convenient expression, in order to avoid confusion with ideas concerning "wisdom" which have been rejected in the earlier part of the book.

attributed to his foreign wives (I Reg 11), based no doubt on historical facts, was elaborated by the Deuteronomic historian for his own purposes.

Besides these various kinds of material there was also a much more popular set of traditions about Solomon. The stories of the two harlots (I Reg 3 16-28) and of the visit of the Queen of Sheba (I Reg 10 1-13) must be regarded as popular tales, unlikely to have originated at court; and the development of this popular legendary tradition is even more clearly seen in the Song of Solomon, where, in addition to the attribution of the whole book to Solomon (1 1), there are references to his magnificent litter and palanquin (3 7-10), the "crown with which his mother crowned him on the day of his wedding" (3 11), and his vineyard (8 11f.). Whatever may be the character of the Song of Solomon[2], there can be no doubt that its author made use of popular legendary material about Solomon.

Solomon's intellectual brilliance was undoubtedly one of the elements in this set of popular traditions: the purpose of the story about the two harlots is to illustrate and to praise him for his brilliant judicial decisions and his understanding of human character. One aspect of this reputation was his unequalled ability to say clever and intelligent things: this is illustrated in the story of the Queen of Sheba. She came to "test him with riddles (*ḥīdōt*)" which he always solved satisfactorily, and she exclaimed that his courtiers were to be envied because they were always in a position to *hear* his wisdom (10 8). Similarly the exaggerated and generalized panegyric of Solomon in 10 23-25 states that "the whole earth sought the presence of Solomon to hear his wisdom, which God had put into his mind" (10 24).

In view of this it is entirely possible that the passage (I Reg 5 9-14) in which Solomon is praised, among other things, for his *authorship of proverbs* is based on a popular tradition — that is, on a tradition unconnected with the court or any other clearly defined group[3]. The author of this passage knows of the existence of non-

[2] For a review of modern discussion on this question see O. Eissfeldt, The Old Testament: An Introduction, 1965, 483—491; also p. 119 f. below.

[3] The date and provenance, as also the unity, of this passage are disputed. A. Alt, Die Weisheit Salomos, ThLZ 76 (1951), 139—144 (= Kleine Schriften, II 1959², 90—99), found here the influence of foreign wisdom literature on the court of Solomon himself; R. B. Y. Scott, Solomon and the Beginnings of Wisdom in Israel, VT Suppl III 1955, 262—279, thought of the passage as post-exilic "folklore". M. Noth, Könige I. 1—16, BK 9/1, 1968, 80f., who regarded it as more or less a unity and possibly pre-Deuteronomic, believed that its provenance and background were uncertain, though like other traditions about Solomon it probably originated in Judah and more specifically at Jerusalem. For J. Gray, I and II Kings, OTL, 1970², 144—146, it comes from a "late popular" source, although it may be based on an earlier tradition.

Israelite "wisdom" (that of Egypt and of the "people of the East"), and knows the names of a number of men renowned for their wisdom (5 11). The possibility that there were in Israel educated men outside court circles who looked back to Solomon as the archetype of writers of such literature cannot be dismissed; and if this is so, it may have been such men who wrote those sections of Proverbs which have been editorially designated as "proverbs of Solomon".

The title of Prov 25 1 does not in any way disprove this. This title undoubtedly testifies to the fact that the Judaean court was a centre of intellectual activity at the time of Hezekiah, and that all or part of the section which follows (ch. 25—29) in its present form is the work of Hezekiah's scribes; but this historical note by no means proves that we are dealing here with a literary tradition continuously handed down at that court from the time of Solomon. The ways in which the names "Solomon" and "Hezekiah" are used in this verse are quite different: the latter is a precise historical reference intended to indicate the date, and in general terms the authorship, of the present collection of proverbs; the former is, as in 1 1 10 1, no more than the expression of a popular belief that proverb-writing in Israel goes back to Solomon. Consequently the material on which Hezekiah's scribes worked was not necessarily of court origin[4].

Thus the only clear reference to a court origin to be found in the titles of Proverbs is the reference to Hezekiah's scribes in 25 1. All the other titles are compatible with the view that the sections of Proverbs to which they refer were composed outside court circles. This applies not only to the "proverbs of Solomon" and "sayings of clever men" but also to the two titles which designate the sections which follow as of foreign origin: the "words of Agur son of Jakeh of Massa" (30 1) and the "words of Lemuel, king of Massa, which his mother taught him" (31 1). If the names of foreign wise men[5] were known to the author of I Reg 5 9-14, it is not inconceivable that collections of their sayings were known, and available for translation, to educated men other than court scribes.

---

[4] Scott, Solomon and the Beginnings of Wisdom in Israel, has also thrown doubt on the view that the references to Solomon's wisdom prove the existence of a continuous tradition of "wisdom" at the Judaean court from the time of Solomon, and has suggested that we should look to the age of Hezekiah for its earliest flowering.

[5] There is great uncertainty about the provenance of the names of Ethan the Ezrahite, and Heman, Calcol, and Darda, the sons of Mahol, who are here mentioned as paragons of wisdom immediately after the statement that Solomon's wisdom surpassed the wisdom of all the people of the east, and all the wisdom of Egypt (I Reg 5 10f.); but some of them are certainly not Hebrew names. See the commentaries, especially J. A. Montgomery and H. S. Gehman, The Books of Kings, ICC, 1951, 132; Noth, Könige, 82f.; Gray, I and II Kings, 147.

The *contents*, as well as the forms, of the material in Proverbs have been frequently scrutinized in recent years with a view to determining their background and so, in general terms, their authorship; but the evidence has proved elusive and ambiguous. In ch. 1—9 the earliest stratum consisted of a series of short Instructions preceded by an introduction[6]. There can be no doubt that these are based on the model of Egyptian Instructions, which served as textbooks in schools; but, as has been argued above[7], this fact does not necessarily mean that they were composed under the same circumstances as the models on which they are based, or by professional schoolmasters. In other respects their purpose is clear: they are educational texts used in the instruction of the young.

The interpretative material which has been added to these Instructions[8] is less susceptible of classification, but it would be reasonable to suppose that most of it was added while the Instructions were still serving their original purpose. In some of these passages, which introduce the concept of *ḥokmā* as equivalent to the teacher's words[9], the appeal to the young is still quite evident, and the tone exhortatory. In others, where this *ḥokmā* is theologically explained as the wisdom of Yahweh himself, it is evident that a theological development has taken place; but it is not possible to say with any certainty when or by whom this was achieved[10].

One other section of Proverbs (22 17—24 22) is also, as is generally acknowledged, partly modelled on Egyptian literature, specifically on the Instruction of Amen-em-opet[11]. But it contains material of various kinds, and can as it stands hardly be intended for the instruction of children, as it contains sayings addressed to parents (23 13f.). Like the Instructions in ch. 1—9, it shows no clear signs of having been composed by professional teachers.

It has been argued that the remainder of the material in ch. 10—29 is instructional material composed for use in a "wisdom school" attached to the court. These sections undoubtedly contain some sayings which might be addressed to boys destined to fill responsible

---

[6] See Whybray, Wisdom in Proverbs, 33—52.

[7] P. 40ff.

[8] See Whybray op. cit. 72—104.

[9] Prov 2 2-4. 10f. 4 5-9 7 4.

[10] E.g. 2 5-8 8 35b. See Whybray, Wisdom in Proverbs, 95ff. For a somewhat different view of ch. 1—9 see McKane, Proverbs, 1—10. 278—280. McKane, however, also refrains from making precise statements on these questions and speaks rather in general terms of the substitution of "the more diffuse, rambling style of preaching" for the "more exact didactic procedures of the wisdom teacher" (279).

[11] See p. 40 and n. 122 above.

functions at court[12]; but, as von Rad has recently pointed out[13], specifically court-oriented proverbs are rare in the book of Proverbs. Von Rad concludes[14] that the collections in their present form have been edited by "the wise men" at court for use in the school, but that the material itself has its origin outside the court and outside the school, in the circles of the educated "bourgeoisie" or the "gentleman farmers"[15]. The theory of a final editing of some parts of Proverbs at court is supported by the title in 25 1[16].

The theory of an educated class, both urban and provincial, capable of reading such books and of producing men capable of writing them is supported by the researches of Skladny[17]. Although Skladny, in his attempt to distinguish the specific characters of the various sections in ch. 10—29, sometimes seems to go beyond the evidence and to draw over-fine distinctions, he has succeeded in showing that the social background of these sections is in the main well-to-do, not aristocratic, partly agricultural and partly urban[18].

From the *forms* of the material in Proverbs it is difficult to draw any definite conclusions with regard to the circles for which it was composed. It is generally agreed that the "statements" (*Aussagewort*) which form the bulk of the single sayings are not simply popular proverbs[19]. Their style, especially their poetical parallelism, shows them to be consciously literary creations, and is quite different from that of the popular sayings which are occasionally found in other books of the Old Testament. However, their form affords no more specific clue to their origin.

Concerning the "admonitions" (*Mahnwort*), a form which occurs with great frequency in the Egyptian Instructions, the most widely held theory is that its origins lie in an imitation by the Israelite "wisdom schools" of the Egyptian style. This view has been challenged by Gerstenberger[20], who finds their origins in codes of "family ethics" (*Sippenweisheit*), closely related to the "prohibitives" of the Old Testament laws, used by patriarchs of the clan as oral instruction; these were only later collected in the "schools". Richter[21] adopts a

---

12 Especially 11 14 13 17 14 35 16 14. 15 18 16 19 12 20 2. 18 25 5. 6f. 15 29 26.

13 Weisheit in Israel 30f.

14 Op. cit. 30f. 35.

15 "eine bürgerlich-grossbäuerliche Schicht" (31).

16 See p. 51f. above.

17 U. Skladny, Die ältesten Spruchsammlungen in Israel, 1962.

18 The work of Gerstenberger and Richter (op. cit.) is in the main not relevant here, since its concern is to enquire into the oral tradition which lies behind Proverbs rather than into the question of the composition of Proverbs itself.

19 Hermisson op. cit. 24ff.; von Rad, Weisheit in Israel, 41—43. 49—51.

20 Wesen und Herkunft des "apodiktischen Rechts".

21 Op. cit.

somewhat mediating position: the *Mahnwort* was developed in fairly late times in schools attended by the sons of upper-class citizens, but the process was a native Israelite one, parallel to that which took place in Egypt but independent of it.

Gerstenberger's arguments are by no means entirely convincing; and in view of the close resemblance between the Egyptian *Mahnwörter* and those of Proverbs[22] it would seem gratuitous to deny the probability of a direct influence by older Near Eastern literatures on that of Israel. The existence of such influence on the longer Instructions in Prov 1—9 22 17ff. can hardly be doubted. But even though this may be regarded as a reasonably certain conclusion, knowledge of the sources of influence does not inevitably dictate conclusions about the nature of the Israelite circumstances which received this influence.

Attempts have been made to isolate other forms occurring in Proverbs and to determine their *Sitz im Leben*. Thus von Rad regards the questions in Prov 6 27f. as "Schulfrage", which "at least indirectly go back to some form of school-teaching method"[23]. It is, however, very doubtful whether this kind of question, which states the absurd in an interrogative form in order to elicit a negative answer, can really be traced back to the school in spite of the parallels in other Near Eastern literature. Such rhetorical devices are frequently found in the literatures of many peoples, and are, as von Rad himself admits, "scattered almost throughout the whole of the Old Testament"[24]. It is, indeed, hardly too much to say that the question form, which lends itself to a great variety of purposes, is the main rhetorical device of Hebrew literature, both poetry and prose[25]. If it was used a teaching method, which is entirely probable, there is no reason to suppose that this was its original function. The fact that it occurs in almost every kind of Old Testament literature makes it probable that it was a regular form of popular speech before it appeared in a literary guise of any kind.

The above survey of the evidence from Proverbs suggests that the material which it contains is of diverse origin. If there is evidence of a strictly educational purpose in some sections and of the activity of court scribes in others, the titles, contents and form of the larger part of the book offer little which points incontrovertibly to either of these, and the contents of the bulk of the material are consistent with the view that it was written for an adult educated class not

[22] See McKane, Proverbs, for a detailed study. The *Mahnwort* also occurs in Mesopotamian literature: see again McKane op. cit.

[23] Op. cit. 32.

[24] P. 32.

[25] See Whybray, The Heavenly Counsellor, 19ff.

confined to court circles, for their instruction and entertainment, by some of the more gifted members of that class, whom their contemporaries and successors honoured with the epithet *ḥākām*.

II. JOB

It is universally agreed that the book of Job occupies a unique place in the literature of the Old Testament. On the other hand, as far as its general theme is concerned, it has a number of parallels in the literature of the ancient Near East. Although no convincing evidence has come to light of a direct literary dependence on any ancient Near Eastern text so far known to us, it is reasonable to suppose that its author was familiar with this literary genre[26]. Job itself is a literary achievement of such magnitude that it seems inconceivable that it was the very first attempt to write this kind of work in an Israelite context; such earlier attempts, however, have been lost.

The independence and audacity of his thought set the author of Job apart from the didacticism of Proverbs, and it is difficult to see him as a member of a tradition-bound class of professional literary men. Yet it has frequently been assumed that this was so: that he belonged to that class of *ḥᵃkāmīm* by whom Proverbs is supposed to have been written, having been trained in the "wisdom schools" and become familiar with their teaching; but that he came to see the fallacy of some aspects of their teaching and reacted against it.

There is no doubt that the author of Job was familiar with the kind of teaching which we find in Proverbs, and with the forms in which it is expressed. The speeches of Job and his "friends" abound in poetical units which would fit well into Proverbs as individual sayings[27]; and also in longer didactic poems[28] whose form and content are comparable with those in Prov 1—9[29]. It is equally clear that the teaching of eudaemonism, according to which men receive, one way or another, before they die, the due reward of their actions, is one of the most characteristic teachings of Proverbs, and that this teaching is expressed in the speeches of the "friends" of Job as a foil to the radical questioning of it which is one of the main themes of Job. However, this teaching is not peculiar to Proverbs, Job and Ecclesiastes, but is presupposed generally in the writings of the Old Testament.

[26] See most recently J. Gray, The Book of Job in the Context of Near Eastern Literature, ZAW 82 (1970), 251—269.

[27] E.g. 5 2. 17 6 14 12 11. 12 14 4 17 5 22 29 24 19.

[28] See von Rad, Weisheit in Israel, 58—60.

[29] Compare, for example, Job 5 12-16 with Prov 3 32-35 and Job 5 17-27 with Prov 3 11f.

A further distinction between Job and Proverbs is that Job is not didactic, at least not in the same sense as Proverbs. The purpose of every section of Proverbs may be described as instruction, even though there is often also an element of entertainment and of problem-setting[30]. On most subjects of importance Proverbs adopts a clear and consistent attitude which, whether by implication, as in the *Aussagewort*, or directly, as in the *Mahnwort*, it recommends to the reader. Where contradictions or differences of attitudes are found, they usually occur in widely separated sayings[31], which may indicate that the authors or editors were unaware of, or had not considered the implications of, these differences. Occasionally we find two apparently contradictory proverbs side by side[32]: here it is clear that the author or editor has arranged them in this way deliberately in order to draw attention to a problem which requires further thought. Nowhere in Proverbs, however, do we find any sustained discussion of these problems. The long poems in ch. 1—9 and in 31 10-31 are as didactic and definite in their teaching as are most of the short sayings[33].

This positive and confident didactic tone, which is imitated, only to be attacked, in the speeches of Job's "friends", is entirely different from that of the book of Job considered as a whole. It has often been remarked that the book offers no clear-cut solution to the problems which it raises. This is surely due not to the author's inability to make his conclusions clear to the reader, but to his basic intention, which was not didactic in any strict sense, but was to air and discuss certain problems to which he knew of no answers, in order to provoke reflection. This may have been the intention of some sayings in Proverbs; but in Job, considered as a single literary work, the method is quite different, and the scale of the enterprise quite beyond comparison with anything in Proverbs. Moreover the confident tone of Proverbs is entirely lacking in Job except where it is imitated for the purpose of showing its falsity[34].

Yet another significant difference between the character of Job and of the various sections of Proverbs is that, whereas only a very limited number of styles are found in the latter, and these are of a rather undefined character as far as *Sitz im Leben* is concerned, Job

---

[30] In so far as many of the sayings are intentionally open to more than one interpretation (see McKane, Proverbs, 22ff. and *passim*) or depend mainly for their point on word-play of various kinds, they cannot be regarded as purely didactic in the sense of an intention to inculcate a particular doctrine.

[31] E.g. 17 8. 23.

[32] Especially 26 4. 5.

[33] 30 4, which has affinities with Job 38—41, especially 38 4ff., may be a fragment of a longer poem of a more reflective kind.

[34] On the speeches of Elihu (Job 32—37) see p. 65f. below.

makes use of a number of clearly defined *Gattungen*, particularly those of the law-court, the individual lamentation and — in the framework — the prose narrative.

So extensive is the use made of these forms that it has even been suggested that Job ought not to be regarded as an example of "wisdom literature" at all: "wisdom" forms are only a few among the many types of literary tradition of which this unique writer availed himself[35]. This suggestion of course begs the question of what is meant by "wisdom forms"; but the fact that it could be made at all emphasizes the width of the gulf which separates the author of Job from the various authors of Proverbs. What is surprising about the book of Job is not that its author was familiar with these various forms, which would be part of Israel's literary and cultural heritage, but that he felt free to use them as he chose. This certainly does not suggest that he was trammeled by the conventions of a narrow group.

The individuality, or at least the uniqueness, of Job is also shown by the very large vocabulary stock of which he disposed. Whatever may be the explanation of this phenomenon, it is a further indication of the author's independent and special place in Old Testament literature.

The form of the book as a whole is perhaps the strongest indication of this. While the device of embedding a poem of a reflective character within the framework of a prose narrative has parallels in Near Eastern literature, and the use of the extended dialogue is also represented in both Egyptian and Babylonian literature, neither is to be found elsewhere in the Old Testament[36].

---

[35] Volz op. cit. 22—26 put this point of view most forcibly. For him, the author of Job is the very opposite of a wisdom teacher. There is no intention to teach or to offer a solution to the problems raised by the book (which accounts for the failure of modern scholars to agree on such a "solution"). Rather the book is a lamentation expressing in a dramatic way the personal experience of the author. C. Westermann, Der Aufbau des Buches Hiob, 1956, and A. Weiser, Das Buch Hiob, ATD 13, 1956[2], 9—12, amplify the views of Volz, adding supporting arguments from more recent form-critical studies of the affinity of Job with the poetry of the cult. H. Richter, Studien zu Hiob, 1959, equally denies the connection of Job with wisdom literature, but stresses rather its forensic element and sees the author as using this mode of speech in much the same way as the prophets. Pope op. cit. xxixf. regards Job as *sui generis* and unclassifiable. Similarly P. Humbert, Le modernisme de Job, VT Suppl III 1955, 150—161, discusses the book as the work of an individual author of genius without attaching it to any "school". All these writers, and many others, strongly emphasize the independence and originality of the author.

[36] The dialogue form was, however, used in later Jewish literature, especially in IV Ezra (II Esdras). See the comments of von Rad in Weisheit in Israel 60—62. The short dialogue between Yahweh and Abraham in Gen 18 22-33 is hardly comparable, though it is, like Job, set in the context of a narrative and concerned with a not dissimilar

It has been suggested that the dialogue form is derived from a practice of holding disputations in the "wisdom schools" by professional teachers. But there is in fact no evidence whatever for such a practice. The theory seems to have originated with Gunkel[37]. It is supported by Eissfeldt[38] and Fohrer[39], both of whom cite as evidence the existence of the dialogue form in Egyptian literature, which is often used to discuss themes not entirely unlike that of Job[40], and the riddling between Solomon and the Queen of Sheba in II Reg 10 1-13. Eissfeldt also refers more specifically to the Egyptian satirical letter of the official Hori to the scribe Amen-em-opet[41], which suggests the existence of scribal disputations in Egypt[42]. It is supposed by these scholars that this Egyptian practice was imitated in the Israelite "wisdom schools", where the teachers disputed with one another as an academic exercise[43]. But an inference of this kind requires support from within the Old Testament itself, and this is entirely lacking. The riddling between Solomon and the Queen of Sheba is hardly a "disputation" in any sense remotely comparable with the dialogue in Job[44]; nor is it legitimate to infer that it reflects a practice of disputation between professional wise men in the hypothetical "wisdom school" of the time of Solomon[45].

---

question, and thus in a limited sense may be a forerunner of Job. In one form or another the argument or discussion is of course an obvious way of making a point: cf., e.g., Gen 3 1-5.

37 H. Gunkel, Hiob, RGG², II 1929.

38 Introduction 468.

39 Introduction to the Old Testament, 1968, 333; Das Buch Hiob, KAT 16, 1963, 50.

40 The Dispute with his Soul of One who is Tired of Life (Erman, The Literature of the Ancient Egyptians, 86—92; ANET 405—407); The Protests of the Eloquent Peasant (Erman 116—131; ANET 407—410); the dialogue et the end of the Instruction of Ani (Erman 241f.). There are also similar dialogues in Babylonian literature, e.g. The Dialogue of Pessimism (Lambert, Babylonian Wisdom Literature, 139—149; ANET 437—438); The Babylonian Theodicy (Lambert 63—91; ANET 438—440).

41 Pap. Anastasi I; ET in Erman 214—234; ANET 475—479.

42 See G. von Rad, Hiob xxxviii und die altägyptische Weisheit, 292—301 (ET 281—291).

43 Cf. G. Hölscher, Das Buch Hiob, HAT 1/17, 1952², 4.

44 Gray, I and II Kings, 260, and Noth, Könige, 224, both point out that battles of wits have frequently been a feature of court life both ancient and modern; but it is difficult to see what there can be in common between court entertainment and the discussion of serious problems by learned men in an academic context.

45 That there were "disputations" of other kinds in Israel, of which the book of Malachi, based on disputations between the prophet and the people, perhaps provides the clearest evidence, is not here called into question; but this has no bearing on the question of the supposed "wisdom disputations".

Moreover, the "dialogue" in Job is not really a disputation at all. Each of the speeches of Job and his "friends" — as also those of Yahweh — is a set piece. There is little attempt by the speakers to seize upon points made by those who have preceded them, and there is little development of thought as the book proceeds, as would be the case if the dialogue were modelled on real disputations[46]. This disconnected method, though a strange one to the modern reader, is adequate to its purpose in the context of a literary work, since the reader is able to draw his own conclusions about the validity of the various points of view which have been set out; but it is inconceivable as a method in real, lively discussion. Either the author of Job was unfamiliar with a custom of "learned disputation", or he deliberately rejected it as unsuitable to his purpose.

It is perhaps significant that the dialogue in Job is represented as taking place not between "learned men" belonging to a professional class, but between a (once) wealthy landowner and his friends: that is, between educated farmers. Since the book is set somewhat vaguely in a remote patriarchal period, it is possible that a tradition that the "fathers" of Israel were especially wise has played a part in the creation of the fiction, although there is little trace of such a tradition in the narratives of Genesis and the other narratives of Israel's early history[47]. In any case the patriarchal setting plays little part in the conduct of the dialogue, and if this is discounted we are left with the significant fact that the author apparently expects his readers to accept as realistic a series of speeches on subjects of great profundity by a group of educated and prosperous farmers.

If a precise context is presupposed, this might well be the *sōd*, or friendly discussion among equals by the elders of the city "in the gate"[48]. This view is perhaps confirmed by Eliphaz' reference to "what wise men have told" in 15 17-19, and by the reference to the conclave in the gate in 29 7-10. It is reasonable to suppose that the handing down of traditional lore, supposed to have come down from patriarchal times, might have taken place on such occasions. It is this traditional lore which Job is represented as, quite exceptionally, criticising.

If, as is probable, the speeches of Elihu (Job 32—37) are to be regarded as interpolations into the book of Job, the question of their background must be considered separately. This is particularly necessary as it has been maintained that these chapters, more than the

---

[46] Von Rad, Weisheit in Israel, 270f., rightly points out that the "dialogue" of Job is presented not as a series of disputes (*Streitgespräche*) but as a series of conversations (*Gespräche*) between an afflicted man and his friends, in which he laments his misfortunes and they try to give him comfort.

[47] See p. 53f. above; p. 108 below.

[48] On this see L. Köhler, Der hebräische Mensch, 1953, 143—171.

remainder of the book, show signs of being the work of professional "wise men"[49].

Elihu's speeches have, it is true, much more the character of a disputation than the rest of the book. They pick up a number of Job's statements (e. g. in 33 9-11 34 5f. 9 35 2f.) and discuss them, seeking to demonstrate their falsity. They have something of the didactic tone of the lecture. Yet here also there is nothing to suggest that their author was a "wise man" in any narrow sense. Not only is the fiction of the discussion between friends preserved, but Elihu's own claim to special inspiration, together with his assertion that God speaks to man in general through direct revelation, shows that this author's thought is far removed from any conventional idea of a "wisdom tradition" based wholly on the principles of inherited professional lore and learned reflexion upon it.

At the outset Elihu puts forward, in defence of his own temerity in speaking before his elders, the view that an understanding of human problems has nothing to do with seniority or length of experience:

> It is not the old that are wise,
> nor the aged that understand what is right. (32 9)

To this view he opposes the assertion that

> It is the spirit in a man,
> the breath of Shaddai, that makes him understand. (32 8)

In its context this statement can hardly mean anything other than that Elihu is claiming for himself a special divine inspiration which gives him the right to speak[50].

In another passage (33 14-18) Elihu goes further, asserting that God speaks generally to men in dreams and visions of the night, if they are open to receive his message. This emphasis on the reality of divine inspiration, which has a parallel in the main poem of Job, where it is Eliphaz who claims to have received a message in the night from "a spirit" (4 12-21), is quite different from the thought of Proverbs, where, although it is often acknowledged that God directs men's thoughts and words in various ways (e. g. 1 7 2 1ff. 16 1), there is never any reference to such direct manifestations of his inspiration.

We are thus led to conclude that the book of Job, though its author (or authors) was familiar with sayings of the kind found in

---

[49] So, e.g., G. Fohrer, Introduction to the Old Testament, 1968, 330 (cf. his Studien zum Buche Hiob, 1963, 87—107) says that Elihu "uses the rhetorical form of the lecture delivered by a wisdom instructor". Weiser op. cit. 217f. also sees him as a wisdom teacher using the form of the *Streitgespräch*. Cf. also Volz, Hiob und Weisheit, 90—95.

[50] So, e.g., Hölscher, Pope, Fohrer; H. H. Rowley, Job, NCB, 1970, 265. 269. Cf. also 32 18: "The spirit within me constrains me."

Proverbs, is unique in the literature of ancient Israel. It makes use of a variety of Israelite traditions besides that of earlier didactic literature, and its fiction of a discussion between mature, independent, prosperous men who are leaders of their community strongly suggests that its author was no professional "wise man" but rather a highly educated man of genius belonging to the same social class as the characters whom he portrays.

III. ECCLESIASTES

This book continues to present enigmas of every kind, and no attempt can be made here to penetrate them. There is no agreement among contemporary scholars concerning the date, authorship, purpose, unity or meaning of the book, and even large portions of the text still present serious problems of detailed interpretation. Nevertheless some general remarks may be made about the relationship of the book to earlier Old Testament literature, and, at least negatively, about the character of the author.

Like Job, Ecclesiastes contains many short proverbs[51] similar to those found in the book of Proverbs, showing that the author was familiar with the style and manner of earlier proverbial literature. Many of these, however, exhibit an individual point of view, and use the characteristic vocabulary of the author of the book, and are probably his own compositions[52].

In spite of obvious similarities with both Proverbs and Job, which are not confined to literary style but include similarities of theme, especially that of the relationship of God to the individual human life, Ecclesiastes is in fact quite clearly not only very different from Proverbs, but also as unlike Job as Job is unlike Proverbs.

This is true, first of all, of the form of the book. Ecclesiastes is neither a well-organized composition like Job nor a mass of unrelated short pieces like the larger part of Proverbs. Although there is no agreement about its structure, it is probably best seen as a collection of pieces of short and medium length[53]. But it has a unity of thought and expression which marks it out — allowing for a few later additions — as the highly individualistic work of a single mind[54]. It neither confines itself to the working out of a single great theme, like

---

[51] E.g. 1 15. 18 4 5. 6 5 3.

[52] E.g. 1 18 4 5.

[53] For a recent survey of the question see O. Kaiser, Einleitung in das Alte Testament, 1969, 307—309.

[54] Cf. most recently von Rad, Weisheit in Israel, 293.

Job, nor concerns itself, like Proverbs, with a multitude of themes ranging over the whole of human life. Rather it returns again and again to a few basic themes which it emphasizes by means of a small number of key-words which either do not appear elsewhere at all in Proverbs and Job or only play a minor role there[55]. With a few exceptions[56] its teaching is entirely consistent.

The forms used by Ecclesiastes are either elaborate developments of earlier forms or forms which are quite original. The autobiographical "I-style" in which the whole book is cast and which is most prominent in the first two chapters may be a development of a style which is already found in embryo in such passages as Prov 4 3ff.; but if so it has been developed beyond all comparison. Similarly the longer sections of which most of the book is composed are quite different from the long sections in Proverbs and Job, being mainly in prose (or possibly rhythmical prose).

Finally, in spite of the partial overlap in theme between Job and Ecclesiastes, the tone of the latter is quite different from that of the former. Its thoroughgoing pessimism and its passionless, detached attitude are unique in the Old Testament.

Some of these differences can perhaps be accounted for by the considerable lapse of time which should probably be allowed between the writing of Job and of Ecclesiastes. This certainly accounts for some of the differences of language between the two books. Nevertheless the impression remains that each work stands on its own as an individual composition having no direct relationship to the other or to any Old Testament book.

What kind of a man was the author of Ecclesiastes? His character seems as impenetrable as the title, Kohelet, by which he appears to have been known. There is, however, perhaps an element of true biography in the "autobiographical" section, 1 12ff. In the sense that the author claims to have been "king over Israel in Jerusalem" (1 12), this is fictitious autobiography: in claiming to be Solomon the author was making use of a common tradition about Solomon's wisdom in order to make it possible for him to claim that he had had the

---

[55] E.g. *hebel*, "nothingness, worthlessness" (34 times in Eccles as against 3 in Prov and 5 in Job); *ʿāmāl*, "toil, trouble" (22 times as against 2 in Prov and 8 in Job — not always in the same sense); *yitᵉrōn* (10 times; not in Prov or Job).

[56] Especially those passages (e.g. 2 26 3 17 5 8 7 18. 26 8 12f. 11 9b) which appear to deny the major contention of the book that "one fate comes to all, to the righteous and the wicked" (9 2). Whether such passages are to be regarded as additions depends, however, on the interpretation of the book as a whole. (See especially K. Galling, Kohelet-Studien, ZAW 50, 1932, 276—299.) It has recently been maintained by F. Ellermeier, Qohelet, I/1 1967, that they are statements of theses which the author then attacks in the sections which follow.

opportunity to "see everything that is done under the sun" and to try out every kind of human activity, and to conclude that it was worthless. But it is obvious from the book that he was in fact a man of great experience, and possible that he was also a man of wealth: his rejection of "pleasure" (*śimḥā*), seen as the fruits of great wealth (2 1-11), does not read like the highminded renunciation of an ascetic, nor like the contemptuous rejection by a poor man of something which he has never been able to possess, but rather like a sober account — expressed in exaggerated terms in accordance with the Solomonic fiction — of the genuine experience of a man of means who has become disillusioned. He may therefore have been, in his own generation, in a similar social class — though more urbanized — to the author of Job.

The appendices to the book (12 9-14), probably written by a number of different hands, add little to what the book itself tells us. Only v. 9f. speak directly about Kohelet himself. V. 9a, as has already been pointed out[57], does not put him into a class of professional "wise men", but says that he "taught the people knowledge", and, either because of this, or quite independently, admiringly calls him "wise", that is, a man of superior intelligence. The remainder of v. 9f. refers to his literary activity, but throws no further light on the question whether his authorship was in some sense a "professional" activity or not.

IV. CONCLUSION

The internal evidence of these three books suggests that in the course of a long period in Israel's history there existed an educated class, albeit a small one[58], of well-to-do citizens who were accustomed to read for edification and for pleasure, and that among them there arose from time to time men of literary ability and occasionally of genius who provided the literature which satisfied their demand. The extant examples of this literature which have come down to us in Proverbs, Job and Ecclesiastes reveal little of the characters of these men, but they provide enough information to make it possible to draw some general conclusions about the nature of Israel's intellectual tradition.

The common interest in these books is an interest in the problems of human life: not the political problems of the nation of Israel, which, though of gigantic and tragic proportions, are never referred to here, but the problems of ordinary individual citizens: their rela-

---

[57] P. 47f. above.

[58] See p. 32 above.

tions with one another within their own communities in their daily lives, their concern about the present and the future, including the fate of their children and descendants, and about the justice or injustice of their personal destinies[59]. These are all perennial problems; and in so far as there were in every generation men who thought about them and made their thoughts known to others, there may be said to have been an "intellectual tradition" in Israel which was distinct from other traditions such as the historical, legal, cultic and prophetic.

But there is no evidence of an *institution* existing through the centuries which acted as the vehicle of this "tradition". These three books themselves bear no marks of having been produced in a "school" of any description. Their authors were admittedly distinguished from the majority of their fellow-citizens by the fact that they were literate and educated; but there was clearly a not inconsiderable number of educated men in Israel who constituted the circle of their readers. These men did not set themselves apart from their fellow-citizens: they were familiar with, and participants in, the other "traditions" of Israel which were concerned with daily and religious life. They constituted a separate "tradition" only in the sense that they concerned themselves more than the majority of their contemporaries in an intellectual way with the problems of human life.

That there should have been some continuity, though of a completely informal kind, of this "intellectual tradition" is natural. It is reasonable to suppose that each generation of educated men will have been familiar with some of the written works — of which many have no doubt perished — of earlier generations, not to speak of the *oral* tradition ("what wise men have told", Job 15 18) which was handed down.

It is as a result of such informal transmission of the intellectual tradition that we find, in Proverbs, Job and Ecclesiastes, an element of common vocabulary, of which the frequent use of the root *ḥkm* is by far the most prominent, and, to some extent, though less evidently, of forms and style appropriate to the expression of thoughts on this particular range of subjects.

Thus we are surely justified in regarding Proverbs, Job and Ecclesiastes as representing a distinct intellectual strand in Israel's life; but it was a strand which needed no formal, concrete vehicle for its transmission.

It is from this point of view that it may now be possible to go a step further and to enquire what evidence there is of this intellectual tradition in other books of the Old Testament.

---

[59] Cf. von Rad's definition (Theology I 418) of the Israelite concept of wisdom as "a practical knowledge of the laws of life and of the world, based upon experience".

Chapter IV: The Intellectual Tradition in the Old Testament

The question which is usually known as the question of "wisdom influence" has recently occupied the attention of a large number of scholars, as the list of publications given at the beginning of this study indicates[1]. It has, however, usually been approached on the basis of the presupposition that "wisdom" in Israel was largely the concern of a class of "wise men" and of "wisdom schools".

I. METHODS FOR IDENTIFYING THE INTELLECTUAL TRADITION

Earlier studies have mainly used three criteria for detecting "wisdom influence": subject-matter, form and style, and vocabulary. The value of each of these methods must be considered.

A. Subject-Matter

A very general description of the problems with which Israel's intellectual tradition concerned itself has already been given[2]. Nevertheless the use of such a description as the sole criterion for the detection of its influence outside Proverbs, Job and Ecclesiastes is extremely precarious and involves a high degree of subjectivism. The description is too broad, and there is no general consensus among scholars which would make a more precise definition possible.

Crenshaw[3] criticises von Rad's definition of the Israelite concept of wisdom as "a practical knowledge of the laws of life and of the world, based upon experience" on the grounds that it is too broad. On the other hand he is certainly right in rejecting the common view of wisdom as "eudemonistic, humanistic, international and nonhistorical" as "both too narrow and false"[4]. But it is not clear that his own definition of "wisdom" as "the quest for self-understanding in terms of relationships with things, people, and the Creator"[5] is more satisfactory: it would be difficult to justify the use of the term "*self-*

[1] P. 1 n. 1.

[2] P. 69f.

[3] Methods in Determining Wisdom Influence 131.

[4] P. 131.

[5] P. 132.

understanding", for example, as a description of the aim of a great deal of the book of Proverbs.

Moreover the problems with which Proverbs, Job and Ecclesiastes are especially concerned are universal human problems which are liable to occur, in one form or another, in almost any writing — for example, in narrative — in which human beings and their mutual relationships are discussed. It would clearly be mistaken to classify all these books and passages as belonging to Israel's intellectual tradition in the sense in which it may be applied to these three books[6]. Other criteria are needed.

B. Form

Form-criticism has come to be more and more widely used in recent years in this connexion. But this method also has a number of disadvantages and limitations, although in some cases it has been used successfully. Generally speaking, form-criticism is inappropriate as a method for the detection of the presence of the intellectual tradition because the enterprise is by definition a search for a particular tradition in books or passages whose form *differs* from that of the books in which it is most clearly at home. The form of a narrative, for example, is necessarily different from that of a proverbial saying[7]; and this is also true of a prophetical oracle. Consequently the forms proper to the intellectual tradition in its classical guise are unlikely to occur in other types of literature except as quotations, imitations or interpolations. Even though it may be accepted that a narrator or a prophet has from time to time borrowed such a form for a particular purpose, the form-critical method only scratches the surface of the problem; for if the intellectual tradition is as much a set of ideas,

[6] See, for example, the well justified criticisms by Crenshaw (p. 140—142) of the thesis of Talmon, "Wisdom" in the Book of Esther, that that book is a "historicized wisdom tale".

[7] It is true that the narrative form is occasionally used in the "wisdom literature", e. g. in Prov 4 3-5 7 6-23 24 30-32 Koh 1 12ff. The use of narrative to express "wisdom" teaching in such works as the Joseph Story (as argued by von Rad, Josephsgeschichte und ältere Chokma) and the Succession Narrative (Whybray, The Succession Narrative) was therefore not incongruous and may have had precedents; but the *type* of narrative employed in those two works is quite different from that found in Proverbs and Ecclesiastes (see Whybray op. cit. 72—76). Consequently the argument that the Joseph Story and the Succession Narrative have "wisdom" characteristics is not based on form-critical methods. In this respect Talmon (op. cit. 427f.) is right in saying that the absence of formal "wisdom" features in Esther does not preclude it from being "wisdom literature", although there are other grounds for rejecting his thesis.

or an attitude to life, as a set of forms, form-criticism is useless in cases — likely to be the majority — where the ideas or attitude may have been borrowed but not the — usually inappropriate — form.

Further, some of the specific form-critical arguments used in this connexion have been subjected to considerable criticism: for example, the arguments of Fichtner[8], Lindblom[9], Terrien[10], Murphy[11], Wolff[12] and others that such forms as the admonition (*Mahnung*), the woe-oracle, the numerical saying, the rhetorical question and the comparative saying are especially characteristic of "wisdom literature" have been seriously questioned[13], and it is more probable that these belong to the common life of Israel in which the "wisdom" writers shared.

A further caveat against over-reliance on form-criticism as a means of detecting significant influence by one tradition upon another has been entered by Fohrer[14], who has pointed out that even when it can be shown that a speaker or writer has in fact made use of extraneous forms, this does not necessarily mean that his thought has been significantly influenced by them. His intention may merely have been to refer to a well known saying or mode of speech in order to communicate more effectively with his audience. "A distinction must . . . be made between the original meaning of a genre and the way in which it is utilized, that is, between the form and its function" in its new context[15]. Fohrer illustrates this point with a striking example of such a borrowing from outside the "wisdom tradition", coupled with one from within it: "In 5 1-7 Isaiah utilizes the type of the love song and in 28 23-29 the type of the wisdom instruction. But as a prophet he certainly did not have the office of a minnesinger or troubadour or that of a teacher of wisdom[16]."

[8] Jesaja unter den Weisen. Although Fichtner anticipates Gerstenberger and Richter in dismissing the "ethischer Mahnung" common both to wisdom literature and some prophetical books as "Allgemeingut der israelitischen — und weithin der altorientalischen! — Geisteswelt" (19) and also regards other supposed "wisdom forms" in Amos, Hosea and Micah as later interpolations, in the case of Isaiah he uncritically refers to the use of comparative sayings and word-play as indications of wisdom influence (22).

[9] Wisdom in the Old Testament Prophets.

[10] Amos and Wisdom.

[11] R. E. Murphy, A Consideration of the Classification, "Wisdom psalms", VT Suppl IX, 1963, 156—167.

[12] Amos' geistige Heimat.

[13] Especially by J. L. Crenshaw, The Influence of the Wise Upon Amos, ZAW 79 (1967), 42—52.

[14] G. Fohrer, Remarks on Modern Interpretation of the Prophets, JBL 80 (1961), 309—319.

[15] Op. cit. 312. [16] P. 311.

This is not to say that form-criticism is entirely useless in this connexion. If we allow that Isa 28 23-29 is an example of the same intellectual tradition as that of Proverbs, Job and Ecclesiastes, this enables it to be interpreted more intelligently, provided that it is recognized that Fohrer's point is valid[17]. The conclusion has been arrived at partly on form-critical grounds.

In fact form-critical study has been able to draw valuable conclusions of this kind in a number of instances. This is particularly true of the study of the Psalms, where entire passages, and even entire psalms, have been identified as belonging formally to this tradition[18]. Nevertheless form-criticism is an inadequate method for detecting the presence of this tradition except where a borrowed form, which is indisputably characteristic of it, and which can be identified with reasonable certainty, accompanies the borrowing of an equally characteristic idea. Such cases are likely to be in the minority.

C. Vocabulary

An approach which has commended itself to a number of writers, but has not yet been used in a completely systematic way, is the examination of the incidence of a *vocabulary* distinctive of Israel's intellectual tradition. It is, of course, not possible to separate the question of vocabulary from those of style and contents, nor is it to be supposed that the presence or absence of certain words *infallibly* indicates the adherence or otherwise of a passage to a particular tradition. All available methods must, as far as possible, be used together, though, as has been indicated above, this will not always be possible.

A certain degree of objectivity does, however, attach to this method, provided that certain safeguards are observed. Unfortunately the vocabulary test has not, up to the present, yielded the assured results which might be expected of it, owing mainly to the fact that no systematic attempt has yet been made to formulate adequate criteria for determining which words are sufficiently characteristic of this tradition to be used for this purpose[19].

---

[17] See p. 149 below.

[18] See, among other works, Jansen, Die spätjüdische Psalmendichtung; Mowinckel, Psalms and Wisdom; H.-J. Kraus, Psalmen I, BK 15/1, 1961², LV and *passim*.

[19] See further p. 121ff. below.

II. CRITERIA FOR DETERMINING THE TERMINOLOGY OF THE INTELLECTUAL TRADITION

In this matter it is clear that the following guiding principles must be observed:

a) It must be clearly established which terms are characteristic of Proverbs, Job and Ecclesiastes and may thus properly be used as criteria.

b) Only words of central significance for the main concerns of these books should be included.

c) A distinction must be drawn between words which are mainly confined to these books and those which, though especially frequently used there, are nevertheless in fairly general use in the other Old Testament books or as the technical vocabulary of another genre (e. g., *tōrā*). The latter, though not valueless as criteria, must be used with especial caution.

d) Attention must be paid to the possibility of changes of meaning or nuance in the use of particular words in different contexts.

e) Attention must be paid to the contexts in which the words are used.

f) Isolated occurrences should be considered significant only if they are especially significant in their contexts; concentrations of occurrences in a single literary unit should normally be regarded as having greater weight.

g) Attention must be paid where appropriate to the demarcations of literary units, and to differences of authorship within a single book.

h) The possibility of interpolations and glosses must be taken into account.

i) The probability or otherwise of the presence of this tradition as suggested by other criteria must be taken into account.

Of the words eligible to be placed in this list, it is obvious that, even among those which are clearly characteristic of these books, some had greater significance than others for their authors. It will generally be agreed that the words which most characteristically express the norm or ideal of human conduct in their eyes are those derived from the root *ḥkm: ḥākam*, "to be wise", *ḥākām*, "wise", and *ḥokmā* (also *ḥokmōt*), "wisdom". These words occur exceptionally frequently in Proverbs, Job and Ecclesiastes, and more frequently there than in the whole of the rest of the Old Testament[20]. It is, indeed, this fact which led to their designation as "wisdom literature".

[20] Including the 22 occurrences of the Aramaic equivalents *ḥokmᵉtā* and *ḥakkīm* (21 in Daniel; 1 in Ezra), the root occurs 346 times in the Old Testament, of which Proverbs, Job and Ecclesiastes account for 189.

At the same time the fact that these words also occur with some frequency in other Old Testament books and in a number of different books affords the opportunity for an investigation into the influence of the intellectual tradition on a scale large enough to permit a judgement to be made about the value of the vocabulary test by comparing its results with conclusions reached on other grounds. It would therefore seem to be methodologically sound to begin with a study of the distribution of the root *ḥkm*, and then to supplement or modify the results by means of a study of the distribution of other elements of the vocabulary of the intellectual tradition.

III. THE DISTRIBUTION OF THE ROOT *ḤKM* IN THE OLD TESTAMENT

A. The Occurrences of ḥkm

The purpose of the following preliminary survey is to eliminate those occurrences which are irrelevant to the present purpose and to discover in which books and passages the root occurs in significant contexts.

Genesis

The only 3 occurrences are in the Joseph Story: 41 8. 33. 39. The incompetence of the *ḥ*^{a}*kāmīm* of Egypt (41 8) is implicitly contrasted with the true *ḥokmā* of a Joseph (41 33. 39).

Exodus

18 occurrences, of which 16 refer to the skill of those engaged in making the priestly garments, Tabernacle, Ark etc. and their furnishings and utensils (28 3 [twice] 31 3. 6 [twice] 35 10. 25. 26. 31. 35 36 1 [twice]. 2. 4. 8), one to the *ḥ*^{a}*kāmīm* of Egypt (7 11) and one to Pharaoh's plans for the control of the numbers of the people of Israel (*nitḥakk*^{e}*mā*, "let us act shrewdly", 1 10).

Leviticus

No occurrences.

Numbers

No occurrences.

Deuteronomy

Of the 8 occurrences, 7 (1 13. 15 4 6 [twice] 32 6. 29 34 9) are found in the framework to the code: 2 (1 13. 15) refer to Moses' choice of able leaders of the people to assist him, and one (34 9), which is universally recognized as belonging to the Priestly source, to Joshua, Moses' successor, who was filled with the "spirit of *ḥokmā*" after Moses laid his hands upon him. In 2 (4 6 [twice]) Israel's special gift of *ḥokmā* is equated with obedience to Yahweh's commandments; and in the remaining 2 (32 6. 29), both of which are found in the "Song of Moses", Israel's disobedience to Yahweh, which led to its rejection by him, is attributed to a lack of *ḥokmā*. The only occurrence in the Deuteronomic code itself (16 19) is in a motive clause attached to a law prohibiting the taking of bribes[21].

Joshua

No occurrences.

Judges

One occurrence: 5 29. The syntax (*ḥakmōt śārōtēhā ta'ᵃnennā*)[22] shows that the reference is to superior intelligence of a general kind: "the ablest of her princesses answered her".

Ruth

No occurrences.

I and II Samuel

The only 6 occurrences are all in the Succession Narrative (II Sam 9—20 I Reg 1f.). Of these, 3 (II Sam 14 2 20 16. 22) refer to "skilful women"; 2 (II Sam 14 20 [twice]) to the *ḥokmā* of the king; and 1 (II Sam 13 3) to that of Amnon's "friend" Jonadab.

I and II Kings

Of the 21 occurrences, 2 (I Reg 2 6. 9) belong to the Succession Narrative and refer to Solomon's *ḥokmā*; the remaining 19 all belong to the history of the reign of Solomon (I Reg 3 12. 28 5 9. 10 [three times]. 11. 14 [twice]. 21. 26 7 14 10 4. 6. 7. 8. 23. 24 11 41). Of these, 18 refer to Solomon's superior *ḥokmā* and 1 (7 14) to the skill of the Tyrian craftsman Hiram.

[21] This clause is almost identical with Ex 23 8 (Covenant Code), except that there it is "officials" (*piqᵉḥīm*) who are blinded by bribes, whereas in the version in Deuteronomy it is "the eyes of wise men" (*'ēnē ḥᵃkāmīm*). It is generally accepted that this is a "wisdom saying" (see, e.g., G. von Rad, Das fünfte Buch Mose: Deuteronomium [ATD 8], 1964, 82 [ET Deuteronomy (OTL), 1966, 115]; P. Buis and J. Leclercq, Le Deutéronome [SB], 1963, 129), although B. Gemser, The Importance of the Motive Clause in Old Testament Law, VT Suppl I, 1953, 64 regards it as "a striking example of the intrinsic coherence of legal practice and wisdom or proverbs".

[22] Or *ḥakmat*; see the commentaries. The syntactical structure is not affected.

I and II Chronicles

All the 17 occurrences are found in the Chronicler's expansion of the story of Solomon. 6 (I Chr 22 15 28 21 II Chr 2 6 [twice]. 13 [twice]) refer to the skill of the craftsmen employed in Solomon's building operations; the remainder (II Chr 1 10. 11. 12 2 11. 12 9 3. 5. 6. 7. 22. 23) to Solomon's own *ḥokmā*.

Ezra and Nehemiah

The only occurrence is in Esr 7 25 (Aramaic), where "the wisdom of your God which is in your hand" in the decree of Artaxerxes is clearly intended to be the equivalent of "the law of your God which is in your hand" in the same decree (v. 14). The reference is to the law-book which Ezra took with him to Jerusalem.

Esther

Of the 2 occurrences here, 1 13 refers to the *ḥ^{a}kāmīm*[23] of Persia. 6 13 refers to the *ḥ^{a}kāmīm* of the official Haman, but the text is uncertain[24].

Psalms

13 occurrences, distributed among 11 psalms (19 37 49 51 58 90 104 105 107 111 119). Psalms 49 and 107 each have 2 occurrences.

In 58 6 the reference is to magic (*ḥōbēr ḥ^{a}bārīm m^{e}ḥukkām*, "skilful enchanter"); in 107 27 the reference is to the skill of seamen.

In 3 cases (19 8[25] 37 30 119 98) the context shows that *ḥokmā* is closely connected with the Law, which gives men *ḥokmā* and inspires their utterances. In 2 instances (51 8 90 12) the context is a prayer that God will give or teach *ḥokmā*.

According to 104 24 it is by *ḥokmā* that God created the world; and in 107 43[26] the *ḥākām* is urged to give heed to God's love mani-

---

[23] On the meaning of the phrase *yōd^{e}ʿē hāʿittīm* see p. 16 above.

[24] It has been suggested, in view of the translations of LXX and Pesh and the incongruity of the word *ḥ^{a}kāmāw* in its context, that it is a corruption of a word meaning "friends", such as might be derived from the root *rḥm*. See BH and also H. Ringgren, Das Buch Esther, ATD 16, 1967[2], 393. 396; E. Würthwein, Esther, HAT 1/18, 1969[2], 188; H. Bardtke, Das Buch Esther, KAT 17/5, 1963, 344.

[25] It is generally agreed that 19 8-15 are a composition distinct from the first part of the psalm. So, e.g., B. Duhm, Die Psalmen, KHC 14, 1899, 61; H. Gunkel, Die Psalmen, HKAT 2/2, 1929, 78; A. Weiser, Die Psalmen, ATD 14/15, 1966[7], 133. 135 (ET The Psalms, OTL, 1962, 197. 201); Kraus, Psalmen I 153.

[26] 107 33-43 are generally, though not universally, regarded as a separate composition (so Duhm, Gunkel, Kraus).

fested in his care for nature and men. This verse is generally regarded as specifically a "wisdom saying", though not necessarily as a later addition to the psalm[27]. The sentiment expressed in 111 10 that "the fear of Yahweh is the beginning (or, "essence") of *ḥokmā*" occurs in slightly different forms in various contexts[28], but the fact that the psalm is an alphabetic acrostic shows that it is an integral part of the composition.

In 105 22 the statement about Joseph, that he taught *ḥokmā* to the elders of Egypt, is clearly based on the Joseph Story in Genesis. In 49 the writer, who proposes (v. 4) to "speak *ḥokmōt*", clearly regards himself as a writer in the intellectual tradition, since he describes his work (v. 5) as "a proverb" (*māšāl*) and "a riddle" (*ḥīdā*). In v. 11 he contrasts the *ḥākām* with the fool, as in Proverbs, Job and Ecclesiastes. It is clear that a number of different concepts of "wisdom" are to be found in these psalms, and that a close investigation of these in relation to the different literary types will be necessary.

Song of Solomon

No occurrences.

I Isaiah (Isa 1—39)

11 occurrences. Of these, 5 (5 21 10 13 29 14 [twice] 31 2) are generally accepted as utterances of Isaiah himself[29]. These are all condemnatory of those, whether Israelites or Assyrians, who claim to possess *ḥokmā*, with the exception of 31 2, which more positively declares that Yahweh himself is *ḥākām*, with the implication that his *ḥokmā* is superior to all human *ḥokmā*.

3 occurrences (19 11 [twice]. 12) refer to the *ḥ^{a}kāmīm* of Egypt in a passage which is probably of later date than Isaiah[30]. The Isaianic authorship of 11 2, in which the "spirit of wisdom" is regarded with approval as one of the divine gifts which will rest upon the future Davidic king, is disputed[31].

[27] E.g. "makes use of the style of wisdom literature" (Weiser); "Weisheitsspruch" (Kraus).

[28] Prov 1 7 9 10 Job 28 28 Sir 1 20.

[29] On 5 21 29 14 31 2 see also p. 18—21 above.

[30] So, e.g., K. Marti, Das Buch Jesaja, KHC 10, 1900, 155; G. B. Gray, The Book of Isaiah, I—XXVIII, ICC, 1912, 321—323; B. Duhm, Das Buch Jesaia, HKAT 3/1, 1922⁴, 140f.; G. Fohrer, Das Buch Jesaja I, ZB, 1960, 208f.

[31] It is opposed by Marti, Gray, Mowinckel (He That Cometh, 1956, 17) and Fohrer but defended by J. Skinner, The Book of the Prophet Isaiah, Chapters i—xxxix, CB, 1930, 104; Duhm 104f.; W. Eichrodt, Der Heilige in Israel: Jesaja 1—12, BAT 17/1, 1960, 137ff.; O. Kaiser, Der Prophet Jesaja, Kapitel 1—12, ATD 17, 1963², 125f.

In 2 passages there are difficulties of text and interpretation. 33 6 takes a favourable view of *ḥokmā*, but Skinner's dismissal of it (264) as "untranslateable" seems not unjustified. It is generally taken to be non-Isaianic. In 3 3 the phrase *ḥᵃkam ḥᵃrāšīm*, if the text is correct, refers to magicians[32]. The phrase occurs in a list of persons who form the mainstay of Judaean life, but who are doomed to destruction.

II Isaiah (Isa 40—55)

3 occurrences. In 40 20 the reference is to a craftsman; in 44 25[33] and 47 10 to the *ḥᵃkāmīm* of Babylon.

III Isaiah (Isa 56—66)

No occurrences.

Jeremiah

17 occurrences. Of these, 2 (9 16 10 9) refer to skill of a non-intellectual kind, and 5 (10 7 49 7 [twice] 50 35 51 57) to the *ḥᵃkāmīm* of foreign nations. Of these, 10 7 is almost universally regarded as non-Jeremianic.

In 6 cases (4 22 8 8. 9 [twice] 9 22 [twice]) the reference is to the prophet's own countrymen who claim *ḥokmā* yet are really wicked or foolish because their *ḥokmā* is not in accordance with the will of Yahweh[34].

9 11 is part of a prose passage (9 11-15) which is generally believed to be a Deuteronomic addition to the book[35]; the phrase "Who is the man so *ḥākām* that he can understand this?" is almost identical

---

[32] See p. 21 n. 43 above.

[33] That the reference here is to Babylonian "wise men" is generally agreed by the commentators. In the context (v. 24-28) a contrast is made between the ineffectiveness of the Babylonian attempts to predict the future through the agency of their soothsayers, diviners and "wise men", whose efforts Yahweh frustrates, and Yahweh's own sure promises, guaranteed by his role as creator of the world and Redeemer of Israel and made through the prophets, to rebuild Jerusalem and the cities of Judah. In v. 25, for *baddīm* read *bārīm*, "soothsayers", with most commentators, e.g. Duhm; Fohrer; C. R. North, The Second Isaiah, 1964; C. Westermann, Das Buch Jesaja, Kap. 40—66, ATD 19, 1966 (ET Isaiah 40—66, OTL, 1969); J. L. McKenzie, Second Isaiah, AB 20, 1968; Kö; BH (but not BHS). The suggestion was originally made by P. Haupt.

[34] See also p. 21—24 above.

[35] So, e.g., J. P. Hyatt, The Book of Jeremiah, IB V, 1956, 891; Rudolph, Jeremia, 61—63; Bright, Jeremiah, 73; Weiser, Jeremia, 81f.; E. W. Nicholson, Preaching to the Exiles, 1970, 60—63.

with Ps 107 43 and similar also to Hos 14 10. In 18 18, where it is Jeremiah's opponents who refer to the *ḥākām*, the meaning, as has already been shown, is neutral, referring to the proclivity of such men for giving advice[36]. Finally 10 12 = 51 15, where the statement is made that Yahweh created the world by his wisdom, is almost universally regarded as non-Jeremianic.

Lamentations

No occurrences.

Ezekiel

8 occurrences, all falling within the section on Tyre and Sidon (chs. 26—28). Of these, 2 (27 8. 9) refer to the skill of the seamen employed by the Tyrians. The other 6 (28 3. 4. 5. 7. 12. 17) all refer to the pretended *ḥokmā* of the prince, or king, of Tyre, and are found in two consecutive poems (28 1-10. 11-19) of which the second makes extensive use of a Paradise myth in some ways parallel to, but differing from, Gen 2—3. According to this myth it was his claim to the possession of the divine *ḥokmā* which led to the downfall of the being placed by God in the garden of Eden[37].

Daniel

24 occurrences, all in the narrative section of the book (ch. 1—6). Of these 3 are in chapter 1 (1 4. 17. 20), which is written in Hebrew, and refer to the God-given *ḥokmā* of the four Judaean youths at the court of Nebuchadnezzar. The remaining 21 are in the Aramaic chapters. 13 (2 12. 13. 14. 18. 24 [twice]. 27. 48 4 3. 15 5 7. 8. 15) refer to the *ḥakkīmīn* of Babylon. 4 (2 20. 21 [twice]. 23) occur in Daniel's prayer (2 20-23) and refer to the *ḥokmā* of the true God, which he gives to the *ḥakkīmīn* and has given to Daniel in particular. The remaining 4 (2 30 5 11 [twice]. 14) also refer to Daniel's God-given wisdom.

Hosea

2 occurrences. In 13 13 Ephraim is referred to in an oracle as "a stupid son" (*bēn lōʾ ḥākām*). 14 10 is universally regarded as a later addition to the book; the phrase "whoever is *ḥākām*, let him understand these things" is similar to Jer 9 11 and Ps 107 43[38].

[36] See p. 24—31 above.

[37] See especially G. A. Cooke, The Book of Ezekiel, ICC, 1936, 315—322; G. Fohrer and K. Galling, Ezechiel, HAT 1/13, 1955, 162—164; W. Zimmerli, Ezechiel II, BK 13/2, 1969, 676—688 and the literature cited there.

[38] See p. 12 above.

Joel

No occurrences.

Amos

No occurrences.

Obadiah

1 occurrence, v. 8. This is a reference to the *ḥ^akāmīm* of Edom.

Jonah

No occurrences.

Micah

No occurrences.

Nahum

No occurrences.

Habakkuk

No occurrences.

Zephaniah

No occurrences.

Haggai

No occurrences.

Zechariah

One occurrence, 9 2. This is a reference to the *ḥokmā* of Tyre and Sidon.

Malachi

No occurrences[39].

---

[39] The above survey includes all occurrences (157) of the root *ḥkm* in the Old Testament apart from Proverbs, Job and Ecclesiastes.

B. Evaluation of the Occurrences

It is evident that some of the occurrences of the root *ḥkm* surveyed above are more significant than others for the detection of a true concern with *ḥokmā* in an intellectual sense. On the one hand its frequent repetition in a fairly short book or passage (as in the 24 occurrences in the space of a few chapters in Daniel), where a contrast is evidently deliberately made between pagan *ḥokmā* and that whose source is the true God, is likely to indicate that "wise" and "wisdom" are used there as key-words or motifs, even though most occurrences are accounted for by the constant repetition of a single phrase ("the wise men of Babylon") which, if it occurred in a different context and in an isolated case, might have little or no significance.

On the other hand, a small number of occurrences in a single short passage (as in Gen 41 8. 33. 39) may, if that passage constitutes an important climactic point in the structure of the whole work, point to a concern with the intellectual tradition in the work as a whole (in this case, the Joseph Story, Gen 37—50). The occurrences in each book must be judged on their own merits. But in general it is possible to eliminate certain types of occurrence as having little or no significance for the present purpose.

i. Passages where *ḥokmā* refers to manual skill or other non-intellectual activities including magic, except where the same literary unit also uses the concept in other senses in order to make a contrast. Such non-significant passages include the 16 occurrences in Exodus where *ḥokmā* is the manual skill of those engaged in making priestly garments, the Tabernacle, the Ark etc.[40], and also probably Ex 7 11[41]. They also include I Reg 7 14, referring to the craftsman Hiram, and the 6 similar references in Chronicles; also Ps 58 6 107 27 Isa 3 3 40 20 Jer 9 16 10 9 Ez 27 8. 9[42].

ii. Passages where the root *ḥkm* is used of human intelligence in a very general sense, with nothing in the context to suggest that the author is especially concerned with the problems of human life: Ex 1 10 Jdc 5 29 Jer 18 18 Hos 13 13.

---

[40] It is not disputed that the "wisdom" of these persons was God-given and thus has religious overtones. But it remains manual skill, and does not raise the problem raised by the intellectual tradition. [41] See p. 15f. above.

[42] The "wise women" of II Sam 14 2 20 16. 22 are not practitioners of magic arts, but women recognized for their exceptional intelligence. Moreover in view of the general concern of the Succession Narrative with the intellectual tradition, indicated by the 4 other occurrences as well as by its general character, it is unlikely that these "wise women" are introduced into the story in a merely incidental way. See further, p. 89ff. below.

iii. References to the *ḥᵃkāmīm* of foreign countries in contexts where there is no attempt to discuss the nature of this *ḥokmā* or to draw any specific conclusions from it. Thus in Jer 49 7 Ob 8 the *ḥokmā* of Edom, which was traditionally one of its main characteristics, is simply a symbol for the Edomite people in passages which prophesy its destruction; the same is true of the reference to the *ḥokmā* of Tyre and Sidon in Zech 9 2. In Isa 47 10, similarly, the *ḥokmā* of Babylon is referred to only because it was this which led to her fall. In other similar passages (Isa 44 25 Jer 50 35 51 57) the *ḥᵃkāmīm* of Babylon are simply items in a list, mentioned together with other classes (princes, warriors, diviners, etc.); no especial significance attaches to the word here.

The same is true of the references to the *ḥᵃkāmīm* of Egypt in Isa 19 11f. Here, although their claim to *ḥokmā* is dwelt on in some detail, the ineffectiveness of Egyptian *ḥokmā* is not used in order to express either praise or contempt of *ḥokmā* itself.

iv. Cases where literary dependence on another source is clearly established: all the occurrences in Chronicles[43].

v. Isolated occurrences in a book or an extended literary unit where the context does not suggest that the word is intended to bear any especial significance. Thus the use of *ḥokmā* as a description of the law-book in Esr 7 25, the reference to the consultation of lawyers or astrologers in Est 1 13[44] and the reference to Joseph's teaching *ḥokmā* to the elders of Egypt in Ps 105 22 — all solitary occurrences in an entire book or psalm — do not suggest that *ḥākām* or *ḥokmā* is being used as a key-word or as a word bearing any notable significance.

The solitary reference in the Code of Deuteronomy (Dtn 16 19) is also hardly to be regarded as indicative of the character of the code as a whole. Indeed, it should perhaps be included among the passages mentioned under ii above. It is a fact that a bribe blinds the eyes (even) of intelligent men; and that this is the sense here is strongly suggested by the absence of the article. If, as has been suggested, the motive clause here is a quotation or reminiscence of a proverbial saying[45], then it proves no more than that the author was familiar with the intellectual tradition. Such a literary allusion does not prove that he was influenced by it in any deeper sense[46].

---

[43] Even in the material in Chronicles which is entirely additional to that provided by Kings there is no evidence of an intention to introduce a new concept of *ḥokmā* going beyond that intended by the Deuteronomic Historian.

[44] See p. 16 above.

[45] See p. 77, n. 21 above.

[46] See p. 73 above.

The statement in Dtn 34 9 that Joshua was "full of the spirit of *ḥokmā*" should probably be eliminated from the discussion on similar grounds. It is universally agreed that the passage in which this statement occurs belongs to the priestly strand (34 1a. 7-9), and that it refers back to Num 27 18-23 (also P), where Moses laid his hands upon Joshua[47]. A similar phrase occurs in Ex 28 3 (also P), where it is stated that Yahweh has "filled with the spirit of *ḥokmā*" (*millē'tīw rūaḥ ḥokmā*) each of the persons who is to make Aaron's garments. There, however, *ḥokmā* is manual skill. Clearly *rūaḥ ḥokmā* belonged to the vocabulary of P, though it was not exclusive to him (cf. Isa 11 2). The fact that he has here combined the *rūaḥ* of Num 27 18 with the *rūaḥ ḥokmā* of Ex 28 3 in this note about Joshua does not suggest that he is under the influence of the intellectual tradition which is under discussion here.

Finally it is necessary to point out that the occurrence in Hos 14 10 is no indication of the influence of the intellectual tradition upon the prophet Hosea. It is universally agreed that this is an addition to the book of Hosea by a reader. It indicates that this reader regarded Hosea as a *ḥākām*, but tells us nothing about Hosea himself.

vi. Cases where the text or interpretation is too uncertain to be used with confidence: Est 6 13 Isa 3 3 33 6 Jer 10 7[48].

C. Analysis of Significant Occurrences

If the above analysis is accepted, the occurrences which remain prove to be restricted to a comparatively small number of books and passages[49]:

1. The Joseph Story (Gen 37—50)
Gen 41 8. 33. 39.

2. The Introductory Section of Deuteronomy (Dtn 1—4)
Dtn 1 13. 15 4 6 (twice) (N. B. There is also an isolated occurrence in the Code of Deuteronomy: 16 19).

---

[47] There is here, however, a curious discrepancy. In Num 27 18-23 Joshua is chosen for ordination because he already possesses the spirit (*'iš 'ašer-ruaḥ bō*); in Dtn 34 9 the "spirit of wisdom" is given to him as a result of the imposition of Moses' hands.

[48] This passage (Jer 10 1-16) is generally regarded as the work of an author or authors later than Jeremiah, and also as being in disorder. V. 6f. are missing not only from LXX but also from the Qumran fragment 4Q Jer[b].

[49] The elimination of particular occurrences does not preclude the possibility that the books or passages in which they appear may be adjudged to be influenced by the intellectual tradition on other grounds.

3. The Song of Moses (Dtn 32)
Dtn 32 6. 29.

4. The Succession Narrative (II Sam 9—20 I Reg 1f.)
II Sam 13 3 14 2. 20 (twice) 20 16. 22 I Reg 2 6. 9.

5. The History of Solomon (I Reg 3—11)
I Reg 3 12. 28 5 9. 10 (3 times). 11. 14 (twice). 21. 26 10 4. 6. 7. 8. 23. 24 11 41.

6. A Small Group of Psalms
Ps 19 8 37 30 49 4. 11 51 8 90 12 104 24 107 43 111 10 119 98.

7. I Isaiah (Isa 1—39)
5 occurrences certainly attributable to Isaiah himself (5 21 10 13 29 14 [twice] 31 2) and 1 of disputed authorship (11 2).

8. Jeremiah
6 occurrences attributable to Jeremiah (4 22 8 8. 9 [twice] 9 22 [twice]) and 3 (2) of later authorship (9 11 10 12 = 51 15).

9. Ezekiel 28
V. 3. 4. 5. 7. 12. 17.

10. Daniel
1 4. 17. 20 2 12. 13. 14. 18. 20. 21 (twice). 23. 24 (twice). 27. 30. 48 4 3. 15 5 7. 8. 11 (twice). 14. 15.

The root *ḥkm* is consequently missing, in any significant sense, from the following:

Gen 1—36 (all strands)

Exodus, Leviticus, Numbers

Deuteronomy (except for the introductory chapters and the Song of Moses)

Joshua and Judges

Samuel and Kings (except for the Succession Narrative and the History of Solomon)

The work of the Chronicler (Chronicles, Ezra, Nehemiah)

141 of the 150 psalms

II and III Isaiah

Ezekiel (except for ch. 28)

The Minor Prophets (apart from the later addition to Hosea [Hos 14 10])

Ruth, Song of Solomon, Lamentations, Esther[50].

---

[50] In the foregoing pages all occurrences of *ḥkm* are accounted for.

The positive results of this analysis contain few surprises, but generally tend to confirm conclusions reached by recent scholars on other grounds. At the same time in some instances they help to clarify literary problems of unity and authorship.

1. The Joseph Story

Gen 41, in which the 3 references to *ḥokmā* all occur, is clearly the turning-point of the story of Joseph. It is in this chapter that his misfortunes at his brothers' hands and in prison in Egypt come to an end, and that his unalloyed success and prosperity begin[51]. The cause of the change in his fortunes is the failure of the *ḥᵃkāmīm* of Egypt to interpret Pharaoh's dreams (v. 8) and Joseph's ability to do so, coupled with the practical advice which he gives (v. 33-36) on the policy to be followed in dealing with the famine. Pharaoh finds that Joseph himself fits the role of the *'îš nābōn wᵉḥākām* whom Joseph advises him to select to carry out this policy (v. 33. 39). These references are therefore key-words in a key-passage; and this conclusion supports the theory of von Rad[52] that the purpose of the Joseph Story as a whole is to present Joseph as an ideal example of the "wise man" whose virtues are rewarded with success[53].

2. The Introductory Section of Deuteronomy

Of the 4 occurrences here, those in 4 6 are the most significant. Here it is stated that obedience to Yahweh's laws promulgated through Moses "will be your *ḥokmā* and your understanding (*bīnā*) in the sight of the peoples, who, when they hear all these statutes, will say, 'Surely this great nation is an able and understanding people (*'am-ḥākām wᵉnābōn*)'." It is clearly the intention of the author of these words to characterize the Deuteronomic Code as the highest *ḥokmā* whose possession is infinitely superior to any *ḥokmā* which other peoples

[51] This is recognized by L. Ruppert, Die Josephserzählung der Genesis, 1965, 68, although he does not consider wisdom to be a leading characteristic of the story.

[52] Josephsgeschichte und Ältere Chokma.

[53] D. B. Redford, A Study of the Biblical Story of Joseph, VT Suppl XX, 1970, 100—105, disagrees with von Rad's thesis that the Joseph Story belongs to the category of wisdom literature; but both he and von Rad are thinking in terms of a literature produced in, or connected with, wisdom *schools*. In fact, Redford's own evaluation is in much broader terms: "in a broad sense" Joseph "resembles the paragon of virtue described by Wisdom Literature", but in the sense of "a common, human ideal, widely disseminated throughout all strata of all ancient Near Eastern societies" (105). This definition is too broad, while von Rad's is too narrow.

may claim to possess. It would, however, be wrong to regard this view as necessarily expressing the point of view of the Deuteronomic Code itself.

Although there is at present no consensus of scholarly opinion regarding the authorship of the "first introduction" to Deuteronomy (1 1—4 43), the view[54] that it comes from the same hand as the Code now has few supporters. Noth[55] and those who accept his thesis of a "Deuteronomic History" regard it as substantially part of that work, while Fohrer[56] believes it to have been written as a secondary introduction to Deuteronomy itself, probably in the exilic period. Although there is some uncertainty about the relationship of 4 1-43 to ch. 1—3, and also about the literary unity of this section itself, Noth[57] includes 4 6 in the basic substratum which comes from the same hand as ch. 1—3. Fohrer[58] does not question its relationship to the previous chapters.

There is therefore general agreement that this author, who regarded wisdom as a significant concept and related it closely to the Law in a way which already foreshadows later theological developments[59], is not to be identified with the author(s) of the Deuteronomic Code itself. If he was the Deuteronomic Historian it is surprising that these are the only, or almost the only, occurrences of the root *ḥkm* in any passages composed by the Deuteronomic Historian himself[60]. The statements in 1 13. 15 that the practical administration of the Law was carried out, under Moses' direction, by men selected for their *ḥokmā* constitute a natural extension of the author's view of the Law itself (or obedience to it) as *ḥokmā*.

3. The Song of Moses

The 2 occurrences in this poem, which is universally recognized as an independent piece, are similar in character. Israel's misfortunes

[54] E.g. that of S. R. Driver, Deuteronomy, ICC, 1896², lxvii—lxxiii.

[55] M. Noth, Überlieferungsgeschichtliche Studien, 1943, 14ff.

[56] Introduction 176f.

[57] Op. cit. 38f.

[58] P. 176.

[59] As seen in, e.g., Sir 24.

[60] See p. 109ff. below. The other possible occurrences are all in the History of Solomon (I Reg 2 6. 9 3 12 11 41), where, since the dominating theme is that of Solomon's wisdom, their occurrence in the editorial material is very natural. Nevertheless the first 3 of them are regarded as non-Deuteronomic by Montgomery and Gehman, The Books of Kings, 87f. 105—107, and as probably non-Deuteronomic by Noth, Könige, 9. 44—48. In 11 41 the word "wisdom" simply summarizes the content of the editor's sources.

are attributed to their lack of *ḥokmā* in failing to understand that Yahweh punishes those who disobey him.

It is possible that this theme, which is the counterpart of the positive statement in 4 6 that true *ḥokmā* consists in obedience to the Law, was at least partly instrumental in the decision of a later editor to place the Song here[61]. Certainly the choice of the concept of *ḥokmā* in the Song as the one thing necessary for Israel's prosperity suggests that this concept was important for the author, and this view corresponds to the conclusion of von Rad on grounds of form, style and language that "we must look for the origin of the poem in the sphere of Wisdom literature"[62].

The presence of "wisdom elements" has been discerned by other writers who, however, do not go as far as von Rad in making "wisdom" the sole significant element in the poem[63]. It should be noted also that the poem is very variously dated: Eissfeldt[64] and Albright[65] ascribe it, on the grounds of historical allusions and language respectively, to the 10th or 9th century, though most scholars have dated it considerably later.

4. The Succession Narrative

8 occurrences in such a relatively short work (14 chapters), when one bears in mind the rarity of the root *ḥkm* in the narrative books of the Old Testament (e. g. its complete absence from the rest of I and II Samuel and from I Reg 12 to II Reg 25), can hardly be put down to coincidence[66]. At the very least they reflect an unusually high preoccupation with the concept and practice of *ḥokmā* in the period when the work was written and especially in the circles within which and for which it was written. Against this view it has been urged by J. L. Crenshaw that the representatives of *ḥokmā* here play a "minor role" and have a "questionable function"[67].

---

[61] On the reason for the present position of the Song and on its supposed relationship to the Deuteronomic Law see O. Eissfeldt, Die Umrahmung des Mose-Liedes Dtn 32, 1—43 und des Mose-Gesetzes Dtn 1—30 in Dtn 31, 9—32, 47, Kleine Schriften III, 1966, 322—334; Introduction, 227.

[62] Deuteronomium 143 (ET 200).

[63] Especially Boston, The Wisdom Influence Upon the Song of Moses; cf. Fohrer, Introduction, 189f.

[64] Die Umrahmung des Mose-Liedes.

[65] W. F. Albright, Some Remarks on the Song of Moses in Deuteronomy xxxii, VT 9 (1959), 339—346.

[66] See R. N. Whybray, The Succession Narrative, especially 56—95.

[67] Method in Determining Wisdom Influence 139.

The former of these claims is hardly borne out by the facts. The advice given to Amnon by his friend Jonadab, who was "an extremely clever man" (*'îš ḥākām me'ōd*, II Sam 13 3) marks the beginning of the entire chain of events by which successively Amnon and Absalom were removed from the line of succession (II Sam 13—19). The advice given to David by the "wise woman" of Tekoa sent by Joab (II Sam 14 2-20) was the cause of David's recall of Absalom (14 21-24), which was in its turn the prelude to the rebellion of Absalom, which ended in his death. These were events of crucial importance for the purpose of the author.

Similarly the *ḥokmā* displayed by Solomon on the advice of David to put Joab and Shimei to death (I Reg 2 6. 9) was regarded by the author as a vital element in the establishment of Solomon's position as David's successor: it is not until he has recorded the execution of these acts that he is able to conclude his narrative with the statement that "the kingdom was established in the hand of Solomon" (2 46b).

Of those who are referred to as possessing *ḥokmā* in the Succession Narrative, only the "wise woman" of Abel (II Sam 20 16-22) can be said to play a minor role[68]. The evidence of the *ḥokmā*-texts in the Succession Narrative of the importance attached by the author to the advice given by "wise men" and "wise women" is strongly supported by the many other occasions in the story when such wisdom is proffered, even though the root *ḥkm* does not occur[69].

The "questionable function" of some of the "wisdom" proffered in the Succession Narrative does not mean that Crenshaw is right in concluding that "wisdom" is not a significant theme in the work[70]. One of the themes of the book is the interplay in human events between "wisdom" and folly; and the author was well aware, as were the authors of Proverbs, that not everything which passes for wisdom should be accepted at its face value, and also that wickedness can assume the character of wisdom for its own purposes[71]. The statement that Jonadab was *ḥākām me'ōd* is hardly to be taken at its face value: it is probably ironical in intention[72], as may also be the flattering remark of the wise woman of Tekoa to David that "my lord has

[68] On the characterization of David as "wise" by the wise woman of Tekoa (II Sam 14 20) see below.

[69] See The Succession Narrative 58—60.

[70] It should be noted, moreover, that Crenshaw's arguments are directed against a supposed thesis that "wisdom influence" is "the *exclusive* background for the . . . succession document" (142; my italics). Such a thesis has not, to my knowledge, been advanced.

[71] The Succession Narrative 59. 60. 64.

[72] The Succession Narrative 85.

wisdom like the wisdom of the angel of God to know all things that are on the earth" (II Sam 14 20). Jonadab's advice was either naive or treacherous: it was superficially "wise" in that it ingeniously enabled Amnon to gain his immediate purpose, but entirely lacking in true wisdom in that it failed to point out the dangerous consequences of success.

In a somewhat similar way, David's cleverness in seeing through the wise woman's mission and in perceiving the hand of Joab behind it showed him to be superficially wise, yet the action which he was prompted to take by the woman's trick, recalling Absalom to Jerusalem, was immediately followed by a terrible act of folly. His refusal, on Absalom's arrival, to be reconciled with him or to restore him to his former position at court and within the family led to disastrous consequences. The narratives which follow (II Sam 14 24—15 6) make it clear that this was how the author regarded it. It is impossible to doubt that in these episodes, as elsewhere, he was deliberately raising the question of the nature of "true wisdom".

Whether there is an ironical intention in I Reg 2 6. 9, where Solomon's ruthless, and, in one case, treacherous elimination of potentially dangerous men is described as "wisdom" is less clear. Such ruthless action is, perhaps, implicitly advocated in Prov 16 14 20 26[73]. But whatever the intention of the author, it is significant that here, in one short passage, the concept of *ḥokmā* should be twice used in referring to policies which, whatever their morality, were of historical importance.

The occurrences of the root *ḥkm* in the Succession Narrative thus confirm the conclusion reached on other grounds that this is a work in which *ḥokmā* plays a crucial rather than merely a minor role.

5. The History of Solomon

The number of occurrences here (18) leaves no room for doubt that *ḥokmā* (always associated, directly or indirectly, with Solomon) is one of the main themes, if not the main theme, of this part of Kings. It is also generally agreed that this *ḥokmā* of Solomon is understood in different passages to mean quite different things, so that the impression given by the history of Solomon in its final form is that Solomon's wisdom was all-embracing, including learning, literary ability, political sagacity (though there may be a hint of irony in ch. 11, with its tale of at least partial failure), administrative skill and an understanding of human nature. Nor is there any dispute over the way in which this impression has been created: the authors or

[73] Cf. The Succession Narrative 90.

compilers have made use of a variety of sources of different kinds, each with its own interpretation of Solomon's wisdom.

Regarding the authorship of the material, however, there is much disagreement. All recent studies of these chapters admittedly agree to a large extent in their view of the main three stages of compilation: pre-Deuteronomic material (whether already mainly gathered into a single work or not) was compiled to form a "Deuteronomic edition" (or editions), and this was eventually supplemented in the post-exilic period by "post-Deuteronomic" additions.

But the precise division of the material into pre-Deuteronomic, Deuteronomic and post-Deuteronomic is a matter on which there is no clear agreement. The numerous occurrences of *ḥkm* are found in passages whose authorship is disputed. It may be noted, however, that in the history of the study of these chapters there is a distinct tendency in recent years to minimize the role of the Deuteronomist Historian as author and to argue for the antiquity of much of the material which was formerly attributed to him[74]. Whereas Pfeiffer[75], representing much older scholarship[76], regarded a large proportion of these chapters as having been partly or substantially rewritten by the Deuteronomist, the major commentaries of recent times[77] are very sparing in the verses which they attribute to him.

The references to Solomon's *ḥokmā* occur in 7 different contexts, each of which is generally recognized as having a separate origin: the story of Solomon's dream (3 4-15); the story of Solomon's judgement (3 16-28); a description of Solomon's international reputation for literary (and possibly scientific) skill (5 9-14); the story of Solomon's relations with Hiram king of Tyre (5 15-26); the story of the visit of the Queen of Sheba to Jerusalem (10 1-13); another short statement about Solomon's reputation for *ḥokmā* (10 23f.); and the Deuteronomic formula which closes the account of the reign (11 41-43).

Most recent commentaries[78] are in agreement that none of the references to Solomon's *ḥokmā* in these passages can certainly be attributed to the Deuteronomist, with the exception of 11 41, which is universally recognized to be part of the Deuteronomic summary of the reign. However, this verse is itself a witness to the fact that the

---

[74] On the other hand, R. B. Y. Scott, Solomon and the Beginnings of Wisdom in Israel' has argued that almost all the "wisdom" passages are *post*-Deuteronomic.

[75] R. H. Pfeiffer, Introduction of the Old Testament, 1941, 383—391.

[76] Cf., e.g., C. F. Burney, Notes on the Hebrew Text of the Books of Kings, 1903.

[77] Montgomery—Gehman, Gray, Noth. However, J. Fichtner, Das erste Buch von den Königen, BAT 12/1, 1964 and Weinfeld, Deuteronomy and the Deuteronomic School, 246, take a different view.

[78] See n. 77 above. Scott, however (art. cit. 270), regards 3 12. 28 5 21 as Deuteronomic. Eissfeldt (Introduction 288) is uncertain about 5 21.

Deuteronomist found a tradition of Solomon's *ḥokmā* in the material which he used: "Now the rest of the acts of Solomon, and all that he did, and his *ḥokmā*, are they not written in the book of the acts of Solomon?" There is no reason to suppose[79] that the phrase "and his *ḥokmā*" has been added to the sentence at a later time. The form of the sentence corresponds exactly to a number of other Deuteronomic summaries concluding the accounts of the reigns of kings of Israel and Judah[80]. In all these cases the Deuteronomist is summarizing in a few words the contents of the written sources to which he specifically refers, in this case the "book of the acts of Solomon". It is, indeed, extremely probable that some at least of the stories about Solomon's *ḥokmā* which he used come from this source[81]. Thus although this verse is to be attributed to the Deuteronomist, it is simply a reference to the tradition about Solomon's wisdom which he found in his source material.

It is therefore reasonable to conclude that the interest in *ḥokmā* displayed by the History of Solomon is not an importation into the story by the Deuteronomist but something which was already present in the Solomon tradition and which the Deuteronomist preserved without adding significantly to it. The significance of this conclusion — as far as the Deuteronomist is concerned — will be considered at a later point in the discussion[82].

6. Psalms

In the case of the Psalms, owing to their poetical form, the form-critical method is more effective than elsewhere in detecting the influence of the intellectual tradition, and the strictures made against it earlier[83] do not apply here, or at least only with much less force.

The book of Psalms is an extremely varied collection of poems, and therefore there is no *a priori* reason why some of these — or parts of them — should not be products of the intellectual tradition like the longer poems in Proverbs and Job. Form-criticism is clearly relevant here. Similarly a psalm may contain, or even be wholly com-

---

[79] As does Gray (I and II Kings 298), who thinks that "and his wisdom" is "possibly an addition to the original note".

[80] Cf. especially "and his might" (I Reg 16 5); "and the conspiracy which he made" (I Reg 16 20); "and the might which he showed" (I Reg 16 27); "and the ivory house which he built" (I Reg 22 39); and also I Reg 22 46 II Reg 13 8 13 12 14 15. 28 20 20 21 17.

[81] So also Noth, Könige, 262f.; Eissfeldt, Introduction, 288.

[82] P. 109ff. below.

[83] P. 72ff. above.

posed of[84], elements identifiable as *Weisheitssprüche* or short "wisdom sayings".

The fact that the Psalms are couched, like Proverbs and Job, in poetical form also makes the criterion of subject matter, also criticised above[85], more readily applicable than in the case of most other Old Testament literature, since identity of thought is more likely than in the case of narrative to be accompanied by similarity or identity of expression, and the danger of subjectivism in the making of comparisons is thereby lessened.

These considerations lead to the conclusion that, in the case of the Psalms, the criterion of the occurrence of the root *ḥkm* is of less consequence than in the literature so far surveyed. This conclusion is further strengthened by the fact that each psalm is an independent composition of relatively restricted length. It is not to be expected that, even in a psalm which may be identified on other grounds as wholly belonging to the intellectual tradition, the root will necessarily occur. Nevertheless it may be of some value to examine those psalms in which it does occur in order to see to what extent this criterion confirms the results obtained by other methods.

In looking for the influence of the intellectual tradition on the Psalms it is important to bear in mind the distinction first made by Gunkel between psalms which belong wholly to the category of "wisdom literature" and those which simply employ "wisdom forms" to a lesser extent[86], and also the dictum of Mowinckel that "the psalm-writer may use the form of the 'wisdom poetry' for his personal expression of the praise of God, or thanksgiving for a blessing received — without his psalm being a wisdom or problem poem"[87].

Of the psalms in which the root *ḥkm* occurs, 37 and 49 are generally recognized as belonging wholly to the category of "wisdom literature", on grounds both of style and contents. Ps 37[88] is concerned wholly with the problem of the prosperity of the wicked, and expresses confidence in their eventual downfall and in the eventual vindication of the righteous: this theme is found frequently in Proverbs and in the speeches of the friends of Job. The lack of progression in the argument is explained by Weiser as due to its compilation, in

---

84 So Weiser, Psalmen, 212f. (ET 314f.), with regard to Ps. 37, and Kraus, Psalmen II, BK 15/2, 819f. with regard to Ps 119.

85 P. 71f. above.

86 H. Gunkel, Einleitung in die Psalmen, 1933, 384ff.

87 The Psalms in Israel's Worship I 31.

88 On the "wisdom" characteristics of Ps 37 see Gunkel, Die Psalmen, 155f.; Einleitung 386f. 389f.; Mowinckel, The Psalms in Israel's Worship II, 111. 138f.; Psalms and Wisdom 213f.; Kraus, Psalmen I, 287f.; Weiser, Psalmen, 212f. (ET 314f.); M. Dahood, Psalms I, AB 16, 1966, 227.

spite of its alphabetic acrostic form, from a series of "wisdom sayings", while Gunkel and Mowinckel point out its use of various forms attested in Proverbs and Job, such as the admonition and the admonitory tale in the first person told by the man of experience to his juniors. It is in this context of thought that v. 30 asserts that "the mouth of the righteous utters *ḥokmā*", an assertion which is followed in the next verse by the confident assertion that "his steps do not slip".

Similarly the "wisdom" character of Ps 49 is shown by the introductory verses (v. 2-5) in which the author makes a general appeal to people of all nations and classes, avoiding any references — as in Proverbs, Job and Ecclesiastes — to any specifically Israelite religious experience, and proposes to speak *ḥokmā* (v. 4) under the inspiration of a "proverb" (*māšāl*) and in response to a "riddle" (*ḥīdā*), and by the theme of the transitoriness of human life, which is strongly reminiscent of parts of the book of Job[89].

The first reference to *ḥokmā* here (v. 4) is thus itself part of a formal statement that the psalm belongs to that tradition. The second reference (v. 11a) poses a problem of interpretation: "Truly he (one) sees that *ḥ^{a}kāmīm* die"[90]. Gunkel saw in this verse, which appears to put the *ḥākām* on the same level as the "fool and the stupid" (v. 10b) as equally futile in view of their common end in death, an interpolation made in the spirit of Ecclesiastes. If this were so, it would be a "wisdom" interpolation into a "wisdom poem" of a different character. But this objection to v. 10 has not been accepted by more recent commentators. If v. 10a is an original part of the psalm it has probably something of an *a fortiori* sense: even the *ḥ^{a}kāmīm* must die, and so for the foolish to live as if they were immortal is a very clear example of their folly. However the line is interpreted, it shows a concern with *ḥokmā* in the sense of a concern with the problems of human life, and the designation of the whole psalm as belonging to this tradition is thereby confirmed[91].

In the case of 5 other psalms (51 90 104 107 111) there is a general agreement among modern commentators that their authors have at particular points found the concept of *ḥokmā* a useful aid in the expression of their thoughts in compositions which are basically of a different kind. It is at such points that the root *ḥkm* occurs.

Thus Ps 51 is primarily an individual lamentation, and Ps 90 a communal lamentation: both are prayers for God's mercy and for the restoration of his loving care for the petitioners. But in the course

---

[89] See the commentaries for details.

[90] The proposed emendation of *yir'e* to *r^{e}'ē* (imv., "see") is hardly necessary.

[91] On this verse see especially Kraus 366.

of the prayer each writer is led to reflect on the state of the human heart which has led to the present alienation from God. Such reflection momentarily brings about in him a desire for, among other things, such an understanding of himself and of the human condition which only the *ḥokmā* which God gives can provide.

For the author of Ps 51 this will enable him to repent of his sins and receive pardon: so he prays, "Teach me *ḥokmā*" (v. 8). In Ps 90 it is as a release from the crushing weight of the realization of the brevity of human life, which makes the misery of the present even harder to bear, that the author prays in v. 12: "So teach us to number our days that we may obtain a heart of *ḥokmā*"[92]. Both these passages take for granted the idea that God is the source of true *ḥokmā*, an idea found elsewhere in the Old Testament[93]; but there is no reason to assume any direct literary dependence on any other passage. Nor should either of these psalms be considered as primarily concerned with the concept of *ḥokmā*: *ḥokmā*, as divinely assisted intelligence, is simply a concept to which each of these authors turns as he considers what he lacks and what he needs in his present distress.

Ps 104 111 belong to the category of the Hymn[94], or as Westermann prefers to call it, the "psalm of praise"[95]. Both praise Yahweh for his gracious actions, though they differ in that Ps 104 speaks only of his creation and preservation of the world, while Ps 111 concentrates on his goodness to his chosen people. As in the lamentation, where the author's reflections on the state of the human heart are capable of leading his thoughts in the direction of *ḥokmā* as the cure for its weaknesses, so here in the "descriptive psalm of praise"[96] the listing of Yahweh's many gracious actions may also lead to thoughts concerning *ḥokmā*, since such creative skill and glorious deeds presuppose that he possesses this quality in the fullest measure.

In Ps 104, which is probably a late psalm in which the classical structure of the psalm of praise has to some extent been modified, the reference to *ḥokmā* occurs as a sudden exclamation (v. 24) inserted into the list of God's providential actions in organizing and maintaining the natural order: "O Yahweh, how great are thy works! In *ḥokmā* hast thou made them all." But in spite of the suddenness of the exclamation, it may be said that here the thought of

[92] Or, perhaps better, "enter the gate of wisdom" (reading *nābō'* for *nābī'* and assuming *bāb* = "gate" [cf. Aram. *bāb*, Acc. *bābu*]); so Wellhausen (cited in Gunkel, Die Psalmen, 402). For the idea of Wisdom's gates cf. Prov 8 34 9 4.

[93] E.g. I Reg 3—11 Prov 1—9.

[94] So Gunkel and most subsequent commentaries.

[95] C. Westermann, Das Loben Gottes in den Psalmen, 1961 (ET The Praise of God in the Psalms, 1966).

[96] A sub-category of the psalm of praise defined by Westermann op. cit.

ḥokmā is not merely incidental, but summarizes the thought of the whole psalm. Although this psalm is not generally classified as a "wisdom psalm", it has close affinities with Job 38—41, and von Rad has shown that this passage is in turn related to the *Listenwissenschaft* or practice of making lists of phenomena in Egyptian "wisdom literature" as exemplified by the "onomastica"[97]. The statement that Yahweh has made the works of creation "in *ḥokmā*", which is found also in slightly different words in Prov 3 19 Jer 10 12 = 51 15, is a confession of Yahweh's infinitely superior intelligence which springs from the contemplation of the greatness and variety of his works.

In Ps 111 the reference to *ḥokmā* occurs in the final section: "The fear of Yahweh is the beginning of *ḥokmā*" (v. 10). Here again it springs from the author's contemplation, in a mood of praise, of the "works of Yahweh"; but here, as in Ps 51 90, the *ḥokmā* which he has in mind is that God-given human *ḥokmā* which is necessary to man's wellbeing. The only true *ḥokmā* comes from the "fear" of the God who is holy and terrible, yet has established the covenant with Israel, within which he dispenses grace towards his people. The acrostic form of this psalm shows that this final verse is not an appendix added by another writer but an integral part of the psalm. This type of "descriptive psalm of praise" has no fixed form of conclusion[98], and this author has chosen to sum up his praise with a formula which is probably not of his own making, since it occurs in slightly different words on several other occasions[99]. In doing so he has worked within the pattern of the psalm of praise discerned by the form-critics.

Ps 107 33-43 is widely regarded as a secondary addition to v. 1-32[100]. Like Ps 104, these verses list, in a hymn-like manner, the providential works of Yahweh in the realm of nature, and end, like Ps 111, with a formula which sums up the whole with a recommendation — here in the form of an exhortation — to show wisdom in giving heed to them. The first lines of this formula — "Whoever is *ḥākām*, let him give heed to these things; let men consider the steadfast love of Yahweh" — strongly resemble the first lines of the formula (Hos 14 10) with which the book of Hosea concludes. However, whereas in Hosea the formula is an addition made subsequently to the book, in Ps 107 43 the whole formula is closely related to the verses which precede it. Whether the author was making use of an already existing phraseology or not, this verse should probably be regarded as the concluding section of a psalm of praise in the same way as Ps 111 10.

[97] Hiob xxxviii und die altägyptische Weisheit.

[98] Westermann op. cit. (ET) 130.

[99] Job 28 28 Prov 1 7 9 10 15 33 Sir 1 14.

[100] Duhm, Die Psalmen, 252; Gunkel, Die Psalmen, 472; Kraus II 736.

Finally in Ps 19 8 119 98 the root *ḥkm* is used in connection with the Law. Ps 19 8-15 are generally regarded as a separate poem unconnected with the earlier part of the psalm, and both this poem and Ps 119 are entirely concerned with the glorification of the Law as the gift of God, given to his people to preserve them from error and to lead them to salvation. Thus when Ps 19 8 declares that "The law of Yahweh is perfect, reviving the soul; the testimony of Yahweh is sure, making wise (*maḥkīmat*) the simple"; and when Ps 119 98 confesses that "Thy commandment makes me wiser (*teḥakkemēnī*) than my enemies, for it is ever with me", this exemplifies that late tradition which identifies *ḥokmā* with the Law. This view of these two psalms is that which is generally held by the commentators.

We may conclude that the occurrences of *ḥkm* in the Psalms, and the manner in which they are introduced, confirm the conclusions reached by other means about the extent to which these psalms ought to be classified as belonging to the intellectual tradition.

7. I Isaiah

It has already been argued that the view that Isaiah was engaged in controversy with an entrenched class known as "the wise men" is a mistaken one[101]. Nevertheless the occurrence of the root *ḥkm* 5 times among his certainly genuine utterances (5 21 10 13 29 14 [twice] 31 2) shows that he must be counted among those who took seriously the concept of *ḥokmā*. To this extent he may be said to have been "influenced" by it.

With one exception, these passages show him concerned entirely with human "wisdom" and as condemning it and identifying it simply with arrogance: to be *ḥākām* in one's own sight is to deserve a condemnation equal to that reserved for the worst sins (5 18-25); the claim of the Assyrian king to *ḥokmā* is blasphemy against the true God (10 13); and the pretended *ḥokmā* of Israel's clever men, far from saving the state, will be swept away when Yahweh once more takes a hand in directing Judah's political affairs (29 14).

The remaining passage (31 2), however, has rightly been seen as of outstanding theological importance and as showing that Isaiah had a positive as well as a negative concept of *ḥokmā*[102]. It is unlikely that it was he who originated the idea of *ḥokmā* as an attribute of

---

101 P. 18—21 above.

102 On its theological significance see, e.g., H. Ringgren, Word and Wisdom: Studies in the Hypostatization of Divine Qualities and Functions in the Ancient Near East, 1947, 132; Fohrer, Weisheit, 263; Whybray, Wisdom in Proverbs, 22. 83. 93f. Fichtner, Jesaja unter den Weisen, appears to take the same view.

Yahweh[103]. What is more likely to be original with him is the implied assertion[104] in this verse that the divine *ḥokmā*, far from being the beneficent source of human wisdom, is irrevocably opposed to its feeble and blasphemous pretensions[105]. However, this assertion, made in the heat of controversy, may not be his final considered thought on the subject. If 28 23-29 is to be attributed to him[106], he was prepared to concede a more positive contribution of Yahweh's wisdom to human affairs.

However 31 2 is interpreted, it is clear that *ḥokmā* was an important concept for Isaiah, though it was not central to his teaching. To this extent, therefore, the occurrences of the root *ḥkm* confirm the views of those who see a "wisdom influence" on Isaiah on other grounds.

8. Jeremiah

Here, if the general consensus of scholars is accepted that 9 11 10 12 = 51 15 are not utterances of Jeremiah, only 3 passages remain to be considered in an assessment of the place of *ḥokmā* in this prophet's own teaching: 4 22 8 8f. (3 times) 9 22 (twice).

In all three cases a negative judgement is made upon human *ḥokmā*: the so-called *ḥokmā* encountered by Jeremiah among his compatriots is used to do evil rather than good (4 22); the claim to be *ḥākām* on the basis of the possession of the law of Yahweh is falsified by the rejection of Yahweh's word and will lead to disaster (8 8f.); and to be proud of one's *ḥokmā*, like pride in might and wealth, is a false pride, which is contrasted with the true pride in knowing Yahweh (9 22).

These passages are remarkably similar to the negative passages in Isaiah; but there is no corresponding positive teaching about

---

[103] If Isa 11 2, where it is stated that the "spirit of wisdom and understanding" will rest upon the Davidic king, is not a word of Isaiah but belongs to the Judaean royal traditions, it may be earlier than Isaiah. If some at least of the texts in I Reg 3—11 in which Yahweh is represented as conferring wisdom on Solomon are pre-Deuteronomic, they also may go back to a very early date in the history of the monarchy. Certainly the comparison of David's wisdom to that of an angel of God in II Sam 14 20, which may imply something of the kind, belongs to such an early source. In view of the currency of such ideas elsewhere in the ancient Near East an early date for its appearance in Israel is not improbable.

[104] Implied by the word *gam*, "also", probably to be understood with Fichtner, Jesaja unter den Weisen, 26 n. 22, as "ironisch gemeint".

[105] In view of the uncertainty about the date and authorship of 11 2 it would be hazardous to draw conclusions from this verse about Isaiah's own teaching.

[106] On this see p. 149 below.

Yahweh as the source of *ḥokmā*. It was left to the authors of 9 11 and 10 12 to add this thought. It would seem that Jeremiah was faced by the same cocksureness among his contemporaries as was Isaiah, and that he reacted, negatively at least, in a similar way. To this extent but no more he also may be said to have been concerned with the problem of *ḥokmā*.

9. Ezekiel 28

The fact that all the occurrences of the root *ḥkm* in the book of Ezekiel are found in two adjacent chapters (27f.) and exclusively in passages condemning Tyre or its ruler is a striking one. Whether these passages are the composition of Ezekiel or not[107], it is clear that *ḥkm* was not part of the ordinary vocabulary of this prophet. He neither accuses Israel of pride in its assumed *ḥokmā*, nor does he castigate Israel for lacking it, though his catalogue of Israel's sins is an extensive one. In this he differs from his predecessors, Isaiah and Jeremiah. The castigation of those who claim to be wise is reserved for the Tyrians.

If, as has been proposed above, the two references in ch. 27[108] are to be dismissed from the discussion as having a purely professional reference to the practitioners of a manual skill, the use of *ḥkm* in Ezekiel is restricted to 2 passages: 28 1-10, an oracle condemning Tyre under the symbol of the "prince of Tyre", and 28 11-19, a mocking dirge pronounced against the king of Tyre. The relationship between these 2 passages is not certain, but recent study[109] inclines toward the view that their juxtaposition is due to later editors. According to Zimmerli it was these who introduced both the occurrences of *ḥkm* into v. 11-19. Originally the cause of Tyre's downfall here was not pride in its *ḥokmā* but in its beauty[110]. The purpose of the additions was to bind the 2 passages into a literary unit.

If this view is correct, we are left with the 4 occurrences of *ḥkm* in 28 1-10 (v. 3. 4. 5. 7)[111]. There is some doubt whether even this poem

---

107 There is no unanimity among the commentators on this point.

108 V. 8. 9. See p. 83 above.

109 E.g. Fohrer, Ezechiel, 159—164; Zimmerli, Ezechiel II, 662.

110 Zimmerli 672. 686. In the case of v. 12, where the phrase "full of wisdom" is missing from LXX, W. Eichrodt (Der Prophet Hesekiel, ATD 22, 1966, 265 [ET Ezekiel, OTL, 1970, 389]) and Fohrer agree with Zimmerli that the reference is not original.

111 Fohrer (159) adds a further occurrence by emending *kol-sātūm* in v. 3 to *ḥ*^{a}*kāmîm*, following LXX. There is some doubt about the text here, but it is not certain that emendation is necessary; or, if it is necessary, that this is the right emendation. See the discussion in Zimmerli 663.

is from a single hand[112]; but whether this is so or not, it is clear from the way in which the theme is developed that the author(s) took the concept of *ḥokmā* more seriously than the authors of other passages in the prophetical books where the *ḥᵃkāmīm* are castigated and their *ḥokmā* treated with contempt as useless. There is clearly a lesson here for an Israelite audience which is in line with the teaching of Isaiah and Jeremiah about the sin of being "wise in one's own eyes"[113].

Finally it may be of some little significance for the question of authorship that the concept of *ḥokmā* is taken so seriously in these few verses while it is totally lacking from the rest of the book.

10. Daniel

Although slightly more than half the occurrences of the root *ḥkm* in this book refer to the *ḥᵃkāmīm* (Aram. *ḥakkīmīn*) of Babylon, the concentration of no less than 24 occurrences within the small scope of 4 chapters (1 2 4 5) makes it clear that *ḥākām* (*ḥakkīm*) and *ḥokmā* are key-words in these stories. Moreover the strong contrast between the failure of the pagan "wise men" and the success of the man to whom the true God has given *ḥokmā* is strongly reminiscent of the situation in the Joseph Story in Genesis, although the theological implications are more specifically drawn out. The similarity between the two is further seen in the themes which they have in common: the young Israelite captive at the court of the foreign king, the interpretation of the king's dreams, the promotion of the young Israelite to a position of power and honour[114]. There can therefore be no doubt that these chapters are the work of an author (or authors) for whom *ḥokmā* was an important concept.

Some qualifications, however, are necessary. It should be observed that the root *ḥkm* occurs only in stories which concern Daniel himself. It does not occur in ch. 3, where he is not mentioned and the heroes are the three companions, Shadrach, Meshach and Abednego, although it occurs in the introductory narrative (ch. 1), where Daniel and the companions are mentioned together.

A further point of interest it that it does not occur in the stories where the theme is not the interpretation of dreams but the suffering and vindication of the faithful Jewish captives: that is, the stories of the three companions in the furnace (ch. 3) and of Daniel in the den of lions (ch. 6).

---

[112] See especially Zimmerli 669f.

[113] On the mythological background see especially Zimmerli 667—669.

[114] On this point see O. Plöger, Das Buch Daniel, KAT 18, 1965, 25f.

These distinctions tend to confirm the now widely held opinion that the stories in ch. 1—6, whether a literary unity or not, have been gathered from different sources. This may perhaps assist in the understanding of the pre-history of the book[115]. The absence of the theme of *ḥokmā* from ch. 3 confirms the view that the tradition of the three companions was originally unconnected with that of Daniel[116]. Again, its absence from ch. 3 and 6 may suggest that the theme of suffering and vindication was also originally a separate tradition.

Ch. 1 presents a further set of problems. It is widely agreed that in its present form its purpose is to weld into a unity the diverse narratives of ch. 2—6. But there is evidence that it is itself far from being a literary unity. Within v. 3-20 there are discernible three distinct layers of narrative[117].

The original story seems to have told simply how Nebuchadnezzar selected a number of young Jewish noblemen and gave them a Babylonian education to enable them to be appointed to his staff. This simple story is clearly discernible in v. 3. (4). 5b[118]. 18. 19. Its point is to be found in v. 19: in the course of a mere three years (v. 5b) these Jewish young men, who began with no knowledge of Babylonian customs and education, were able to master these things so well that they became the equals, or the superiors, of even the most accomplished Babylonians[119].

A second theme, which perhaps never existed independently but is a midrashic elaboration of the original story, is that of the faithfulness of Daniel (and his companions) to the food laws of the Pentateuch, and the vindication of this faithfulness. It is clear that in the original version of this theme Daniel alone was the hero. It is he and he alone who takes the initiative. This theme is found in v. 5a. 8-16, and is entirely separable from the rest of the story. V. 11b, which

---

115 See, e.g., J. A. Montgomery, The Book of Daniel, ICC, 1927, 93; Plöger 27; M. Delcor, Le Livre de Daniel, SB, 1971, 10—13.

116 Cf., e.g., A. Bentzen, Daniel, HAT 1/19, 1952², 5. 34; N. W. Porteous, Das Danielbuch, ATD 23, 1962, 42 (ET Daniel, OTL, 1965, 55); Plöger 61f.

117 Whether this problem should be solved by literary criticism or by traditio-criticism or redaction-criticism is a question which cannot be pursued here, though it may be remarked that literary analysis at least partly meets the case.

118 The grammatical anomaly of *l^egadd^elām* disappears once it is recognized that v. 5a is a later addition.

119 The story has received a number of additions. It is unlikely that all of the many epithets in v. 4 can be original; some of them are simply "embellishments" which in fact spoil the narrative style; and the reference to *ḥokmā* here belongs to a later stage in the redaction (see p. 103 below). It is also doubtful whether the names of the four young men are those which originally stood here. Their present purpose — that of the final redactor — is of course to prepare for the chapters which follow.

associates the names of the three companions with that of Daniel, belongs to the final stage of the redaction.

The third theme, which attributes God-given *ḥokmā* to Daniel (and his companions), appears only in v. 4. 17. 20. It also is quite separable from the remainder and consists of a series of additions which belong to the final stage of the redaction, anticipating the events of the chapters which follow in the present arrangement of the book. It is only in these verses that the root *ḥkm* appears. This *ḥokmā* is referred to in a way which makes it clear that it is to be distinguished from the Babylonian education which is the motif of the first theme.

To sum up, there are three stories in the first part of Daniel in which *ḥokmā* plays an essential role: ch. 2 4 5. In these stories it is clear that *ḥokmā* has always played an essential role: without it there would be no story. In addition, the theme of *ḥokmā* has been inserted by an editor, who may be the editor of ch. 1—6 or of the whole book[120], into the introductory chapter. This prominence of *ḥokmā* in certain chapters of the first half of the book has to be taken into account in an assessment of the thesis put forward, in particular by von Rad[121], that apocalyptic is the child, not of prophecy, but of wisdom.

The question which needs to be asked is not whether there is "wisdom" in ch. 1—6, but whether there are the characteristics of apocalyptic there. This cannot be said to be fully the case in ch. 4 5. Although the dreams and their interpretations are related in a style similar to that of apocalyptic, they are not in themselves apocalyptic visions, as they do not predict the end of the world and the setting up of God's kingdom, but only future events *within* history.

It is, as has been recognized by others, ch. 2 which has all the characteristics of an apocalyptic vision, and is, in fact, as is well known, similar to the vision in ch. 7. Thus here "wisdom" and apocalyptic are closely connected. Daniel himself receives a revelation of the mystery of the king's dream in a "vision of the night" (v. 19), and then praises God who "gives wisdom to the wise" (*yāhēb ḥokmᵉtā' lᵉḥak-kīmīn*, v. 21) and in particular for giving "wisdom and strength" (*ḥokmᵉtā' ūgᵉbūrᵉtā'*) to him personally (v. 23). In view of the fact that Daniel's visions in the latter part of the book are also called night visions (7 1) it would seem that the final author or editor intended to imply that these were of the same kind; and, indeed, the revelation made to him through the man Gabriel is described in 9 22 as giving him "wisdom and understanding".

In 9 22 however, the root *ḥkm* is not used. The phrase employed is *lᵉhaśkīlᵉkā' bīnā*. Both of these roots occur fairly frequently in both parts

---

120 See the commentaries.

121 Theologie II 314—328 (ET 301—315).

of Daniel, and the participle *maśkīlīm* occurs also, in a nominal sense, in 11 33. 35 12 3. 10. Whether these "wise men" are to be envisaged as teachers of the eschatological mysteries like Daniel himself[122], or as wise leaders of the Jewish people in a more general sense during the persecutions of Antiochus Epiphanes[123], or as the faithful Jews as a whole, who are to be rewarded with resurrection to life in return for their faithfulness[124] is not certain.

We may conclude that ch. 2, with its connections with the latter half of the book, does give some support to von Rad's thesis. At the same time, the fact that the vocabulary used differs in the two halves of the book may be of some significance. In ch. 2 4 5 the derivatives of *ḥkm* are key-words, while in ch. 7—12, the book of the visions, they do not occur at all. Moreover the root *śkl*, though used elsewhere in the literature of the intellectual tradition, is not confined to it[125]. This difference of vocabulary is unlikely to be without significance. However much the author (or authors) of ch. 7—12 may have seen these stories as suitable to his purpose, their vocabulary was not entirely the same as his. This fact may be of some significance in attempting to solve the complex problem of the origin of the apocalyptic literature.

D. Non-occurrences of ḥkm

We now turn to those books and passages, constituting the major part of the Old Testament, from which the root *ḥkm* is absent, at least in any significant sense[126].

1. Narratives

a) Gen 1—36

In Genesis it is only in the Joseph Story that the root occurs; and, as has been suggested already[127], this tends to confirm the view that that narrative does not belong to the main strands of tradition in the book (J, E, P) but is a literary unit which stands apart from the rest[128]. If this is accepted, *ḥkm* is entirely absent from all the main

[122] So Plöger 171f.

[123] So N. W. Porteous 141f. (ET 168).

[124] So Bentzen 82f.

[125] See p. 137f. below.

[126] See p. 86f. above. [127] P. 87 above.

[128] Von Rad (Josephsgeschichte; Das erste Buch Mose, ATD 4, 1953 [ET Genesis, OTL, 1961]) does not take this step. See, however, R. N. Whybray, The Joseph

strands of tradition in Genesis. In view of the subject-matter of the book this is somewhat surprising.

i. The Primeval History (ch. 1—11)

As is well known, the creation stories in Genesis (1 1—2 4a [P] 2 4b-8 [J]) both belong to different traditions from those found in the "wisdom books". Although in both of the Genesis accounts God's creative actions are described in such a way as to arouse the reader's admiration for a skill which far exceeds human wisdom, the words *ḥākām* and *ḥokmā* are not used, and there is no real equivalent here to the expression "Yahweh by *ḥokmā* founded the earth" (Prov 3 19)[129].

If the Genesis creation stories are demythologized versions of older myths, the omission of references to God's wisdom may be part of the demythologization. Both in Enuma Elish and Atrahasis[130] the "wisdom" of the gods is much in evidence, and is closely allied to magic. The effortlessness — or so it is made to seem — with which God creates the world in the two Genesis creation stories is far removed from the atmosphere of the myths, and it may therefore be that what we have here is an "anti-wisdom" bias, or at least a deliberate avoidance of the word *ḥokmā* in order to avoid a misunderstanding of the nature of Yahweh's creative work and divine nature. A similar bias is perhaps to be found in Ex 7 11 (P), where Pharaoh's *ḥᵃkāmīm* are closely associated, if not identified, with magicians[131], and are helpless before the divinely sent Moses and Aaron. Here again Aaron's action might be called *ḥokmā*, but the word is not used.

A similar "anti-wisdom" bias has been claimed for the story of the Fall of Man in Gen 3 (J); but there the problem is somewhat different. The absence of *ḥkm* from this story has frequently been remarked upon. The themes with which it is concerned, especially those of human knowledge and of life and death and their relationship to obedience and disobedience, are prominent in the tradition represented by Proverbs, Job and Ecclesiastes, and the way in which they are treated here is clearly intended to stimulate serious reflexion upon them. Moreover the fact that the creator-god El in the Ugaritic

---

Story and Pentateuchal Criticism, VT 18 (1968), 522—528, where it is argued that his view of the character of the Joseph Story demands this conclusion.

129 The statements in 1 4. 10. 12. 18. 21. 25 that God "saw that it was good" and in 1 31 that the whole creation was "very good" come nearest to this, but the obliqueness with which the author speaks of the thing made rather than directly of the maker may be significant.

130 Translation in W. G. Lambert and A. R. Millard, Atra-ḫasīs: The Babylonian Story of the Flood, 1969.

131 See p. 15f. above.

myths[132] is credited with wisdom suggests that wisdom may have been an important feature of the mythical material which lies behind the J narrative.

It has been suggested by some scholars that J deliberately avoided the use of *ḥkm* in Gen 3 for theological or polemical reasons[133]. It is argued that at two crucial points in the story where *ḥkm* might have been expected, another word is used: in v. 1, where the serpent is called *ʿārūm* rather than *ḥākām*, and in v. 6, where, in speaking of the woman's perception that the tree of the knowledge of good and evil is "desirable for making one wise", the word used is *lehaśkīl*. There is, however, no reason to suppose a deliberate avoidance of *ḥkm*, since the words used are entirely appropriate.

ʿārūm appears to have been originally a word without specific moral connotations denoting shrewdness of a purely practical kind. In Proverbs it is used always in an approving though morally neutral sense of that innate shrewdness which ensures worldly success; in Job, however, it has acquired a pejorative sense: it refers to the crafty man whose tricks are designed to injure other men and who is the enemy of God[134]. It is therefore entirely appropriate as an epithet applied to the serpent. It is true that *ḥākām* also can have the sense of "shrewd, cunning", and that it is so used to describe Jonadab, whose cunning is of a similar order, in II Sam 13 3; but there is no reason to suppose a deliberate avoidance of *ḥākām* in Gen 3 1, since the meanings of the two words clearly overlap.

Similarly *hiśkīl*, whether in the sense of "to be wise" or "to make wise", is a word which occurs frequently in a sense indistinguishable from the qal. and pi./hi. respectively of *ḥākam*, and is closely associated with the root *ḥkm* in a number of passages[135]. Consequently the use of the one instead of the other in Gen 3 6 would hardly be perceived by the reader as having especial significance.

132 For the references see p. 7 n. 5.

133 Thus F. Hvidberg, The Canaanite Background of Gen. I—III, VT 10 (1960), 285—294, suggests that the choice of *ʿārūm* rather than *ḥākām* to describe the cleverness of the serpent in v. 1 is part of a polemic against Baalism: the serpent is the symbol of Baal (289). Alonso-Schökel, Motivos sapienciales y de alianza en Gen 2—3, who argues that wisdom motifs are present in Gen 2f., goes further: not only in 3 1 but throughout these chapters *ḥkm* is avoided, either because Adam before the Fall knew only good and evil and so cannot be called "wise", or in a polemical interest: the only true wisdom is that which God gives (and had clearly not given to Adam), and which results in obedience. He refers to Dtn 4 6-8 for this concept.

134 In Prov 1 4 8 5. 12 the noun *ʿormā* is regarded in a quite opposite positive sense as the possession and gift of the "wisdom" teachers and of wisdom herself. On the "vocabulary of old wisdom" see McKane, Proverbs and Wise Men; Proverbs, especially 262ff.

135 Dtn 32 29 Ps 119 98f. Prov 16 23 21 11 Dan 1 4. 17.

It may then be concluded that Gen 3 is a passage where the absence of the root *ḥkm* does not indicate the absence of Israel's intellectual tradition. Indeed — to anticipate a later chapter[136] — it should be noted that, while *hiśkīl*, though it occurs more frequently in the "wisdom books" than elsewhere, is by no means entirely confined to them, *ʿārūm* is one of the few words in the vocabulary of biblical Hebrew which occurs almost exclusively there[137], and therefore constitutes as effective a confirmation of the influence of the intellectual tradition on Gen 3 as would the occurrence of the root *ḥkm* itself.

The remainder of the Primeval History might seem to offer other occasions for the use of *ḥkm*, especially the references to the rise of civilization in 4 17-22 and the story of the Tower of Babel (11 1-9). Both of these passages are concerned, in different ways, with the advance of the human intelligence. But in neither does *ḥkm* occur. In the former, the laconic statements about the activities of Cain, Jabal, Jubal and Tubal-cain clearly imply that these men are regarded as the first among mankind to practice these civilized arts. It is possible that ultimately there lie behind these statements traditions, known to us from Philo Byblius and elsewhere, of the bringing of the arts of civilization to mankind by the gods — in other words, of a "wisdom myth"; but, as is now generally recognized, the resemblance of Gen 4 17-22 to the Sumerian King List, in which brief statements of this kind are incorporated into dynastic tables of rulers of various cities, makes it probable that the material used by J here was already in this abbreviated and "demythologized" form[138]. Consequently there is no reason to suppose the existence here either of a mythical or of a "wisdom" tradition, whatever may have been the remote origins of these statements.

The story of the Tower of Babel (J) is of a different kind. Like the story of the Fall, it is in its present form a story with a theological moral which is stated quite plainly. It is in fact a kind of parable showing what will be the fate of those who are "wise in their own eyes" and who, in that confidence, dare to match themselves with God. V. 6 makes it plain that the problem is that of the virtually unlimited possibilities of human achievement — what, in fact, might very well be called man's *ḥokmā*. The passage is, however, too short for the absence of that word to be necessarily significant. If J was thinking of

[136] See p. 137f. 148 below.

[137] Apart from Gen 3 1 it occurs only in Job 5 12 15 5 Prov 12 16. 23 13 16 14 8. 15. 18 22 3 27 12.

[138] See T. Jacobsen, The Sumerian King List, 1939, and the commentaries on Genesis, especially U. Cassuto, A Commentary on the Book of Genesis, I 1961, 187—189. A translation of part of the Sumerian King List is given in ANET 265f.

the problem of human "wisdom" when he wrote ch. 3 he may also have had it in mind when he wrote 11 1-9.

From the above discussion of the Primeval History it appears that, although *ḥkm* does not occur there, there is no reason to suppose that it was deliberately excluded. Indeed, there is a strong possibility that this theological question was in the mind of J, though it does not appear explicitly in his creation story. There is no trace of it in P.

ii. The Patriarchal Stories (ch. 12—36)

Here it suffices to say that, in contrast to the Joseph Story, *ḥokmā* plays no part at all. None of the patriarchs, Abraham, Isaac or Jacob, and no other person, is called *ḥākām*. In the case of Jacob this is surprising, since he is portrayed in a number of incidents as displaying an unusual degree of shrewdness. It is clear that, although in the Primeval History, where the human figures are representative of mankind as a whole, the author of one of the strands of material (J) seems to have seen an opportunity to discuss the problem of wisdom, which is a human problem in the widest sense, the thoughts of the authors of all the strands in ch. 12—36 (J, E and P alike) were concentrated on other matters when they came to describe the origins of Israel.

The shrewdness of Jacob was an element which was already present in the material, where it is accorded neither praise nor blame, except in the sense that Jacob is a "folk hero", the ancestor of Israel, the one who is accorded the blessing. The authors of the narratives in their present form have not fundamentally altered the impression given by the original tales: thus "wisdom" in any significant sense is not an issue here. It is simply a coincidence that Jacob is not explicitly called *ḥākām* or *'ārūm*; but even if this were the case, this designation would have no theological significance. The ancestors of Israel are neither presented to the reader as outstanding examples of "wisdom" who for this reason received the blessing, nor are they taken as examples of men who endangered their possession of the blessing by an overweening confidence in their own "wisdom". This kind of thought is not discernible in this part of Genesis at all.

b) Exodus and Numbers

The lack of interest in *ḥokmā* on the part of the J, E and P strands in the patriarchal narratives is, not surprisingly, also a characteristic of the narratives in Exodus and Numbers. The root *ḥkm* is found here in Pharaoh's phrase "Let us act prudently" (*nitḥakkᵉmā*, Ex 1 10), in the reference to Pharaoh's *ḥᵃkāmīm* in Ex 7 11, and in the 16 references in Ex 28 31 35 36 where *ḥokmā,* in some cases God-given, is attributed to Bezalel and to other persons who made the vestments, Tabernacle and their furnishings; but it has already been argued that in none of these cases is *ḥkm* used in anything but the most general senses[139].

In Ex 1 10 Pharaoh's proposed *ḥokmā* is nothing more than common sense applied to politics, and nothing in the context suggests that the choice of the word is intended to have special significance. In 7 11, as has been suggested, the *ḥᵃkāmîm* of Pharaoh may simply have been "skilled" magicians; the contest between the Egyptian magicians and Aaron, whose rod "swallowed up their rods" (v. 12) is conducted on a level far removed from *ḥokmā* in any intellectual sense; and nothing is made of the word *ḥākām* here which might suggest an interest in the intellectual concept.

The very large number of occurrences of *ḥkm* in Ex 28—36 might suggest that *ḥākām* and *ḥokmā* are intended to be key-words in this part of Exodus, but an examination of the verses in question shows that this frequency is entirely due to the extraordinarily repetitive style of the author(s). The statement about the skill (*ḥokmā*) of those who built and furnished the Tabernacle and made the vestments is mentioned first in the command which God gives to Moses, again in Moses' command to the people, and again in the statement that the work was completed. Moreover, separate statements are made to convey the information that this skill was possessed by Bezalel, Oholiab, "all able men" and "able women"; and these are repeated with regard to different aspects of the work. But *ḥākām* and *ḥokmā* are only two of a large number of words which are constantly repeated in this way: consequently in the context their repetition has no especial significance. The author is saying no more than that the skill in question was in some cases a natural endowment, and in others specifically given by God.

We may therefore conclude that in the narratives in Exodus and Numbers no interest in *ḥokmā* in any significant sense is shown. Neither Moses nor any other leader in these stories is said to have possessed *ḥokmā* in his work of guiding and teaching the children of Israel.

c) Joshua, Judges, Samuel, Kings

Here the significant occurrences of *ḥkm* are confined exclusively to two sections: the Succession Narrative and the account of the reign of Solomon. Otherwise, apart from the reference to Sisera's mother's "wise woman (or women)" in the Song of Deborah (Jdc 5 29) it does

139 See especially p. 11. 13. 15f. 83 above.

not occur at all, either in the sources which the Deuteronomist used, or in the editorial material contributed by the Deuteronomist himself.

This is a very remarkable fact which can hardly be without significance for an understanding both of the Deuteronomist and of the other literary traditions which he incorporated into his work. It would appear that at no stage in the development of the historiography of Israel concerning the period from Joshua to the Exile, culminating in the Deuteronomic History itself, did it occur to any of the authors, compilers or editors of the historical material, with the exception of the author of the Succession Narrative and of those who were responsible for the traditions about Solomon, to attribute *ḥokmā* to any king or leader of Israel or to any other historical personage whose deeds they recorded and interpreted, or to comment on their lack of *ḥokmā*, or to refer in any way to the concept of *ḥokmā* in considering the trends of Israelite history as a whole.

This is particularly extraordinary in view not only of the immense length of the material, which makes it improbable that the absence of *ḥkm* is a mere accident, but also of the great variety of the backgrounds from which these authors and compilers came, and the length of the period which they represent[140]. In Joshua and Judges there are local stories and sanctuary legends, tribal stories and hero-stories; in Samuel, special collections of traditions connected with Samuel, Saul, David, and the Ark; in Kings, extracts from the archives of the kingdoms of Israel and Judah, presumably the work of court scribes, to whom some of the narratives also are probably to be attributed. There are also probably records of the Temple at Jerusalem, drawn up by the Temple scribes; there are the prophetic stories, formed originally in the circles of Elijah, Elisha and Isaiah.

The implications of the absence of any reference to *ḥokmā* in any of these sources ought to be given careful consideration. For these narratives comprise the bulk of pre-exilic Israelite narrative available to us, both of a "popular", a "sacral" (to use von Rad's word) and a court or scribal character. In particular we need to consider how far theories of a "Sippenweisheit" and of a strong "court-wisdom" need to be modified in the face of this silence.

Finally it is necessary to consider the implications of this silence for an understanding of the character of the Deuteronomic History itself. The silence of the Deuteronomist is as remarkable as that of the material which he used. We might have expected that the compiler who included in his book the Solomonic material with its

---

[140] The brief survey of the sources of Joshua-Kings which follows is broadly accepted by the majority of scholars. It is not intended to be exhaustive. For details and alternative theories see the commentaries and Introductions.

emphatic praise of Solomon for his *ḥokmā* would have also included *ḥokmā* among the virtues which he ascribes to such men as Hezekiah or Josiah; but he did not do so. Hezekiah is praised for loyalty to Yahweh (II Reg 18 5f.), and Josiah for turning to Yahweh and obeying the Law of Moses (II Reg 23 25); but there is no mention of their *ḥokmā*, nor of the lack of *ḥokmā* shown by other kings, in the Deuteronomic comments on their reigns. Nor in the condemnation of the nation as a whole (e.g. II Reg 17) is lack of *ḥokmā* mentioned as one of the causes of its fall.

This total silence about *ḥokmā* in the parts of Joshua-Kings written by the Deuteronomist himself may throw light on the composition of Dtn 1—4. As has already been pointed out[141], the only significant references to *ḥokmā* in the introductory section of Deuteronomy occur in Dtn 4 6. Here the Deuteronomic Code, itself innocent of occurrences of *ḥkm* except for one motive clause, is commended to the people as "your *ḥokmā*", and as the envy of other peoples. We may presume that it is this code which is the "law that my servant Moses commanded them" which Israel is accused of breaking under the influence of Manasseh (II Reg 21 8f.), and it is generally believed that it was the "book of the Law" which was the basis of Josiah's reform. Since, however, the Deuteronomic Historian in Joshua-Kings is not only silent about the sapiential character of this law when he refers to it specifically, but also makes no use of the *ḥokmā* concept at all, it may be suggested that the passage in which 4 6 occurs is not the work of the Deuteronomic Historian but of another writer who *did* see the Deuteronomic Code as *ḥokmā* and wrote an introduction to it in order to stress this point of view.

d) Chronicles, Ezra and Nehemiah

A similar avoidance of the root *ḥkm* is observable in the work of the Chronicler. In Ezra-Nehemiah the word *ḥokmā* (in Aramaic) occurs once, in the rescript of Artaxerxes (Esr 7 25). Here, as a comparison with v. 14 shows, the phrase "the *ḥokmā* of your God with which you are entrusted" (literally, "which is in your hand") clearly refers to the Law of Moses which Ezra was to take with him on his journey to Jerusalem[142]. This appears to be the only passage in the Old Testament where *ḥokmā* is used in this precise and narrow sense, and it foreshadows a usage which became common in later times[143]. This

---

141 See p. 87f. above.

142 So, e.g., W. Rudolph, Esra und Nehemia, HAT 1/20, 1949, 74; J. M. Myers, Ezra-Nehemiah, AB 14, 1965, 59.

143 On this narrowing of the meaning of the term see W. Bousset and H. Gressmann, Die Religion des Judentums im späthellenistischen Zeitalter, 1966⁴, 164ff.

late development lies outside the scope of this book; but it is clear that the Chronicler had no use for the concept of *ḥokmā* in a more general sense. Neither Ezra nor Nehemiah is credited with *ḥokmā*, and in Chronicles the root is found only in passages where the author is following or expanding material from Kings: that is, in passages concerning Solomon and the craftsmen who were engaged in the construction of the Temple[144].

e) Other Narrative Books

In *Esther* there is only one certain occurrence of *ḥkm*: in 1 13 Ahasuerus consults the *ḥakāmīm yōdeʿē hāʿittīm* about the action to be taken in view of Queen Vashti's disobedience. There is some doubt about the meaning of *ʿittīm* here; but whether the men in question are astrologers, lawyers or political counsellors, the reference is purely incidental to the story and part of its "local colour"; the question of the nature of *ḥokmā* is not raised. In 6 13 the word *ḥakāmāw* occurs, but the text is doubtful[145].

The absence of any significant occurrence of the root *ḥkm* in a book of this length must be taken into account in an assessment of the validity of the contention of S. Talmon[146] that the book of Esther is an example of "wisdom literature", being "a historicized wisdom-tale"[147]. The weaknesses of Talmon's thesis have already been cogently pointed out by J. L. Crenshaw[148].

Although Esther in its setting and some of its motifs resembles other stories — such as the Words of Ahiqar and the Joseph Story — which may be classed as "wisdom literature", the crucial question is whether it is concerned to depict "wisdom" and folly in order to draw a lesson which raises the question of the nature of true wisdom. If this is not the case, it cannot properly be called a "wisdom-story". Crenshaw has shown that the purpose of the story is quite other than this, and that "wisdom" is not a significant characteristic of any of the characters in the story. Here, then, there is no question of a deliberate avoidance of the root *ḥkm* in a narrative where one might expect it to occur. It is absent because there is in fact no such concern here at all. As Crenshaw says, "It is difficult to conceive of a book more alien to wisdom literature than Esther[149]".

---

144 I Chr 22 15 28 21 II Chr 1 10. 11. 12 2 6. 11. 12. 13 9 3. 5. 6. 7. 22. 23.

145 On both the meaning of *ʿittīm* and on the text of 6 13 see the commentaries. Cf. also p. 16. 78 above.

146 "Wisdom" in the Book of Esther.

147 Talmon 426.

148 Method in Determining Wisdom Influence upon "Historical" Literature 140—142.

149 Crenshaw 141.

The root *ḥkm* is also entirely absent from *Ruth* and *Jonah*, where also there are no other grounds for supposing the existence of the influence of the intellectual tradition.

2. Laws

It has already been noted that there is no significant occurrence of *ḥkm* in Exodus or Numbers, either in the narratives or in the laws. It is also entirely absent from Leviticus. In the Code of Deuteronomy it occurs only once, in 16 19, where the law "You shall not pervert the course of justice or show favour, nor shall you accept a bribe" is followed by the motive-clause, "for bribery blinds the eyes of *ḥᵃkāmīm* and subverts the cause of innocent men". Some reference to this case has already been made[150]. If the motive-clause is to be regarded as an addition to the original law, it represents a rapprochement made by an editor of the intellectual tradition with the legal tradition. The theory of Gemser that it belongs from the very first to the legal tradition and "points to an archaic, traditional element in the formulation of the laws"[151] is improbable in view of its rhythmic character, which is not that of the laws as a whole.

Although Gemser argues that its rhythmic character indicates its antiquity, its strict metre and parallelism, which are precisely the same as those of innumerable sayings in the book of Proverbs, show, on the contrary, that it belongs to the highly sophisticated literary intellectual tradition. Von Rad rightly says that it "can be classified as a wisdom saying and the original parallelism can still be clearly recognized"[152]. Von Rad goes on to contrast its form with that of the next verse, which "on the other hand . . . is . . . an example of the homiletic guise in which the old earlier material in Deuteronomy is so often presented"[153]. If this is so, then this sole occurrence of *ḥkm* in the laws of the Old Testament is no indication of the influence upon them of a significant concern with *ḥokmā*.

The problem of Dtn 16 19 does, however, raise the question of a possible original common source of the legal and intellectual traditions. This theory has been put forward especially by Gerstenberger, with regard to the "apodictic" laws[154]. He argues that the apodictic laws in the Decalogues, Covenant Code, Deuteronomy and Holiness Code,

150 P. 77 n. 21 above.

151 B. Gemser, The Importance of the Motive Clause in Old Testament Law, 64.

152 Deuteronomium 82 (ET 115).

153 Op. cit. 82 (ET 115).

154 Wesen und Herkunft. See also his Covenant and Commandment, JBL 84 (1965), 38—51.

which in their present contexts are represented as spoken by God through the medium of Moses, were originally part of a stock of precepts and prohibitions which originated in the semi-nomadic period before the Israelite settlement in Canaan. These precepts were the basic principles which governed the life of the clan, and they were enunciated by the leader or "father" of the clan[155]. This material was then later drawn upon separately by two distinct classes in the more highly organized nation of Israel which succeeded the semi-nomadic society: by the priests, who incorporated it, together with the casuistic laws[156], into the legal corpora associated with the cult, and by the new class of "wise men" which produced the "wisdom literature"[157].

Gerstenberger stresses the numerous similarities between the motifs found in the apodictic laws and in the commands and prohibitions (*Mahn- und Warnwort*)[158] in the book of Proverbs. He explains one of the most obvious differences between the two — the absence of cultic laws in the latter — as due to the fact that when the collections of proverbs came to be written, cultic matters had passed wholly into the hands of the priests whose especial province they were, and consequently were no longer suitable or necessary for inclusion in the literary works of the "wise men"[159]. He does not, however, deal satisfactorily with another difference between the two bodies of literature which is equally obvious: the fact that, while in the laws the theme of *ḥokmā* is totally ignored, in Proverbs *ḥokmā* plays a dominant and decisive role as the norm of all human conduct[160].

It is true that the great majority of the occurrences of *ḥkm* in Proverbs are in statements (*Aussage*) rather than in commands and prohibitions, but they are by no means absent from the latter[161]. But in any case, in his attempt to demonstrate the similarities between

[155] Wesen und Herkunft 110ff.

[156] On the distinction between the two types of law see A. Alt, Die Ursprünge des israelitischen Rechts, BSAW 86/1, 1934 = Kleine Schriften I, 1959, 278—332 (ET The Origins of Israelite Law [Essays on Old Testament History and Religion, 1966, 79—132]). Gerstenberger, however, uses the term "apodictic" in a much narrower sense than Alt (see his remarks on p. 19ff.), and restricts his discussion to the so-called "prohibitive".

[157] Wesen und Herkunft 141ff.

[158] Unlike Richter (Recht und Ethos), Gerstenberger (p. 50—54) does not regard the prohibition (beginning with *lō'*) as significantly different in kind from the admonition or vetitive (beginning with *'al*).

[159] Wesen und Herkunft 63f.

[160] The 101 occurrences of *ḥkm* in Proverbs are well distributed. The root occurs at least once in each chapter, and is well represented in ch. 1—9 22—24, where the majority of commands and prohibitions occur.

[161] E.g. Prov 2 2 3 7 4 5. 7 5 1 6 6 8 33 9 8. 9 19 20 22 17 23 19. 23 27 11.

the two types of literature, Gerstenberger does not always confine himself to comparing the apodictic laws with the commands and prohibitives in Proverbs, but makes use of the entire range of material in Proverbs when he is concerned to point out the range of themes which are common to both[162]. It would seem, therefore, that he claims to have found evidence of the influence of *Sippenweisheit* in Proverbs as a whole; and if this is so, the absence from the laws and predominance throughout Proverbs of *ḥkm* remains a significant fact which requires an explanation.

It might be argued that many of the occurrences of *ḥkm* in Proverbs are found in the introductory formulae or generalized admonitions in which the master urges his pupil to pay attention to his words[163], rather than in the more specific commands to follow or to avoid particular kinds of behaviour, and that these belong to the setting of the material in a new intellectual context rather than to the basic material itself — in other words, that such formulae correspond, in Proverbs, to the equally secondary formulae in the laws, such as the frequently repeated "And the Lord said to Moses": they merely show that the material has been taken over, in the one case by the priests and in the other by the class of "wise men". Gerstenberger, however, does not adopt this view.

It is, indeed, essential to his argument that the "father-son" formulae belong, not to the later stage of written "wisdom literature", but to the original material. It is this, he argues, which shows that the prohibitions and commands in Proverbs in their original form[164] constituted the instruction given in the semi-nomadic period by one who was in a literal, or at least, in a very real, sense the "father" of the clan[165]. But if this is so, the frequency of the occurrence of *ḥkm* in the "father-son" formulae would indicate that the norm of conduct required was already summed up in the word *ḥokmā* in the clan-society of the semi-nomadic period[166]. We should therefore expect to find some reference to this norm of *ḥokmā* in the laws as they now stand in the Pentateuch, even though the father-son formulae have disappeared from the legal collections; and the more so because *ḥkm*

---

162 Thus on p. 65 he speaks of "Mahnungen, Warnungen und Sprüche" in this context.

163 E.g. 4 5. 7 5 1 8 33 23 19. 23 27 11.

164 That is, without the secondary additions of motive-clauses and of clauses added for the sake of poetical parallelism.

165 P. 121.

166 Gerstenberger (130) speaks of the absence of references to the "*institution* of the 'wise men' " (my italics) from the early proverbial sayings as a proof that the origin of the prohibitive in Proverbs is anterior to that of the "class of wise men" (*Weisenstand*). It has already been argued (p. 15ff. above) that such a class did not exist.

in Proverbs is *not* in fact entirely confined to these formulae, but appears also in a number of more specific commands[167]. The absence of *ḥkm* from the laws therefore appears to constitute a strong argument against Gerstenberger's thesis[168].

3. Psalms and Lamentations

It has already been pointed out[169] that the criterion of the occurrence of *ḥkm* is less readily applicable to the *Psalms* than to other types of Old Testament literature. Since each psalm is an independent composition of no more than moderate length, and since there is no evidence concerning the identity of the authors which could make it possible to say whether any author composed more than one of the psalms extant in the Psalter, no conclusions can safely be drawn from the absence of *ḥkm* in any one case. The concept of *ḥokmā* may have been important to the author of a given psalm, and yet in such a short composition it might well be that the occasion for using the words *ḥākām* or *ḥokmā* did not arise. There may therefore be — and it is generally agreed that there are — psalms where the intellectual tradition associated with the root *ḥkm* is present even though the root itself does not occur[170].

There is, however, something more which may be said on this subject. If it is legitimate to draw conclusions from groups of psalms which clearly belong to well-defined types and represent distinct traditions, it may be observed that the concept of *ḥokmā* appears to have been foreign to what may be called the classical cultic tradition of Israel, at least in pre-exilic times. The absence of *ḥkm*, in any significant sense, from no less than 141 of the 150 psalms is impres-

---

[167] See especially 3 7 (on conceit); 6 6 (on diligence); 9 8. 9 (on the value and limitations of giving advice and reproof). It is true that it appears much more frequently in the statements than in the commands and prohibitions.

[168] Criticism of the thesis might be offered on other grounds, but these are not relevant to the present discussion. The work of W. Richter (Recht und Ethos), which offers an alternative theory of a relationship between law and wisdom in the Old Testament, equally fails to explain the absence of the norm of *ḥokmā* from the apodictic laws.

In the case of Deuteronomy especially, in view of the fact that an increasing number of writers have claimed to discover "wisdom influence" in that book on grounds other than those of vocabulary (see p. 1 n. 1) it is perhaps necessary here to repeat my earlier statement (p. 74) that the absence of the vocabulary of the intellectual tradition does not *necessarily* preclude the possibility that a book or passage (in this case, the laws of Deuteronomy) may have been affected by that tradition. Nevertheless the absence of *ḥkm* from those laws is a significant fact which requires explanation.

[169] P. 93f. above.

[170] See p. 153 below.

sive evidence of this. It never occurs in any psalm in which there are clear and undoubted references to the use of that psalm in the temple cult[171]. Although some of the 9 psalms in which it does occur are related formally to types of psalm which were used in the cult[172], and although the suggestion that in the post-exilic period it was the temple singers who became the heirs of Israel's intellectual tradition has some plausibility, there is no certainty that any of these was properly cultic in character or intention[173]. This conclusion is, of course, in no way novel, nor is it unexpected. Public worship is, in general, declarative rather than reflective. Reflection on the nature of the universe or on human problems, whether general or personal, which is characteristic of the intellectual tradition, belongs in general to private prayer and meditation rather than to the public worship of a community.

What has been said above applies also to the book of *Lamentations*. It is generally agreed that the 5 poems which comprise this book belong to the type of the lamentation, and were composed for cultic use[174]. The absence of the root *ḥkm* from this book is therefore in no way surprising.

4. The Prophetical Books

The fact that *ḥkm* does not occur in any significant sense in the teaching of the prophets apart from I Isaiah, Jeremiah and Ez 28 is remarkable[175].

[171] I accept the view, generally held by the older commentators, and still maintained by Weiser (Die Psalmen, 277; ET The Psalms 410) and Kraus (Die Psalmen I 383. 390f.) that Ps 51 18f. imply that sacrifice is unnecessary or unacceptable, and that v. 20f. are a later addition to that psalm, expressing a different attitude. E. J. Kissane (The Book of Psalms, 1964², 224), M. Dahood (Psalms II, AB 17, 1968, 2) and J. H. Eaton (Psalms, TC, 1967, 141f.) regard v. 20f. as an integral part of the psalm and interpret v. 18f. in other ways.

[172] Ps 51 belongs to the category of the individual lamentation; Ps 90 is a communal lamentation; and Ps 104 107 33-43 111 are either Hymns or contain hymnic elements (see p. 95—97 above). But their literary classification is not necessarily a reliable guide to the purpose for which they were written or to the use to which they were first put.

[173] See, among other treatments of the subject, S. Mowinckel, Die Psalmdichter, Psalmenstudien 6, 1924; Psalms and Wisdom; Jansen, Die spätjüdische Psalmendichtung; M. J. Buss, The Psalms of Asaph and Korah, JBL 82 (1963), 382—392; Murphy, A Consideration of the Classification, "Wisdom Psalms".

[174] See the commentaries. It is generally recognized that other *Gattungen* are used in at least some of these poems, but wisdom is not one of them.

[175] See p. 83—85 above for reasons for excluding the few occurrences from the discussion.

In the case of II Isaiah it has come to be widely believed that there is "wisdom influence"[176]. Yet on the two occasions (44 25 47 10) when he uses the terms *ḥākām* and *ḥokmā* in reference to the "wise men" of Babylon, this prophet makes no attempt to develop the theme in any significant way. In 40 12-28, where it has been argued by many scholars that "wisdom influence" is most clearly seen, and where it might have been expected that he would speak of Yahweh's wisdom, he does not use the root *ḥkm* at all.

The view that this passage, especially v. 12-17. 28, shows the influence of "wisdom thought" is based mainly on two features: the use of the question to introduce a discussion (*Disputationswort* or *Diskussionswort*), and the presence of so-called "wisdom vocabulary". I have argued elsewhere[177] that the use of questions as a rhetorical device, though frequently found in the so-called "wisdom books", is by no means confined to them, but was regularly used in common speech as well as in other types of literature. The question of the vocabulary of this tradition will be considered in a later chapter[178]; here it may be remarked that such words as *ʿēṣā, yāʿaṣ, hēbīn, daʿat,* and *derek* and *ʾōraḥ* used in a metaphorical sense, though frequently found in these books, are by no means confined to them[179]. The only word in this passage which might claim not only to be a distinctive feature of this tradition but, in view of its associations in other Old Testament books, virtually an equivalent of *ḥokmā*, is *tᵉbūnā*, which occurs here twice (v. 14. 28). However, as will be shown in a later chapter, even *tᵉbūnā* is not exclusively confined to the intellectual tradition[180].

The fact that, apart from Isaiah and Jeremiah (the two prophets who were especially associated with the Judaean court and engaged in controversy with the "clever men" of that court whose "wisdom" they contested) the prophets make no use whatever of the root *ḥkm*

---

176 See, among other works, H.-E. von Waldow, Anlaß und Hintergrund der Verkündigung des Deuterojesaja (unpublished dissertation, Bonn), 1953, 47ff.; Der traditionsgeschichtliche Hintergrund der prophetischen Gerichtsreden, 1963, 47ff.; The Message of Deutero-Isaiah, Interpretation 22 (1968), 259—287; Lindblom, Wisdom in the Old Testament Prophets, 198; McKane, Prophets and Wise Men, 81—83; von Rad, Weisheit, especially 34. 143—145; and recent commentaries, including J. Muilenburg, Isaiah, Chapters 40—66, IB V, 1956; Fohrer, Das Buch Jesaja III; McKenzie, Second Isaiah; K. Elliger, Jesaja II, BK 11/1. 2, 1970/1.

177 Whybray, The Heavenly Counsellor, 19ff.

178 P. 121ff. below.

179 See also Whybray, The Heavenly Counsellor, 26f.

180 See p. 138—140 below. *tᵉbūnā* also occurs in 44 19, but it is very improbable that this passage belongs to the genuine utterances of Deutero-Isaiah.

except very occasionally as an element of common speech[181] or in referring to the *ḥakāmīm* of foreign countries raises difficulties for the recently propounded theory that some prophets show the influence of a popular "tribal wisdom" (*Sippenweisheit*)[182].

The problem is analogous to that posed by Gerstenberger's attempt to derive the apodictic laws from this "tribal wisdom"[183]. It is not disputed that the prophets — and perhaps especially Amos — were familiar with, and made use of, forms of speech which were current among the common people of their day, and which — though there is virtually no possibility of proving this — may already have been in use in semi-nomadic times. But to argue from this, and from the occasional similarities between prophetic forms of speech and those of the book of Proverbs, that both are derived from an *institutional* tribal wisdom enunciated by the "father" or leader of the clan is to over-interpret the evidence. This conclusion is strongly supported by the fact that neither Amos nor Hosea — nor, indeed, any of the minor prophets — ever uses the root *ḥkm* in any significant sense. Clearly the theory of "clan-wisdom" put forward by Gerstenberger in his work on the laws, and by Wolff and others in their studies of the prophets, receives no assistance from this quarter[184].

It is not only the theory of *Sippenweisheit* which is invalidated by this avoidance of the *ḥokmā* concept on the part of the prophets. Other theories of wisdom influence on the prophets, which suppose them to have been influenced by a distinct class of "wise men", are similarly affected[185].

5. The Song of Solomon

This book has been classified among the "wisdom literature" of the Old Testament since ancient times, probably owing to the fact that it is ascribed to Solomon (1 1), and that the name of Solomon occurs in it a number of times[186]. This classification has been retained by some modern Catholic scholars, though little serious effort has been made to defend it in recent times.

---

181 E.g. Hos 13 13, where Ephraim's lack of "wisdom" (*bēn lō' ḥākām*) consists merely in his awkwardness as an unborn baby in presenting himself at the mouth of the womb.

182 Gerstenberger, The Woe Oracles of the Prophets; Terrien, Amos and Wisdom; Wolff, Amos' geistige Heimat.

183 See p. 113ff. above.

184 See the remarks of Fohrer, Remarks on Modern Interpretation of the Prophets, on the misuse of form-criticism in this connexion.

185 E.g. Lindblom, Wisdom in the Old Testament Prophets; McKane, Prophets and Wise Men.

186 1 5 3 7. 9. 11 8 11. 12.

It has been pointed out in the most thorough recent study of the subject[187] that the traditional allegorical interpretation, according to which the principal theme of the book is the operation of the grace of God on the human soul, symbolized by the figures of the bridegroom and the bride, places it in the prophetic rather than the "wisdom" tradition. The most generally held opinion, that the book is a collection of love-songs or marriage-songs, with or without a religious purpose, equally detaches it from the category of "wisdom literature"; nor do other modern theories suggest a "wisdom" provenance. The lyrical character of the poems is also far removed from the reflective mood of *ḥokmā*.

Audet suggests that the reason why the book came to be classified among the "wisdom" books at an early date is that it was "adopted" by the "wise men", who saw it as a means of teaching the virtues of marital fidelity. He finds proof of this in such passages as 8 6f. ("Love is as strong as death"), which seem to him to have the flavour of "literary wisdom", and in the close similarity between certain phrases in the book and parts of Prov 5 15-23, which suggests to him that the author of that section of Proverbs was familiar with the Song.

It may well be thought that Audet's arguments are based on evidence which is both slender and also capable of other interpretations. Moreover, they presuppose the existence of a distinct class of "wise men" which, as has already been shown, did not exist. But it is to be observed that even if Audet's explanation of the Song's later "wisdom" connexions is correct, he does not argue that it was *composed* by the "wise men": they merely preserved it and made a small number of additions to it. Audet sees it as originally a collection of songs sung by the bridegroom and the bride at the moment of the exchange of nuptial vows.

No doubt it was the ascription to Solomon which led to the classification of this book with the "wisdom" books; but this ascription does not necessarily indicate an original attachment to any specific "wisdom" tradition: there may have been, as has already been suggested[188], a popular Solomonic tradition which remembered Solomon for characteristics other than his "wisdom"; certainly his wisdom is never referred to here.

There is therefore no reason to suppose a connection between the author(s) of the book and the intellectual tradition, and the absence of the root *ḥkm* from it is in keeping with this view.

---

[187] J.-P. Audet, Le sens du Cantique des Cantiques, RB 62 (1955), 197—221.

[188] See p. 55ff. above.

IV. OTHER CHARACTERISTIC TERMINOLOGY

A. Criteria

The criterion of "wisdom vocabulary" apart from the root *ḥkm* has been and is widely used in works concerned to demonstrate the presence or otherwise of "wisdom influence" in the various books of the Old Testament. However, no serious attempt has yet been made to compile a list of relevant terms, or to formulate the principles by which such terms should be selected. The few attempts which have been made to draw up such a list illustrate the chaotic situation which prevails.

Duesberg and Fransen, in Les Scribes Inspirés, discuss a large number of terms, and append to their work a list entitled "vocabulaire des termes sapientiels"[189]; but this list of some 200 Hebrew words and phrases is not intended, nor is it suitable, for use in determining "wisdom influence"; its intention is to "permettre au lecteur studieux de composer à son usage une petite concordance des différents sens de ces mots et des différents contextes où ils sont enchâssés". Even for such a purpose the list is far too inclusive, and contains such words as *ᵓᵉlōhīm, dābār* and *nābīᵓ* — the last of these having been included simply because it occurs in passages which are used in the book to illustrate the supposed relationship between the *ḥākām* and the prophet. This list is of no use whatever for the present purpose.

R. B. Y. Scott[190] provides a list which ought to be more useful: he claims, indeed, that it "will be useful in assessing wisdom influence in other parts of the Old Testament such as the prophetic writings and the Psalms". But his list, comprising 77 items, includes such words as *ḥaṭṭāᵓ*, "sinner", *yādaᶜ*, "know", *limmad*, "teach", and *rīb*, "dispute, accusation" — words in such common usage in the Old Testament as to be useless for determining a specific literary tradition unless it can be shown that they have a distinctive meaning in particular contexts. Scott provides no evidence of this.

A number of other studies also make use of the criterion of "wisdom vocabulary", using lists of words and phrases which they declare, frequently without giving any reason, to belong to that category[191].

---

[189] Op. cit. 934f.

[190] R. B. Y. Scott, The Way of Wisdom in the Old Testament, 1971, 121f.

[191] Humbert, Recherches, discusses a number of terms, but only in relation to possible Egyptian equivalents. Studies which make extensive use of the vocabulary test include Alonso-Schökel, Motivos sapienciales; A. Robert, Les attaches littéraires bibliques de Prov. I—IX, RB 43 (1934), 42—68. 172—204. 374—384; 44 (1935),

If this method is to be acceptable, it is essential that some principles of selection be formulated. Two such principles would seem to be appropriate:

a) It must be established that the terms selected are characteristic of the "wisdom" or intellectual tradition as exemplified by Proverbs, Job and Ecclesiastes. It is theoretically possible that there may be other words which are equally characteristic of that tradition which, by chance, are less prominent in those books, or even do not appear there at all; but to include any such words would be to add to the element of subjectivism and to be in danger of arguing in a circle[192].

b) The terms selected must be restricted to those which express a concern with the main interests of the intellectual tradition: that is, with the problems faced by mankind in society or as individuals. If this restriction is not observed, chance elements may enter into the selection. For example, in their discussion of these problems, and in illustrating them with metaphors and similes, the writers of this tradition may employ terms which were in common everyday use, although the other books of the Old Testament, not being specifically concerned with the minutiae of social life as such, may, by chance, not employ them, or only occasionally so.

An example of such a word is *ḥābal*, "to seize as a pledge". This word occurs 3 times in Proverbs and 3 times in Job, and 6 times elsewhere in the Old Testament. Statistically it might be argued that, since half the number of its occurrences are to be found in "wisdom" books, it should be regarded as "wisdom vocabulary"; but in fact it clearly denotes a common social custom and was therefore a term in common use throughout Israelite society; no conclusions may be drawn from its distribution in the Old Testament ("wisdom" books, laws, prophets).

An examination of the vocabulary of Proverbs, Job and Ecclesiastes shows that these books do in fact contain a large number of words which refer to the problems of the individual and his place in society[193]. This distinctive terminology comprises, in general terms, the following range of topics:

344—365. 502—525; Malfroy, Sagesse et loi dans le Deutéronome; Fichtner, Jesaja unter den Weisen; Terrien, Amos and Wisdom. The list of phrases given by Weinfeld (Deuteronomy and the Deuteronomic School 362f.) indicates similarities of phraseology between the three "wisdom books" and the Deuteronomic literature, but few of these phrases are peculiar to any one tradition, and many belonged to the common speech of Israel.

[192] For a clear example of this see p. 140—142 below.

[193] It is interesting to note, however, that each of these books has its own specific vocabulary; and that in particular Ecclesiastes has far less specific "wisdom"

i. Wisdom and folly; virtue and wickedness; human conduct in general.

ii. The consequences of the possession of these qualities, e. g. prosperity, happiness, friendship; disaster, poverty, punishment.

iii. The search for knowledge and for prosperity: intelligence, knowledge, education, advice, thought, planning.

The above categories have been widely drawn. Many other Old Testament books use terminology of this kind without qualifying for inclusion within the intellectual tradition, and it is the purpose of the analysis which follows to discover which words are distinctive of that tradition. But it is clearly impossible to investigate all words which might conceivably qualify for a place there. These categories, which undoubtedly correspond in general to the concerns expressed in Proverbs, Job and Ecclesiastes, are simply intended to mark out a range of ideas within which the vocabulary characteristic of the intellectual tradition may reasonably be sought.

In such an investigation there is no question of drawing up a list which is complete and objective in a scientific sense: this would be an impossibility. The selection of words is inevitably, in the last resort, a matter of human judgement.

The method of procedure will necessarily differ from that used in the investigation of the occurrences of *ḥkm*, whose cognates, in spite of their relatively frequent occurrences outside the context of the intellectual tradition, nevertheless are incontrovertibly the key-words of that tradition. No other word is basic to it in this sense, as will be shown in the list of occurrences below. It is therefore necessary to use great caution in determining the eligibility of each word, and to exclude as doubtful any which may have been in common use or shared with other traditions. Only such a rigorous procedure can guard against the danger of a subjectivism which would render the investigation useless.

B. Analysis

Of the large number of words occurring frequently in Proverbs, Job and Ecclesiastes which fall within the range of ideas mentioned above, some occur with equal frequency throughout the range of Old Testament literature, and are clearly words which were in common use, e. g. *ṣaddīq*, *ṭōb*, *limmad*, *yāda'*. The ideas which they express are ideas without which civilised life would be inconceivable. So far are

vocabulary in common with the other two than is the case with Proverbs and Job. These facts add further support to the argument against the theory of a rigid "wisdom tradition" (see p. 69 f. above).

they from being in any sense a specialised vocabulary that no investigation of their frequency of occurrence is necessary.

The remaining words, selected from the Hebrew lexicon, many of which have been used by various writers as indications of "wisdom influence", may be divided, according to their occurrence within and outside the 3 "wisdom books", into 4 general categories.

1. Words Occurring Only in Proverbs, Job and/or Ecclesiastes

'lp

qal "to learn", once in Prov; pi. "to teach", 3 times in Job.

ḥ^a^sar-lēb

"One who lacks sense". 9 times in Prov. Cf. also *ḥ^a^sar-t^e^būnōt*, Prov 28 16.

sik^e^lūt

"Folly". 7 times in Koh.

'āṣēl

"Sluggard". 14 times in Prov; once in Koh.

taḥbullōt

"Guidance". 5 times in Prov; once in Job.

These words are clearly of no use in determining the influence of the intellectual tradition, since they occur only in the 3 "wisdom" books. It may, however, be pointed out that it is doubtful how far even these can be regarded as especially characteristic of that tradition. None of them occurs in all 3 books, and 2 of the 5 are found only in one book. Moreover one of them, *'āṣēl*, was, as far as is known, the only word in biblical Hebrew to denote a sluggard or lazy man, and must presumably, therefore, have been in common use, even though it happens that no other Old Testament writer had occasion to employ it.

2. Words Occurring Frequently Both in Proverbs, Job and/or Ecclesiastes and Also in Other Old Testament Traditions

'āwen

"Mischief, evil". 10 times in Prov; 15 times in Job; not in Koh. 55 times in other books (Num I Sam I II III Isa Jer Ez Hos Am

Mi Hab Zech Ps). Always in poetry with the exception of Ez 11 2. Especially frequent in Ps (29 times), by no means only in psalms considered on other grounds to be influenced by the intellectual tradition.

'ᵉnōš

"Man". 18 times in Job; not in Prov or Koh. 24 times in other books (Dtn 32 I II III Isa Jer Ps Chr). Always in poetry with the exception of Isa 8 1 II Chr 14 10. In the latter case the context is that of the elevated language of prayer; in the former, the meaning of *ḥereṭ 'ᵉnōš* is uncertain, and an emendation of *'ᵉnōš* has been proposed[194]. The word is clearly not especially characteristic of the intellectual tradition.

'ōraḥ

In the metaphorical sense of "human (or divine) behaviour" in moral and religious contexts, this word occurs 18 times in Prov; 4 times in Job; not in Koh. In the other books it occurs in this sense 17 times: I Isa (4 times) II Isa (once) Mi (once) Ps (11 times). Of the occurrences in the Psalms, 5 are in Ps 119. If Ps 119 is counted, in view of the occurrence there of *ḥkm*, as belonging to the intellectual tradition, its occurrences in that literature are frequent; but it cannot be regarded as peculiar to it. Both in its literal and its metaphorical senses it is mainly a poetical word equivalent to *derek*, with which it frequently stands in poetical parallelism.

'ašᵉrē

"Blessed!". 8 times in Prov; once in Job; once in Koh. 35 times in the other books (Dtn 33 I Reg I III Isa Ps Dan Chr). Of these occurrences 26 are in Ps.

Although the majority of occurrences are in the cultic setting of the Psalms, it has been argued[195] that this expression originated in "wisdom" contexts, mainly on the grounds that it is generally an impersonal expression rather than one addressed to particular persons. This view is rendered doubtful by the context in which it is used in I Reg 10 8. Here the references are to specific persons, and in a narrative context. It is true that this narrative, of the visit of the Queen of Sheba to Solomon, is one in which *ḥokmā* plays a prominent part; but it is improbable that even in such a context words would be put into the mouth of a speaker (here the Queen of Sheba)

[194] See Wildberger, Jesaja, 312.

[195] Gerstenberger, Woe-Oracles, 260f.; Wolff, Amos' geistige Heimat, 18—20.

which were not appropriate to the matter in hand, which is the making of a compliment to Solomon. It seems probable, therefore, that *'ašerē* was used in conversation, whether common or elevated. But even if it was originally derived from the intellectual tradition, the fact that the majority of its occurrences are in contexts of a quite different kind would render it useless as a criterion of the influence of that tradition.

Here some comment on the word *hōy* is necessary. This word, often translated "Woe!", although in some passages "Alas!", or simply "Ha!", drawing attention to some person or thing, would be more appropriate, has been regarded by some scholars as the antithesis of *'ašerē*, the two forming a pair, although only in one passage[196] do they appear in juxtaposition. *hōy* has also therefore been thought to be "wisdom vocabulary"[197], although it never occurs in Prov, Job or Koh. Elsewhere it occurs 47 times, almost exclusively in the prophetical books. Crenshaw[198] has rightly pointed out that its absence from Prov, Job and Koh argues conclusively against its origin in the "wisdom" tradition, and that all the evidence points to its belonging rather to that of the prophets[199].

bōgēd

"Treacherous person". 9 times in Prov; not in Job or Koh. 12 times in other books (I Isa Jer Hab Ps Thr). As in the case of *'āṣēl*, the frequency of occurrences in Prov is due to the fact that certain types of man are inevitably frequently mentioned in literature concerned with human society and its problems. But the variety of the other contexts in which this word occurs shows that it was in common use, at least in poetry.

bīn

qal and intrans. hi., "understand". (The trans. hi. is not under consideration here; the participle *mēbīn* used as a noun is treated separately below.) The qal occurs 12 times in Prov; 13 times in Job; not in Koh. 38 times in other books (Dtn 32 I II Sam I II Isa Jer Hos Ps Dan Esr Neh Chr). The intrans. hi. occurs 12 times in Prov; once in Job; not in Koh. 14 times in other books (I Reg I II III Isa Mi Ps Dan Neh Chr). Thus although this word is characteristic of the intellectual tradition in the sense that it appears frequently in Prov

[196] Isa 32 20—33 1.

[197] By Wolff, Amos' geistige Heimat, 12—23; Gerstenberger, Woe-Oracles.

[198] The Influence of the Wise Upon Amos 47f.

[199] See also G. Wanke, אוי und הוי, ZAW 78 (1966), 215—218, where it is pointed out that the arguments of Wolff and Gerstenberger are weakened by a failure to make a distinction between *'ōy* and *hōy*.

and Job, it clearly cannot be used as a criterion for determining the influence of that tradition in view of its wide distribution in other books[200].

daʿat

"Knowledge". 40 times in Prov; 11 times in Job; 8 times in Koh. 31 times in other books (Gen Ex Num Dtn Jos I Reg I II III Isa Hos Mal Ps Dan). In view of the wide variety of occurrences, this word clearly cannot be said to be especially characteristic of the intellectual tradition[201]. It was clearly the most common word for "knowledge", and must have been in common use.

derek

"Road, way". This word was in common use not only in its literal but also in its metaphorical sense, when it is the equivalent of *'ōraḥ*. In its metaphorical sense it occurs 65 times in Prov; 16 times in Job; twice in Koh. Some 230 times in a wide variety of other books.

hebel

"Worthlessness". 3 times in Prov; 5 times in Job; 33 times in Koh. 27 times in other books (Dtn 32 I II Reg I II Isa Jer Jon Zech Ps Thr). In 15 instances in these books it refers to the worthlessness of idols; in 12 instances to the worthlessness of men or of man's hope or work. It is clear that it is a key-word in Koh, but not in Prov or Job. It cannot be regarded as characteristic of the intellectual tradition as a whole.

ḥāqar

"Explore, investigate". Taking qal, ni. and pi. together, this word occurs 4 times in Prov; 6 times in Job; once in Koh. 16 times in other books (Dtn Jdc I II Sam I Reg Jer Ez Ps Thr Chr). It was clearly the primary word denoting man's exploratory activity, and the contexts in which it occurs suggest that it was in common use.

yʿl

hi., "profit, benefit". Twice in Prov; 4 times in Job; not in Koh. 16 times in other books (I Sam I II III Isa Jer Hab). Clearly not especially characteristic of the intellectual tradition.

[200] Against Fichtner, Jesaja unter den Weisen, 23; Malfroy, Sagesse et loi dans le Deutéronome, 53.

[201] Against Alonso-Schökel, Motivos sapienciales, 302; Fichtner 23; Lindblom, Wisdom in the Old Testament Prophets, 199; Malfroy 51.

ka'as

"Vexation, grief". 4 times in Prov; 4 times in Job; 5 times in Koh. 12 times in other books (Dtn 32 I Sam I II Reg Ez Ps). It belonged to the vocabulary of the psalm of lamentation (Ps 6 8 10 14 31 10 85 5), but is also found in prose narratives (I Sam 1 6. 16). It is a rather rare word, but clearly not especially characteristic of the intellectual tradition.

mēbīn

"Understanding, intelligent". In this adjectival sense this word appears to occur 6 times in Prov; not in Job or Koh. 6 times in other books (I Isa Est Chr). In view of the fact that it occurs neither in Job nor in Koh it can hardly be regarded as characteristic of the intellectual tradition.

mūsār

"Discipline, instruction, punishment". 30 times in Prov; 4 times in Job; not in Koh. 16 times in other books (Dtn I II Isa Jer Ez Hos Zeph Ps). In Prov this word is used mainly in an educational context, whereas in almost all other cases it denotes the discipline or punishment imposed on Israel by God. The former meaning is clearly primary: the word belongs originally to the vocabulary of the education of children. Hence it has frequently been regarded[202] as belonging to the terminology of "wisdom". But this is not so unless "wisdom" is equated with the educational system. That this is an erroneous view of the nature of the intellectual tradition has already been demonstrated. The absence of the word from Koh and the fact that Job only once (20 3) uses it in the sense of instruction given by men confirms the view that *mūsār* in its original sense is not characteristic of the intellectual tradition as a whole; and its frequent use in its derived sense in a variety of other books shows that it was not confined in this sense to any one tradition.

m^ezimmā

"Plan, thought". 8 times in Prov; twice in Job; not in Koh. 9 times in other books (Jer Ps). Only in poetry. There is a polarization of the meaning of this word into good and bad: in Prov 1—9 it is used 5 times in a good sense, and, in the remainder of Prov, 3 times in a bad sense. The other occurrences are also divided between the two senses: in Ps (5 times) it is used of the thoughts of evil men; in Jer it is used once of evil thoughts, but 3 times of God's purpose.

[202] E.g. by Lindblom 203; Malfroy 57; Humbert 68; Duesberg and Fransen 229—231.

Of the occurrences in Ps, one (37 7) is in a psalm which has already been classified as belonging to the intellectual tradition; 3 (10 2. 4 139 20) are in lamentations; and one (21 12) in a royal psalm. In the passages in Jer (11 15 23 20 30 24 51 11) there is nothing in the contexts to suggest the influence of the intellectual tradition. It seems clear that this word is a poetical term which cannot be attributed to any one tradition[203].

maʿgāl

"Path, track". 7 times in Prov; not in Job or Koh. 6 times in other books (I III Isa Ps)[204]. All the occurrences in Prov are found in ch. 1—9 (2 9. 15. 18 4 11. 26 5 6. 21). This word is virtually always used in the metaphorical sense of "conduct, behaviour"[205], good or bad, and appears to be synonymous with *ʾōraḥ* and *derek* in their metaphorical usage[206]. In Ps, where it occurs 4 times, it is found in lamentations (17 5 140 6), in a psalm of confidence (23 3) and in a hymn (65 12). It is thus clearly as much at home in cultic contexts as in the intellectual tradition, and its relatively varied distribution suggests that it belonged to a common poetical vocabulary.

māšāl

"Proverb, saying, taunt" etc. 6 times in Prov; 3 times in Job; once in Koh. 29 times in other books (Num Dtn I Sam I Reg I Isa Jer Ez Mi Hab Ps Chr).

There has been much discussion about the fundamental meaning of this word and on the relationship between the various senses which it has in various contexts[207]. Even within the literature of the intellectual tradition itself there are divergences of meaning: while the titles in Prov 1 1 10 1 25 1, together with Koh 12 9, probably refer to short literary proverbial sayings, Prov 26 7. 9 Job 13 12 may refer to some less formal sayings in common speech, while Job 27 1 29 1, which refer to Job's "taking up his *māšāl*" (*wayyōsep ʾiyyōb śeʾēt mešālō*), introduce long speeches of a different kind altogether.

The similar phrase *wayyiśśāʾ mešālō* occurs 7 times in the story of Balaam, introducing oracles which have nothing whatever to do with the intellectual tradition; and still other meanings of the word

[203] Against Malfroy 50.

[204] *maʿgāl* also occurs in I Sam 17 20 26 5. 7, probably in the sense of "enclosure, encampment"; but this is probably a separate word (so Kö 544).

[205] The only possible exception is Ps 140 6, where the wicked lay snares "by the side of the path" (*leyad-maʿgāl*).

[206] In Isa 59 8 it is parallel with *derek*.

[207] See among other works O. Eissfeldt, Der Maschal im Alten Testament, 1913; A. R. Johnson, מָשָׁל, VT Suppl III, 1955, 162—169 and the literature there cited; Hermisson op. cit. 38ff.

māšāl are to be found in the Old Testament which need not be discussed here.

It is clear that *māšāl* is by no means a term exclusively characteristic of the intellectual tradition, and that consequently its occurrence by itself gives no guide to the influence of that tradition in any particular passage. Thus although in Ps 49, which has already been shown to be related to that tradition, the author refers (v. 4f.) to his composition in terms both of *ḥokmōt* and *māšāl*, it does not follow that Ps 78, whose author (v. 1f.) also refers to his composition as a *māšāl*, but where the root *ḥkm* does not occur, is also to be so classified. The two psalms are in fact quite unlike, the latter being a cautionary tale of Israel's past history and the former of a meditative character.

nābāl

"Stupid, impious". 3 times in Prov; twice in Job; not in Koh. 13 times in other books (Dtn 32 II Sam I Isa Jer Ez Ps). This word is one of several used by the authors of Prov to denote various types of fool, and refers to a particular kind of folly allied to wickedness and destructive of society. It is therefore in a sense a technical term in Proverbs, and it may be significant that is found also in other books and passages which have been assigned by some scholars to the intellectual tradition, especially Dtn 32 6 21 Isa 32 6 Jer 17 11.

On the other hand it is not confined to the literature of the intellectual tradition, and, what is more important, it did not originate there. When Tamar warns Amnon that if he violates her he will be "as one of the *nᵉbālīm* in Israel" (II Sam 13 13) she is referring to the type of crime known as *nᵉbālā* (v. 12), or, more fully, "*nᵉbālā* in Israel". That this was a specifically Israelite concept referring to certain breaches of Yahweh's fundamental law laid down for Israel is clear from the use of the expression "she has wrought folly in Israel (*ʿāśᵉtā nᵉbālā bᵉyiśrāʾēl*)" in Dtn 22 21 in a law concerning the investigation of a sexual irregularity similar to that with which the passage in II Sam 13 is concerned. That this is so is confirmed by ther passages in which *nābāl* and *nᵉbālā* occur[208]. It must theorefore be concluded that, although *nābāl* occurs a number of times in the literature of the intellectual tradition, the word and the concept which it denotes were known to the Israelite people in general, and the occurrence of the word is not necessarily an indication of the influence of that tradition[209].

---

208 See also p. 135 n. 224 below.

209 Against Malfroy 55. The fact that the Succession Narrative, in which II Sam 13 13 occurs, belongs to the intellectual tradition is not relevant here, since the author,

n^etībā

"Path". Like *'ōraḥ* and *derek*, with either or both of which it stands in parallelism or close association in the majority of occurrences, this word, which is found only in poetry, has both a literal and a metaphorical sense. The two senses are not always easy to distinguish, but a metaphorical sense is probably to be found 5 times in Prov and 3 times in Job. It does not occur in Koh. A metaphorical sense is also discernible in 6 passages in other books: Isa 59 8 Jer 6 16 18 15 Hos 2 8 Ps 119 105 Thr 3 9. Of these, Ps 119 has already been classified as belonging to the intellectual tradition. But the occurrences in Isa Jer Hos Thr make it clear that the word was not especially characteristic of it. Its occurrence in Jdc 5 6 shows that in its literal sense it was part of the poetical vocabulary of the earliest Hebrew poetry. It occurs far less frequently than either *'oraḥ* or *derek*, and seems to have been used mainly to fulfil the need for parallel expressions in poetry.

sōd

"Meeting, friendship, discussion, consultation, plan, secret"[210]. 5 times in Prov; 3 times in Job; not in Koh. 13 times in other books (Gen Jer Ez Am Ps). The same varieties of meaning are found in Prov and Job as in the other books, and there is therefore no reason to regard the word as in any sense peculiar to the intellectual tradition.

The argument of Terrien[211] that *sōd* in the sense of "intimate secret" is peculiar to the "wisdom literature", and that its use in Am 3 7 in the phrase *gillā sōd*, "reveal a secret", shows the influence of "wisdom" on that prophet cannot be substantiated. While it is true that the phrase *gillā sōd* occurs elsewhere only in Prov 11 13 25 9, his view that *sōd* "is par excellence a sapiential term, conveying the idea of confidential and intimate exchange in an atmosphere of friendship and mutual trust" is belied by such passages as Ps 25 14 55 15, where that intimate relationship is shown to exist between Yahweh and the worshipper specifically within the covenant relationship rather than in a "wisdom" context.

'awlā

"Wickedness". Once in Prov; 10 times in Job; not in Koh. 21 times in other books (II Sam III Isa Ez 28 Hos Mi Hab Zeph

---

in putting the words *nābāl* and *n^ebālā* into Tamar's mouth, is clearly making use of words which would be familiar to such a person.

[210] See further Whybray, The Heavenly Counsellor, 51f.

[211] Amos and Wisdom 112. Cf. also Wolff, Amos' geistige Heimat, 5 n. 3.

Mal Ps Chr). This word is found mainly, though not exclusively, in poetry. Since in the literature of the intellectual tradition it is found almost exclusively in Job, and is widely distributed in the other poetical books, it cannot be claimed that it belongs to that tradition.

ʿēṣā

"Counsel, plan". 10 times in Prov; 9 times in Job; not in Koh. 68 times in other books (Dtn 32 Jdc II Sam I II Reg I II Isa Jer Ez Hos Mi Zech Ps Esr Neh Chr).

The view, accepted with little or no discussion by some[212] and argued by others[213] that this word in pre-eminently a "wisdom word" depends largely upon the identification of the "wise men" with political counsellors which has already been dismissed in an earlier chapter of this book[214].

In the majority of occurrences outside Proverbs and Job the word refers to political advice or consultation in the formal context of the royal court (at least 38 times). In at least 15 other cases, mainly in Isa Jer Ps, it refers to the advice or plan of Yahweh, and in a few cases to the plans or plots of the wicked against the righteous.

The frequency of the political references, and the contexts in which they occur[215], make it clear that the word became a technical term in political circles during the monarchy. It may well be, as Fichtner and McKane have argued[216], that the religious sense, in which Yahweh is spoken of as possessing *ʿēṣā*, is derived from this usage.

Yet these specialized senses of the word appear hardly at all in Proverbs and Job. Of the 10 occurrences in Prov, only one — 20 18, which refers to the planning of military campaigns — finds its obvious interpretation in political terms. In 6 cases (12 15 19 20. 21 20 5 21 30 27 9) *ʿēṣā* is most naturally interpreted, once the identification of "wise men" with politicians has been abandoned, of advice given and plans formed by individuals and groups of individuals in private life[217]. In the three remaining cases (1 25. 30 8 14) it is, by extension, the personified wisdom who is credited with the ability to give the best advice of this kind.

In Job there is one passage (29 21) where a meaning similar to the usage in Proverbs is to be found: Job was the man to whose advice,

---

[212] E.g. Lindblom 194f.; Malfroy 52.

[213] E.g. McKane, Prophets and Wise Men, especially 15—47.

[214] P. 5ff. above.

[215] See Whybray, The Heavenly Counsellor, 27—29. 31—33.

[216] J. Fichtner, Jahwes Plan in der Botschaft des Jesaja, ZAW 63 (1951), 16—33 = Gottes Weisheit 27—43; McKane op. cit. See also De Boer, The Counsellor.

[217] The meaning of 27 9b is obscure.

in the days of his prosperity, the men of the village listened. In 5 other passages (5 13 10 3 18 7 21 16 22 18) *ʿēṣā* is used, as in the Psalms, of the plots of the wicked. In 12 13 it is an attribute of Yahweh. Finally in 38 2, echoed in 42 3, the "counsel" which is darkened by words without knowledge is probably also a reference to Yahweh's *ʿēṣā*[218].

The political use of *ʿēṣā* is, then, almost totally absent from Proverbs and Job. The evidence suggests that the difference between the non-political use of the word in those books and its primarily political use in II Sam Reg Isa Jer lies in the degree of the formality of the occasions on which advice was given and plans formed. Proverbs and Job, together with some of the Psalms, have preserved the evidently original sense of private, or at most, local decision-taking, while the usage in the other books reflects the formal royal council-meeting with its professional counsellors. The one group of passages reflects private or village life, while the other reflects the national life.

The original setting of *ʿēṣā* is well illustrated by Job 29 21:

> Men listened to me, and waited,
> and kept silence for my counsel (*lᵉmō ʿᵃṣātī*).

The setting is the city gate of Job's village (v. 7), when Job's advice on local matters was recognized as decisive. This private, or informal, giving of advice is also illustrated in Prov 12 15, where a distinction is made between the very general categories of the sensible man and the fool:

> The way of a fool (*ʾᵉwīl*) is right in his own eyes;
> but it is a wise man (*ḥākām*) who listens to advice (*lᵉʿēṣā*).

The fact that these two passages occur in "wisdom" books does not mean that *ʿēṣā* is originally a specialized term of the intellectual tradition. The scene depicted in Job 29 is clearly based on everyday life. *ʿēṣā* is, in the Old Testament, by far the most common word meaning "advice", and must have been in common use.

rāṣōn

"Favour, delight". 14 times in Prov; not in Job or Koh. 42 times in other books (Gen Ex Lev Dtn II III Isa Jer Mal Ps Est Dan Esr Neh Chr). The absence of this word from Job and Koh suggests that it does not belong to the specific vocabulary of the intellectual tradition, and this is also indicated by its distribution in the other books. In the great majority of cases it refers to Yahweh's favour or

---

218 So, e.g., E. Dhorme, Le Livre de Job, EB, 1926, 525f. (ET Job, 1967, 575); H. H. Rowley, Job, 1970, 309.

delight; but its use in connexion with kings (Prov 14 35 16 13. 15 19 12 etc.) and occasionally with ordinary men shows that its religious use is derived from that of ordinary life. Where it is used in Prov of God's favour it has a moral connotation: God shows his favour to men of good conduct. Elsewhere it is most frequently found in Lev (7 times) and Ps (13 times), where God is said to be pleased with human actions either ritual or moral. It is clear, however, that in itself the word has no moral or religious connotation, and that its use in Proverbs in similar to the way in which it is employed elsewhere.

We may conclude that none of the words discussed in this section belongs properly to the vocabulary of the intellectual tradition, and so none can be used as a criterion for determining the influence of that tradition outside Prov, Job and Koh.

3. Words Characteristic of Proverbs, Job and/or Ecclesiastes, but Occurring Occasionally in Other Old Testament Traditions

'ᵉwīl

"Fool". 19 times in Prov; twice in Job; not in Koh. 5 times in other books (Isa 19 11 35 8 Jer 4 22 Hos 9 7 Ps 107 17). This word belongs to the catalogue of types of fool which is a notable feature of Prov. In Jer 4 22 also, a verse which has already[219] been characterized as belonging to the intellectual tradition, it occurs in a list of synonyms or near-synonyms: *lō' yādā'ū, sᵉkālīm, lō' nᵉbōnīm,* and the ironical *ḥᵃkāmīm . . . lᵉhārā'*. Similarly in Isa 19 11 it is used in contrast with *ḥākām*.

Nevertheless two occurrences make it doubtful whether it should be considered as exclusively a term of the intellectual tradition. In Hos 9 7 it occurs, as is generally agreed by the commentators, in a phrase which is a quotation of words spoken by the people: *'ᵉwīl hannābī' mᵉšuggā' 'īš hārūāḥ*: "The prophet is a fool, the man of the spirit is a madman". This can hardly be said to be a proverbial saying in the intellectual tradition: it is simply a contemptuous and insulting slogan, presumably expressed in the common speech of the people[220]. Again in Isa 35 8, where the text is uncertain[221], there is nothing in the context to suggest the influence of the intellectual tradition[222].

---

[219] P. 99f. above.

[220] On Hos 9 7-9 see the commentaries, especially T. H. Robinson, Hosea, HAT 1/14, 1954², 36f.; H. W. Wolff, Dodekapropheton I, BK 14/1, 1965², 193ff.; W. Rudolph, Hosea, KAT 13/1, 1966, 173f. 178—180; J. L. Mays, Hosea, OTL, 1969, 128—131.

[221] See the commentaries.

[222] The text of Ps 107 17 is also uncertain.

'iwwelet

"Folly". 23 times in Prov; not in Job or Koh. Twice in other books (Ps 38 6, 69 6). Only in poetry. In spite of its absence from the other two "wisdom books", it might be supposed that the large number of occurrences in Prov would suffice to show that this word belongs specifically to the intellectual tradition. However, its occurrence in two psalms of lamentation where there is no other evidence of the influence of that tradition shows that it does not belong exclusively to it.

ḥānēp

"Godless". Once in Prov; 8 times in Job; not in Koh. 4 times in other books (Isa 9 16 10 6 33 14 Ps 35 16). The frequency of the expression in Job is presumably due to the fact that godlessness is part of the indictment which Job's friends bring, at least by implication, against him. It thus denotes one of the great issues with which the book is concerned. Apart from this the word occurs only once in the "wisdom books" (Prov 11 9), and there it refers to the godless man who slanders his neighbour, a situation similar to that depicted in Ps 35 16 in a psalm which is a lamentation not otherwise associated with the intellectual tradition[223]. In I Isa it is used to describe the state of the nation of Judah or of Zion (9 16 10 6 33 14). In these denunciatory passages also there is no reason to suspect the influence of the intellectual tradition[224].

ḥēqer

"Investigation, examination". Twice in Prov; 7 times in Job; not in Koh. 3 times in other books (Jdc 5 16 Isa 40 28 Ps 145 3). In more than half of the occurrences (7 times) it is used negatively in the phrase *'ēn (lō') ḥēqer*, referring to that which is beyond human power to investigate; 6 times of God's purpose or deeds, and once (Prov 25 3) of the minds of kings. The theme of man's power to investigate the universe and of the limitations of that power is clearly germane

[223] The text of Ps 35 16 is uncertain.

[224] It is true that in Isa 9 16 *ḥānēp* is closely associated with "folly"; but the word used here (*n^ebālā*) is not primarily a term belonging to the intellectual tradition. It occurs in the "wisdom books" only once (Job 42 8), but 12 times in other books (Gen Dtn Jos Jdc I II Sam I Isa Jer), and is closely linked with specifically Israelite traditions: see on *nābāl*, p. 130 above. In more than half its occurrences (Gen 34 7 Dtn 22 21 Jos 7 15 Jdc 20 6. 10 II Sam 13 13 Jer 29 23) it is found in the phrase "folly in Israel" or an equivalent expression, and it is never used of crimes committed outside Israel.

to the intellectual tradition; but the idea of searching the heart (in this case, one's own) already occurs in the Song of Deborah (*ḥiqᵉrē lēb*, Jdc 5 16); and it also occurs in a Hymn (Ps 145 3) where there is no indication of the influence of the intellectual tradition. It therefore cannot be used as a criterion for this purpose.

ʿiqqēš

"Perverse, crooked". 7 times in Prov; not in Job or Koh. 4 (3) times in other books: Dtn 32 5 II Sam 22 27 = Ps 18 27 Ps 101 4. The occurrence in the Song of Moses (Dtn 32 5) would tend to support the view that this word is characteristic of the intellectual tradition. On the other hand the two occurrences in Ps show that the word was also at home in the cult. Both Ps 18 21-27 and Ps 101 have been significantly compared[225] with the so-called "Torah-liturgy" (e.g. Ps 15 24) in which the worshipper was required to testify his innocence and virtuous way of life with regard to a number of specific points. So in Ps 18 27 the worshipper acknowledges that Yahweh would have punished him if he had been "crooked", and in Ps 101 4 he promises to avoid "crookedness". In view of these clearly cultic contexts in which the word occurs, it cannot be definitely classified as specifically characteristic of the intellectual tradition.

ʿormā

"Shrewdness, cunning". 3 times in Prov; not in Job or Koh. Twice in other books: Ex 21 14 Jos 9 4. In these last two cases the word has a pejorative sense and occurs in the phrase *bᵉʿormā*, "with cunning". The occurrences in Prov are all in ch. 1—9, and *ʿormā* is there regarded as a highly desirable quality; though probably, before the addition to these chapters of references to Yahweh which have given them a more religious character[226], a morally neutral quality: the shrewdness required for success in life. The small number of occurrences hardly makes it possible to draw definite conclusions about the history of the word's usage in detail, but its occurrence in the early laws of Israel (Ex 21 14) and in an ancient narrative (Jos 9 4) suggests that it belonged to the common speech of the people[227].

petī

"Simple". 14 times in Prov; not in Job or Koh. 4 times in other books: Ez 45 20 Ps 19 8 116 6 119 130. Of these occurrences, 2 (Ps 19 8

[225] By Kraus, Psalmen, I 146. II 689.

[226] See Whybray, Wisdom in Proverbs.

[227] Against Malfroy 50.

119 130) are found in psalms which have already been classified as belonging to the intellectual tradition.

On the other hand, Ps 116 is a psalm of thanksgiving, and shows no signs of the influence of that tradition. The meaning there is somewhat different from its meaning in Proverbs: the simple man is the unassuming, modest man whom Yahweh protects.

About the text of Ez 45 20 there is some difficulty[228]. If it is correct, this would be a further example of a cultic or legal use of *petī*. The context is that of the cultic laws, and sacrifice is commanded on behalf of those who have committed actions which are technically sins but for which they were not fully responsible. The phrase *'īš šōge*, "man who errs", is to be understood in terms of such passages as Lev 4 13 Num 15 22, where the verb *šāgā* refers to unwitting sin[229]. The *petī* in Ez 45 20 is presumably the simpleminded, who is not wholly responsible for his actions.

It would seem, therefore, that although the word is used frequently in Prov — especially in ch. 1—9 — to denote a particular class of fool, its use was not confined to the intellectual tradition.

śkl

hi. "be wise, consider, be successful, make wise, teach". If the 13 instances in which this verb probably has the meaning of "be successful" are excepted, we are concerned with the following occurrences: 12 times in Prov; 3 times in Job; not in Koh. 31 times in other books (Gen Dtn 32 II Isa Jer Am Ps Dan Neh Chr). The Aramaic cognate *śᵉkal* also occurs once in the hitp. in Dan 7 8.

There is no doubt that this word was part of the regular vocabulary of the intellectual tradition. This is clear from its frequent occurrence in Prov, where it mainly has the meaning of "be wise", and in Dan (10 times); also from its occurrence in Dtn 32 29 Jer 9 23 Ps 119 99, that is, in passages which have already been classified as belonging to that tradition, and in Ps 94 8, whose connexion with that tradition will be demonstrated below[230]. Moreover it has already been pointed out in connexion with its occurrence in Gen 3 6 that it is frequently associated with *ḥkm*[231]; and the occurrence in the same chapter (v. 1) of *'ārūm*, which, as will be shown below[232], belongs exclusively to that tradition, adds further support to this view.

On the other hand there is clear evidence that the word was not the exclusive possession of the intellectual tradition. The clearest

228 See Zimmerli, Ezechiel, II 1158. 1161.

229 Zimmerli 1158.

230 P. 146. 153.

231 P. 106f. above.

232 P. 148 below.

examples of its use in other traditions are Ps 2 10 41 2 64 10. Ps 2 is universally recognized as a "royal psalm". In v. 10 the speaker, who is probably the king, uses the word in commanding the kings of the earth to "show prudence" and worship Yahweh.

In Ps 41 2 *śkl* appears in a psalm of thinksgiving: *'ašerē maśkīl 'el-dāl.* There is uncertainty among the commentators about the meaning of this phrase and about the relationship of this verse to the rest of the psalm; but there is no reason to regard the psalm as influenced by the intellectual tradition; and, as has already been pointed out[233], *'ašerē* is not a term which belongs specifically to that tradition.

In Ps 64 10 the word occurs in a passage in which, in a psalm which begins as an individual lamentation and then continues on a note of certainty, the speaker expresses his confidence in God's help. The contexts of all these three psalm passages are cultic, and there is no reason to suppose that these psalms have been influenced by the intellectual tradition. This is also true of a number of other psalms in which the word occurs[234].

tebūnā

"Understanding". 19 times in Prov; 4 times in Job; not in Koh. 19 times in other books (Ex Dtn 32 I Reg II Isa Jer Ez 28 Hos Ob Ps). In 17 of the total of 42 passages this word is paralleled or closely associated with *ḥokmā.*

In 2 passages the text is uncertain. In Hos 13 2 the interpretation of *tebūnām* is difficult, and the grammar anomalous[235]. A number of commentators have proposed an emendation on the basis of LXX[236]. In Ob 7 the phrase *'ēn tebūnā bō* may be a gloss[237].

Like *ḥokmā, tebūnā* sometimes refers to manual skill, and the two appear together in Ex 31 3 35 31 36 1 I Reg 7 14 in that sense. In Ob 8 *tebūnā* is used in parallelism with *ḥakāmīm* in a reference to the "wisdom" of Edom. It also occurs in 3 other passages already classified as influenced by the intellectual tradition: Dtn 32 28 I Reg 5 9 Ps 49 4. It is clear that within the intellectual tradition *tebūnā* was frequently regarded as synonymous with *ḥokmā.* This is particularly clear in Prov 8 1, where *ḥokmā* and *tebūnā* occur in parallelism, designating a single, personified figure of "Wisdom".

---

233 P. 125f. above.

234 The occurrence in Am 5 13 appears to be a further example of its appearance in a context other than that of the intellectual tradition; but this verse is regarded by some commentators as an interpolation or as a gloss.

235 *kitebūnām*, where *kitebūnātām* is to be expected. See G.-K. § 91e.

236 LXX κατ' εἰκόνα. The emendation most frequently proposed is *ketabnīt.*

237 So, e.g., **A.** Weiser, Das Buch der Zwölf Kleinen Propheten I, ATD 24, 1967[5], 208; BHS.

Again in the prose passage Isa 44 9-20, which is probably not the work of Deutero-Isaiah[238], the satirical polemic against idolatry concludes with the comment that the idolators lack the *t^ebūnā* which would enable them to see the folly of their enterprise. This passage is frequently[239] classified as "wisdom literature" on account of its rationalistic approach to the subject of idolatry, and because it is in the later literature of this tradition that this theme finds its further development[240].

In Jer 10 12 = 51 15 also, where in a statement about Yahweh's creation of the world *bit^ebūnātō* has *b^eḥokmātō* as its parallel, there can be no doubt that the doctrine of creation is here informed by the intellectual tradition: a similar phrase is found in Proverbs itself (3 19).

But it does not necessarily follow that when Yahweh's *t^ebūnā* is mentioned *without* the accompaniment of a reference to his *ḥokmā*, in creation passages, the influence of that tradition is always present. Indeed, the absence of *ḥokmā* from some of these passages may be significant. This view finds some support in the fact that *bīnā*, which, as will be shown, belongs exclusively to the intellectual tradition[241], is never used in creation passages in the Old Testament. Since the time of Gunkel[242] it has been recognized that the participial form which is used in many creation passages — including Jer 10 12 Isa 40 28 Ps 136 5, with which we are here concerned — is characteristic of a different tradition: that of the Hymn or Song of Praise. It is therefore basically a cultic form of expression. Since *t^ebūnā*, like *ḥokmā*, can denote creative skill such as that of an artificer, it is quite possible that the statement that Yahweh created the world by means of his *t^ebūnā* owes nothing to the intellectual tradition; and indeed it is possible that in some passages, such as Isa 40 28 Ps 136 5, the omission of a reference to Yahweh's *ḥokmā* is deliberate, since *ḥokmā*, as has been seen[243], might imply the use of magical practices, an implication which it was necessary to avoid.

A similar reluctance to employ *ḥokmā* and *bīnā* may perhaps also be seen in Isa 40 14 Ps 78 72 147 5. In Isa 40 14, where the question is asked whether Yahweh needed a counsellor to teach him the *'ōraḥ mišpāṭ*, *da'at* and *t^ebūnōt* in order to create the world, the absence of

---

238 The commentators, however, are divided on this question.

239 Most recently by Fohrer, Jesaja, III 77f.; von Rad, Weisheit, 231ff.

240 For Fohrer (78) it is v. 19, with its confidence that "enlightenment will triumph over idolatry", which most clearly indicates the "rationalistic thought of the wisdom teacher".

241 See p. 142—145 below.

242 H. Gunkel, Einleitung in die Psalmen, 1933, 44f.

243 P. 105 above.

both *ḥokmā* and *bīnā* is conspicuous. In Ps 147 5, where the context contains elements which are reminiscent of II Isa[244], only *tᵉbūnā* is used from this group of words, in parallelism with *kōaḥ*, "strength". Finally in Ps 78 72, where the account of Yahweh's guidance of Israel is summed up in the statement that he "guided them by the *tᵉbūnōt* of his hands", there is no reason tu suppose that the single occurrence of *tᵉbūnōt* indicates the influence of the intellectual tradition, since there is no other indication of it in this psalm[245]. The phrase is a strange one, and it is probably best translated adjectivally: "with his skilful hands".

We should therefore probably conclude that, although *tᵉbūnā* occurs frequently in contexts which betray the influence of the intellectual tradition, its use is not entirely confined to such contexts, and its occurrence cannot be used as a certain indication of such influence.

tōkaḥat

"Rebuke, punishment". 16 times in Prov; twice in Job; not in Koh. 6 times in other books: Ez 5 15 25 17 Hab 2 1 Ps 38 15 39 12 73 4. (The cognate noun *tōkēḥā*, which has a similar meaning, does not occur in Prov Job Koh, but occurs 4 times elsewhere: II Reg 19 3 Isa 37 3 Hos 5 9 Ps 149 7.) In spite of the preponderance of occurrences in Prov and Job it is clear that *tōkaḥat* was used in a variety of contexts and was not exclusively confined to the intellectual tradition.

We may conclude that although all the words discussed in this section occur more frequently in books known to belong to the intellectual tradition than elsewhere in the Old Testament, and although some of them may be said to be characteristic of that tradition, none of them was entirely confined to it.

A Note on nākōaḥ

S. Terrien[246] and H. W. Wolff[247] have argued that *nākōaḥ*, "right, upright", is a "wisdom" term and that its use in Am 3 10 is an indication of the influence of "wisdom" on that prophet. This word occurs 8 times in the Old Testament: twice in Prov (8 9 24 26)[248] and 6 times in other books (II Sam 15 3 Isa 26 10 30 10 57 2 59 14 Am 3 10). It does

[244] Cf. Kraus, Psalmen, II 955f.

[245] On the supposed "wisdom character" of Ps 78 see p. 130 above.

[246] Amos and Wisdom 112f.

[247] Amos' geistige Heimat 38—40. Cf. also Crenshaw, The Influence of the Wise Upon Amos, 49.

[248] It is incorrectly stated by Terrien (112) that it also occurs in Prov 26 28.

not occur in Job or Koh, but is found once (*nkḥ*) in the Apocrypha (Sir 11 21)[249].

A total of 3 occurrences in the "wisdom books" of the Old Testament and Apocrypha as against 6 in the rest of the Old Testament provides only very slender evidence for any discussion of the history of a word's usage; yet this evidence has been made to carry a great deal of weight in the thesis that Amos was influenced by "wisdom".

The main arguments used by Terrien and Wolff are those from silence: *nākōaḥ* is never found in the literature of the covenant or legal traditions, nor is it used by any pre-exilic prophet except in Isa 30 10, where the prophet is not using words of his own choice but quoting the words of the opponents of the prophets: "Do not prophesy to us what is right (*neḵōḥōt*)". Therefore, since Amos in 3 10 was not using the terminology of any of these traditions, he must have been following the "wisdom tradition".

This argument from silence is vitiated by the very small number of occurrences of the word in any tradition of the Old Testament. Moreover the explanation given of the occurrence in Isa 30 10 is based upon the identification of the "wisdom tradition" with the court and its "wise men": it is argued that the word is appropriate on the lips of Isaiah's adversaries, because they belonged to this class of "wise men". This identification has been shown to be false[250].

The same dependence on the theory of "court wisdom" also appears in Wolff's explanation of the occurrence of the word in II Sam 15 3, where Absalom, in his campaign to supplant David, assures litigants coming to the court that their claims are "good and right (*ṭōbīm ūneḵōḥīm*)". It is supposed that Absalom, who had been educated at court, was here using vocabulary which was peculiar to his class. It would be more reasonable to suppose that the eminently skilful author of the Succession Narrative would put into Absalom's mouth words which would be readily understood by his listeners, who had not been educated at court but spoke the language of the people.

Wolff seeks to strengthen his case by pointing to other supposed signs of "wisdom influence" in the immediate context of the occurrence of *nākōaḥ* in Am 3 10. He finds significance in the fact that in the same verse Amos uses the — in reality extremely common — verb *yāda'*,

---

249 See the text in F. Vattioni, Ecclesiastico, 1968, 59 (where this verse appears as 11 19). On the reconstruction of the text see R. Smend, Die Weisheit des Jesus Sirach, 1906, 108f.

250 See p. 15ff. above. This argument puts Wolff in a difficulty, since it is his purpose to argue that the wisdom which influenced Amos was not court wisdom but tribal wisdom. He is forced to suppose that the word *nākōaḥ* was common to both; but this admission weakens his whole argument. It would be simpler to suppose that *nākōaḥ* was a word not confined to any particular tradition.

"know", in close connection with *nākōaḥ* ("and they do not know how to do right"), because in Prov 8 9 *n*^{e}*kōḥīm* occurs in the same sentence as *daʿat*, "knowledge". He also finds a similar connection between Sir 11 21 and Amos: the former has, in the LXX, the verb θαυμάζω, which might be the translation of the hitp. of the Hebrew verb *hūm*, which Amos uses in 3 9. The Hebrew text of Sir 11 21 is, however, defective, and this reading not certain.

Finally Wolff finds it significant that the passages in Sir and Am both show a concern for the poor. He rules out, however, as improbable the theory of a direct literary influence of Am on Sir, which would seem to be an obvious explanation of these supposed coincidences, were an explanation required. Such does not seem to be the case, since these very superficial resemblances hardly merit the status of coincidence.

The arguments of Wolff and Terrien should be regarded as a salutary warning against the dangers of an unrestrained determination to discover "wisdom influence" in the books of the Old Testament. It is improbable that anyone examining the evidence objectively would conclude from it that *nākōaḥ* belongs to that tradition. The evidence, in so far as it exists, strongly suggests that this was a word in use in common speech (compare its use, in prose, in ordinary conversation in II Sam 15 3 and in the mouths of Isaiah's opponents in Isa 30 10), which for some reason has found its way only occasionally into the literature of the Old Testament. Such cases are not unusual, and are, indeed, to be expected in view of the limited quantity and range of that literature.

4. Words Apparently Exclusive to the Intellectual Tradition

There remain a few words whose occurrences are restricted to books and passages whose attachment to the intellectual tradition is certain or where such an attachment cannot be ruled out *a priori*. It is these words alone which may be of use in providing clues to the influence of that tradition, although even here it must be stressed that in some cases their absence from other traditions may merely be due to coincidence.

bīnā

"Understanding". 14 times in Prov; 8 times in Job; not in Koh. 15 times in other books (Dtn I Isa Jer Dan Chr), together with one occurrence of the Aramaic *bīnā* (Dan 2 21). The distribution is significant: 8 of the occurrences (Dtn 4 6 Isa 11 2 29 14 Dan 1 20 2 21 8 15

9 22 10 1) are found in books and passages already classified as influenced by the intellectual tradition. Of the remainder, Isa 29 24, which is generally recognised as a late addition expressing the idea of the conversion of Israel in "wisdom" terms, contains, besides *bīnā*, also the word *leqaḥ*, "instruction", which is also found exclusively in the intellectual tradition[251]. In Isa 27 11, which belongs to the late "Isaiah Apocalypse", the phrase "for it is a people without understanding (*lō' 'am-bīnōt hū'*)" is probably an echo of Dtn 4 6 32 6. 28, all of which belong to the intellectual tradition.

Isa 33 19, which promises Israel that they will "see no more the insolent[252] people, the people of an obscure speech which you cannot comprehend, stammering in a tongue which you cannot understand (*nil'ag lāšōn 'ēn bīnā*)" is probably late, but belongs to the Isaiah tradition in that it is clearly intended to be a reversal of Isaiah's threat about the Assyrian invasion in 28 11: "by men of strange lips and with an alien tongue Yahweh will speak to this people"[253]. The context of the latter (v. 7-13), although neither *bīnā* nor *ḥokmā* occurs in it, has an affinity with the intellectual tradition in that it is concerned with the problem, frequently treated in Proverbs, of the fool — in this case the drunken fool — who is heading for destruction because he is incapable of accepting, or unwilling to accept, instruction[254].

In Jer 23 20 it is uncertain whether the final words, "in the latter days you will understand it clearly (*titbōn^{e}nū bāh bīnā*)" are a genuine utterance of Jeremiah or a later insertion[255]. The unusual use of *bīnā* here sets the passage apart from the rest: the noun appears to be used as the equivalent of the inf. abs[256]. But it is also possible that it may be a dittographical addition. The same line recurs in 30 24, but with the omission of *bīnā*, which is not necessary to the sense. Moreover, *bīnā* does not appear to be represented in either LXX or Pesh. Consequently it would be hazardous to use this passage as an example of either the "wisdom" or the "non-wisdom" use of *bīnā*.

Of the 4 occurrences in Chr, 3 are in passages where the Chronicler has elaborated the tradition of Solomon's wisdom in I Reg. I Chr 22 12 occurs in David's charge to Solomon to build the Temple and is a prayer that Solomon may be given "discretion and understanding (*śēkel ūbīnā*)". This phrase is simply a variation of similar phrases in

---

[251] See p. 47f. below.

[252] The meaning of this word is uncertain.

[253] Compare *'am 'im^{e}qē śāpā miššemōa' nil'ag lāšōn 'ēn bīnā* (33 19) with *b^{e}la'^{a}gē śāpā ūb^{e}lāšōn 'aḥeret* (28 11).

[254] E.g. especially v. 9, "To whom can he teach knowledge? (*yōre dē'ā*) and whom can he make to understand the message? (*yābīn š^{e}mū'ā*)."

[255] Some commentators regard the whole of v. 19f. as an interpolation.

[256] So Rudolph, Jeremia, 140.

the account of Solomon's reign in I Reg: *lēb ḥākām wᵉnābōn* (I Reg 3 12); *ḥokmā . . . ūtᵉbūnā* (I Reg 5 9). Similarly in II Chr 2 11, Huram king of Tyre's description of Solomon as *bēn ḥākām yōdēaʿ śēkel ūbīnā* is an elaboration of *bēn ḥākām* in I Reg 5 21, and the whole passage (II Chr 2 3ff.) is a more elaborate version of I Reg 5 15ff. Again, the description of the craftsman Huram-abi in II Chr 2 12 as *ʾīš-ḥākām yōdēaʿ bīnā* is a variation of the description of the craftsman Hiram in I Reg 7 14. All these occurrences, therefore, are part of the Chronicler's further elaboration of the material in I Reg about Solomon's wisdom.

The remaining occurrence in Chr is of a different kind, and presents a difficult problem to which no satisfactory solution has been found. In I Chr 12 33, in a list of the troops who came to join David at Hebron, it is said that the men of Issachar were *yōdᵉʿē bīnā laʿittīm*, "men who had understanding with regard to the times"[257]. The phrase *yōdēaʿ bīnā*, as has been seen, occurs also in II Chr 2 12; the Aramaic equivalent, *yādᵉʿē bīnā*, also in Dan 2 21[258]. The whole phrase is reminiscent of *laḥᵃkāmīm yōdᵉʿē hāʿittīm* in Est 1 13[259].

By this mysterious phrase the Chronicler may have meant simply that the men of Issachar were pre-eminently able to discern that the time to establish the kingdom in Israel had now, in the purpose of Yahweh, arrived. But some commentators have suggested that this singling out of the men of Issachar meant that he was making use of a genuine piece of information about the tribe of Issachar which was of a somewhat different character.

Since the time of the composition of the Targum on Chronicles[260] it has been suggested that the special knowledge possessed by the men of Issachar was astrological[261]. There is, however, no positive proof that this is what is meant by *ʿittīm*. Wellhausen[262] suggested, on the other hand, that it may refer to a tribal reputation for practical "wisdom" similar to that which II Sam 20 18 seems to attribute to the city of Abel Beth-Maacah. This theory also is incapable of proof. But it seems clear that the men of Issachar are here credited with an intellectual capacity of an exceptional kind, for which they were famous, and which is called, not *ḥokmā*, but *bīnā*.

---

[257] 1 MS has *lᵉʿittām*, "with regard to their time". See also Pesh.

[258] See also *lādaʿat bīnā*, Prov 4 1; *ʾim-yādaʿtā bīnā*, Job 38 4.

[259] See p. 16 above.

[260] See the text of the Targum of I Chr 12 32 in A. Sperber, The Bible in Aramaic, IVA 1968, 17.

[261] See, e.g., E. L. Curtis and A. A. Madsen, The Books of Chronicles, ICC, 1910, 202; W. Rudolph, Chronikbücher, HAT 1/21, 1955, 109.

[262] J. Wellhausen, Prolegomena zur Geschichte Israels, 1883², 181 (ET Prolegomena to the History of Israel, 1885, 174).

As has already been observed, almost all the occurrences of *bīnā* in the Old Testament are of a fairly late date. However, Isa 11 2, in which *ḥokmā ūbīnā* appear among the characteristics of the Judaean king, is probably pre-exilic; and if this is so, it is an indication that *bīnā*, though a comparatively rare word in early times, was already regarded as similar or identical in meaning to *ḥokmā*. Thus whether the Chronicler, in using the word of the men of Issachar, is applying to them an ancient title, or whether he is using the terminology of his own day, there is reason to suppose that *bīnā* was virtually interchangeable with *ḥokmā*, and so an item in the specific and exclusive vocabulary of the intellectual tradition. This is supported by the fact that, in no less than 16 of the total of 37 occurrences of the word, it occurs in the same context with *ḥokmā* in parallelism or in very close association, and that in a number of other cases it is associated with other words belonging to that tradition.

baʿar

"Stupid". Twice in Prov; not in Job or Koh. 3 times in Ps (49 11 73 22 92 7); not elsewhere in the Old Testament. A total of 5 occurrences is a slender basis on which to reach an objective conclusion; but all the references outside Prov occur in psalms where the influence of the intellectual tradition is certain or probable on other grounds.

In Ps 49 11 *baʿar* occurs together with *ḥākām* and also with *kᵉsīl*, a word which also occurs only in books and passages belonging to that tradition[263]. It has already been pointed out[264] that this psalm wholly belongs to it.

The character of Ps 73, in which the author uses the word *baʿar* of himself (v. 22) in confessing his earlier stupidity in failing to recognize that God does in fact reward the righteous and punish the wicked, is disputed[265]. But, whether or not it was written for use in worship, its sustained reflection on man's life in this world and on God's justice clearly associates it with the intellectual tradition, and the occurrence of *baʿar* supports this view. The description of the fate of the wicked (v. 18-20. 27f.) adds further plausibility to this opinion, since similar descriptions are found both in Job and in Ps 37[266].

Ps 92 is most commonly regarded as a psalm of thanksgiving with hymnic elements; but the influence of the intellectual tradition in v. 7 is generally admitted. This verse contains the word *kᵉsīl* as

---

263 See 146f. belowe.

264 P. 95 above.

265 For a summary of views see Kraus, Psalmen, I 364—369.

266 See p. 94f. above on Ps 37.

well as *baʿar*, and the thoughts which follow (v. 8-10) on the fate of the wicked are reminiscent of Ps 37 49 73. It is the thought of the greatness of God's works and thoughts (v. 6) which leads this writer into reflections which find their natural expression in the vocabulary of the intellectual tradition.

keṣīl

"Stupid". 49 times in Prov; not in Job; 18 times in Koh. 3 times in Ps (49 11 92 7 94 8); not elsewhere in the Old Testament. This word was used to denote one of the main types of fool in Prov, and is a favourite word of Koh in the same sense. It is therefore not surprising to find it in Ps 49 11 92 7 in company with *baʿar*.

In the remaining occurrence (Ps 94 8) it stands in parallelism with *bōʿēr*, the ptc. of the verb *bāʿar*, whose meaning is virtually the same as the noun or adjective *baʿar*[267]. The character and unity of Ps 94 are disputed; but it is clear that v. 8-11 constitute a distinct section in which the writer turns from his denunciation of, and complaint against, the wicked in the third person and addresses them directly, seeking to convince them of their folly by argument. The address (v. 8) is reminiscent of Wisdom's call to the "simple" and "foolish" in Prov 1 22 8 5, and the argument in v. 9 bears some resemblance to the argument of Prov 20 12. There are thus sufficient grounds for regarding these verses — though not the remainder of the psalm — as influenced by the intellectual tradition, and *keṣīl* is entirely at home here.

lēṣ

"Scoffer, arrogant man". 14 times in Prov; not in Job or Koh. Twice in other books: Isa 29 20 Ps 1 1. This word is often contrasted in Prov with *ḥākām*, and also stands in parallelism with *keṣīl* in Prov 19 29. The description of the *lēṣ* in Prov 21 24 shows that the characteristics of this type of man are pride and insolence.

In Ps 1 1 the word is associated with *rāšāʿ*, "wicked", and *ḥaṭṭāʾ*, "sinner". This psalm, although the root *ḥkm* does not occur, is regarded for a variety of reasons as belonging, like Ps 19 8-15 119 which it resembles[268], to the category of late "wisdom" psalms in which wisdom is identified with, or closely associated with, the Law. *lēṣ* is one of a series of words which characterize the attitude of the man who lives in open contempt of the Law. The purpose of the psalm is to commend the study of the Law and to contrast the blessing which devotion to it will bring with the evil fate of the wicked.

---

267 The consonants (*bʿr*, pl. *bʿrym*) are the same. LXX makes no distinction, translating by ἄφρων both here and in the 5 places where the Hebrew has *baʿar*.

268 See p. 98 above.

The remaining occurrence (Isa 29 20) is found in a passage (29 17-21) which is generally regarded as very late and as owing its inspiration to a variety of older biblical sources[269]. It lacks unity and a positive character of its own, and this makes it impossible either to affirm or deny that the use of *lēṣ* here indicates the influence of the intellectual tradition. In view of its late date, however, it is probable that it is used in a sense similar to that in which it is used in Ps 1 1.

leqaḥ

"Understanding, teaching, persuasiveness". 6 times in Prov; once in Job; not in Koh. Twice in other books: Dtn 32 2 Isa 29 24. Both of these occurrences are in passages already designated as belonging to the intellectual tradition[270].

nābōn

"Intelligent". 9 times in Prov; not in Job; once in Koh. 11 times in other books: Gen 41 33. 39 Dtn 1 13 4 6 I Sam 16 18 I Reg 3 12 Isa 3 3 5 21 29 14 Jer 4 22 Hos 14 10. This word appears to be virtually a synonym of *ḥākām:* it appears in parallelism with it, or joined to it by the copula, or otherwise associated with it or with *ḥokmā,* in no less than 18 of its 21 occurrences.

Like *ḥākām, nābōn* originally had a wider sense, denoting ability of any kind: this is seen in Isa 3 3, where the phrase *nebōn lāḥaš,* "expert enchanter", appears in a list immediately following *ḥakam ḥarāšîm,* "skillful magician"[271]. Elsewhere, however, it always denotes intellectual ability. In all but one of the remaining passages outside Prov Job Koh it is found in contexts already classified as influenced by the intellectual tradition: the Joseph Story; the Story of Solomon; the introductory chapters to Dtn; Isa 5 21 29 14 Jer 4 22; and the late addition to Hos (14 10).

There remains I Sam 16 18, where a member of Saul's entourage praises David for his various virtues, one of which is that he is *nebōn dābār,* "skilled in speech". Skill in speech — and in knowing when to keep silent — is one of the most important of the virtues extolled by the writers of the intellectual tradition, especially in Proverbs. It is specifically attributed to the *nābōn* in Prov 10 13: *beśipetē nābōn timmāṣē' ḥokmā,* "It is on the lips of the *nābōn* that wisdom is to be found"; cf. also Prov 16 21 17 28. It must therefore be concluded, in view also of the contexts of the other occurrences of *nābōn,* that the

269 See, e.g., R. B. Y. Scott, The Book of Isaiah, Chapters 1—39, IB V, 1956, 327f.; Fohrer, Jesaja II, 1962, 82.

270 See p. 87f. 143 above.

271 See also p. 21 n. 43 above.

phrase *n^ebōn dābār* here is an isolated reference to the ideals of the intellectual tradition. The author himself, however, gives no other indication of having been influenced by it[272].

sākāl

"Senseless, foolish". Not in Prov or Job; 5 times in Koh. Twice elsewhere: Jer 4 22 5 21. This word, like its cognates *sik^elūt, sēkel,* both meaning "folly", which are peculiar to Koh, seems to be a relatively late word, although the verb *sākal* occurs in relatively early texts. Of the two occurrences outside Koh, Jer 4 22 has already been identified as under the influence of the intellectual tradition. Jer 5 21, which is probably also a genuine utterance of Jeremiah, is similar to 4 22: in both texts Yahweh castigates his people for their folly, which is the cause of their suffering, and in similar terms: *'^ewīl ʿammī ... bānīm s^ekālīm,* 4 22; *ʿam sākāl w^e'ēn lēb,* 5 21. Since 4 22 is influenced by the intellectual tradition, it is reasonable to suppose that this is true of 5 21 also.

ʿārūm

"Prudent, shrewd, cunning". 8 times in Prov; twice in Job; not in Koh. Once elsewhere: Gen 3 1. The fact that this word is always used in an approving sense in Prov, yet in a disapproving sense in Job suggests that, like its cognate *ʿormā*[273], it was originally neutral in character. To some extent its meanings overlap those of *ḥākām;* but the fact that it occurs outside Prov Job only once suggests that it came to be exclusively associated with the intellectual tradition, although the difference between its use in Prov and Job shows that it had its own history within that tradition. The reasons for regarding its occurrence in Gen 3 1 as indicative of the influence of the intellectual tradition have already been given[274].

tūšiyyā

"Wisdom, success". 4 times in Prov; 6 times in Job; not in Koh. Twice in other books: Isa 28 29 Mi 6 9. In Mi 6 9 the text is in disorder. The phrase *w^etūšiyyā yir'e š^emekā* presents syntactical difficulties and bears no relation to the context, and is generally regarded[275] as a gloss.

---

[272] On the literary problems of this and the adjacent chapters of I Sam see Eissfeldt, Introduction, 268ff.

[273] See p. 136 above.

[274] See p. 106f. above.

[275] See BHS and the commentaries.

The remaining occurrence (Isa 28 29) comes at the end of a passage (v. 23-29) which speaks of the techniques of agriculture as communicated to man by God, to whom it attributes *tūšiyyā* and *ʿēṣā*. This passage, which is attributed by most commentators to Isaiah himself, is generally considered to be an imitation by the prophet of "wisdom" forms and themes[276].

The interest which it shows in the details of the farmer's occupation is uncharacteristic of prophecy, and reminiscent of "wisdom books" both Israelite and non-Israelite[277]. The combination of the account of the farmer's activity with the statement that the rules of agriculture were given by God has a parallel in a Sumerian document[278] which has been classified as "wisdom literature"[279]; and the parabolic form is also characteristic of this type of writing[280]. The opening formula (v. 23), in which the author appeals for attention to his words[281], though not confined to the literature of the intellectual tradition in the Old Testament, is paralleled in two other passages which have been so classified: Dtn 32 1 Ps 49 2-5. The statement in v. 29 that Yahweh is "excellent in wisdom" (*higdīl tūšiyyā*) has been compared with Isa 31 2, where it is stated by Isaiah that "Yahweh also is wise (*wᵉgam-hūʾ ḥākām*)"[282]. Indeed, the choice of *tūšiyyā* in 28 29 to denote Yahweh's supreme skill might suggest that for Isaiah *tūšiyyā* and *ḥokmā* were virtually synonymous, a conclusion which tends to be confirmed by the association of the two words and their synonyms in Prov and Job[283].

The accumulated evidence suggests that *tūšiyyā* should be regarded as belonging exclusively to the intellectual tradition.

V. CONCLUSIONS

The results of the above investigation may now be applied to supplement the results of the earlier investigation into the occurrences of *ḥkm*.

---

[276] E.g. by Fohrer, Jesaja II, 64; Scott, Isaiah 1—39, 321; Fichtner, Jesaja unter den Weisen, 22; von Rad, Weisheit, 32f. 185f.

[277] Von Rad, Weisheit, 185f., compares it to Prov 27 23-27, though he stresses that the purposes of the two passages differ. For non-Israelite literature see n. 278 below.

[278] The so-called "Farmer's Almanac" (S. N. Kramer, History Begins at Sumer, 1961², 109—113).

[279] Cazelles, Débuts, 32.

[280] See the most recent study of the passage in Whedbee, Isaiah and Wisdom, 51—67.

[281] On this *Lehreröffnungsruf* see Wolff, Hosea, 122f.

[282] By Scott 321 and Fichtner 26, among others.

[283] In Prov 2 6f. Job 11 6 26 3 *tūšiyyā* is associated with *ḥokmā* and in Prov 8 14 with *bīnā*.

Of the 4 categories of words whose occurrences have been analysed in section IV above, only category 4 comprises words probably exclusive to the intellectual tradition. These may be regarded as of equal importance with *ḥkm* as constituting a criterion for the detection of the influence of that tradition.

The words in category 3, which occur extensively in Prov Job and/or Koh, but also in some other books and passages which do not belong to that tradition, may be used with caution as supporting evidence in passages where there are other reasons to suppose that that tradition is present, especially if they occur there with some frequency or occupy key positions there; but it would be hazardous to postulate such influence solely on the basis of such occurrences.

The words in category 2 are of far less value as criteria in view of their wide dissemination in various traditions of the Old Testament. In general they are quite useless in this respect by themselves, though there may be cases even here where their occurrence may, for special reasons, be of use in confirming previous conclusions.

A. Passages Already Designated as Belonging to the Intellectual Tradition on the Basis of the Occurrence of ḥkm

Here in some cases confirmation is provided of earlier results; in others little or nothing is added to conclusions already reached.

1. The Joseph Story (Gen 37—50)

The only addition is *nābōn* (category 4), which occurs twice (Gen 41 33. 39) in close association with *ḥākām.* (49 6, in which *sōd* and *rāṣōn,* both from category 2, occur, belongs to the Blessing of Jacob and not to the Joseph Story.)

2. Introduction to Deuteronomy (Dtn 1—4)

Here *nābōn* (1 13 4 6) and *bīnā* (4 6) (both in category 4) occur in close association with *ḥkm.*

3. Song of Moses (Dtn 32)

leqaḥ (category 4) occurs (v. 2) in the introductory section or *Lehreröffnungsruf*[284] in which the author uses the term, with others, to describe the character of his poem. In addition *ʿiqqēš* (v. 5) and

---

[284] See p. 149 above.

t^{e}būnā (v. 28) (both category 3) occur, together with a few words from category 2.

4. Succession Narrative (II Sam 9—20 I Reg 1f.)

No words from categories 3 or 4 occur here, but only some words from category 2, especially *bīn* and *ʿēṣā* (frequently).

5. History of Solomon (I Reg 3—11)

nābōn (category 4) occurs in association with *ḥākām* in I Reg 3 12 and *t^{e}būnā* (category 3) in 5 9 7 14; otherwise only a few occurrences of words in category 2 are found.

6. Psalms

In 19 8-15 *petī* (category 3) occurs in v. 8. In 49, *baʿar* and *k^{e}sīl* (both from category 4) occur in v. 11. In 37 51 90 104 107 111 only words from category 2 occur to supplement *ḥkm*. In 119 *petī* occurs in v. 130. But it should be noted that in this psalm there are no less than 26 occurrences of words in category 2.

7. Isa 1—39

Here it is difficult to be certain which passages are to be attributed to the prophet himself. But the view that he was familiar with the terminology of the intellectual tradition and made use of it is confirmed. In 3 passages where *ḥkm* occurs in a significant sense other terms peculiar to that tradition (category 4) occur: *nābōn* (5 21 29 14); *bīnā* (11 2 29 14). As has already been indicated[285], the occurrence of *tūšiyyā* is one of the factors which suggest that 28 23-29 should be regarded as belonging to that tradition. In 3 3, whose Isaianic authorship is doubtful, *nābōn* probably has a non-intellectual sense similar to that which *ḥokmā* sometimes possesses — a particular skill[286]. The occurrences of words from category 3 in the genuine utterances of Isaiah are relatively isolated, and, like those from category 2, cannot be regarded as evidence.

8. Jer

In Jeremiah's genuine utterances the occurrences of *nābōn* and *sākāl* (both from category 4), together with *'^{e}wīl* (category 3) in 4 22 in conjunction with *ḥkm*, and of *sākāl* in 5 21 confirm the view that Jeremiah was acquainted with the terminology of the intellectual

[285] P. 148 f. above.

[286] See p. 21 n. 43. 147 above.

tradition; the occurrence of *bīnā* (category 4) in 23 20 further confirms this, if this is Jeremiah's own utterance. In 10 12 = 51 15, the connexion of this later addition with the intellectual tradition is to some extent confirmed by the occurrence of *t^ebūnā* (category 3) in company with *ḥkm*.

9. Ez 28

The only additional evidence here is the occurrence of *t^ebūnā* (category 3) in v. 4.

10. Dan

The occurrence of *bīnā* (category 4) in 1 20 8 15 10 1 confirms the connexion of this book with the intellectual tradition. Its occurrence in both sections of the book may necessitate some modification of the conclusion reached above (p. 104f.) about the relationship between the two sections.

11. The Minor Prophets

nābōn in Hos 14 10 in association with *ḥākām* confirms the connexion of this late addition to the book of Hosea with the intellectual tradition.

B. Passages to be Added to the List of Those Belonging to the Intellectual Tradition

1. Gen 2f.

Reasons for regarding *ʿārūm* (3 1) as a term exclusively belonging to the intellectual tradition have already been given[287]. This makes it probable that the whole narrative complex concerning the garden and its trees in Gen 2f. should be so regarded, even though the J creation narrative itself (2 4b-8) shows no signs of such influence. This in turn suggests that the word *daʿat*, which occurs in 2 9. 17 in the phrase "the tree of the knowledge of good and evil" has a special significance here, even though *daʿat* (category 2) is by no means restricted to that tradition. The whole story is specifically concerned with the question of the nature of human wisdom and its limits. (J's concern with the intellectual tradition is also perhaps to be seen in 11 1-9 — see p. 107f. above.)

---

[287] P. 148f. above.

2. Psalms

In addition to those psalms already classified as influenced by the intellectual tradition in view of the occurrence there of *ḥkm*, 4 others (1 73 92 94) make use of vocabulary from category 4.

Ps 1, as has already been pointed out[288], is generally regarded as an example of the late development which identifies "wisdom" with the Law. This is confirmed by the occurrence of *lēṣ* in v. 1. In 73 22 *baʿar* similarly connects this psalm with the intellectual tradition[289]. This is also true of the occurrence of *baʿar* and *kᵉsīl* together in 92 7 and of *kᵉsīl* in 94 8[290].

3. Isa 1—39

Apart from the genuine utterances of Isaiah, words in category 4 occur in 4 verses in these chapters: 27 11 (*bīnā*) 29 20 (*lēṣ*) 29 24 (*bīnā*, *leqaḥ*) 33 19 (*bīnā*). It would seem that the collection of Isaiah traditions has been supplemented by late additions, some of which attempt to interpret the prophet's own teaching in terms of the intellectual tradition[291].

27 11, in which the inhabitants of an unnamed city, perhaps Jerusalem, are called "a people without discernment (*lōʾ ʿam-bīnōt hūʾ*)", belongs to the late "Isaiah Apocalypse"; but in view of the uncertainty of the relationship of this verse to its context[292] it would be hazardous to suggest that this implies the influence of the intellectual tradition on these chapters as a whole, especially since the phrase may be simply an echo of Dtn 32 6.

4. The Minor Prophets

The only occurrence of a word from category 4 in a passage where *ḥkm* does not occur is Mi 6 9 (*tūšiyyā*). As has already been stated, this phrase is probably a gloss[293].

---

288 P. 146 above.

289 P. 145f. above.

290 P. 145—146 above.

291 29 20. 24 33 19. See pp. 143f. 147 above.

292 See the commentaries.

293 P. 148 above. With regard to the remaining occurrences of words in category 4, it has already been pointed out that I Sam 16 18 (*nābōn*) may be an isolated reference to the intellectual tradition; that I Chr 12 33 (*bīnā*) is an allusion to the reputation of certain persons for "wisdom" rather than an example of the influence of the intellectual tradition upon the Chronicler; and that I Chr 22 12 II Chr 2 11. 12 (*bīnā*) merely show the literary dependence of the Chronicler on the History of Solomon in I Reg 3—11.

C. Results of the Terminological Investigation

The foregoing study of the evidence provided by the terminology of the intellectual tradition apart from *ḥkm* thus tends to confirm conclusions previously reached, and makes only a few additions to the passages already considered. The final list of books and passages in which the influence of this tradition may be detected by this means is as follows.

1. Gen 2f. (possibly also 11 1-9)
2. Gen 37—50 (the Joseph Story)
3. Dtn 1—4
4. Dtn 32 (the Song of Moses)
5. II Sam 9—20 I Reg 1f. (the Succession Narrative)
6. I Reg 3—11 (the History of Solomon)
7. Ps 1 19 8-15 37 49 51 73 90 92 94 104 107 111 119
8. Isa 1—39, both in the genuine utterances of Isaiah and in a number of later additions and glosses
9. Jer, also with some later additions and glosses
10. Ez 28
11. Dan
12. 2 late additions or glosses to the Minor Prophets (Hos 14 10 Mi 6 9).

Concluding Remarks

In assessing the contribution made by this study of Israel's intellectual tradition and its vocabulary it must be borne in mind, as has already been emphasized[1], that vocabulary is by no means the only valid criterion for identifying the literature of that tradition. On the other hand it is equally true that no method yet devised is entirely satisfactory: all are subject to a considerable degree of subjectivism. This is no less true of the vocabulary test, which depends entirely on the reliability of the process by which the selection of the relevant vocabulary is carried out.

It will be apparent from the foregoing pages that the dangers of the circular argument are very great. In order to determine which words, occurring both in the acknowledged "wisdom books" and in some passages in other books, are characteristic of the intellectual tradition, it has been necessary to some extent to pre-judge the question whether those passages belong to that tradition or not. The only way to break out of this circle is to make use of other criteria, and this has been done whenever those criteria seemed to merit confidence; but in some cases at least this is merely to replace one subjective criterion by another.

It is clear that the elements of subjectivism and arbitrariness cannot be wholly excluded from the argument, and that any conclusions which are reached can never achieve more than the status of probability. It may be that the attempt made in this study, more thorough than any known to the writer, to use the criterion of vocabulary to determine the influence of the intellectual tradition will lead some readers to conclude that this criterion is, in the end, unusable. If this is indeed to be the conclusion something will still have been gained: many theses as yet unwritten may remain so, while many works already published will now be read with a more critical eye.

Yet the main results of the investigation do in fact tend to support a number of currently held views, while they cast doubt on others. It is the unexamined assumptions found in a number of earlier studies about what constitutes "wisdom vocabulary" which have led the present writer to err on the side of caution. Caution is undoubtedly one of the most important prerequisites for any study of this subject.

---

[1] P. 74 above.

Finally, a word must be said about the other aspects of "wisdom study" and the relation of the present work to them. Little has been said here, especially in the second half of the book, about the *history* of the intellectual tradition in Israel. The first half concentrates mainly on the pre-exilic period, with regard to which the question whether there was at that time in Israel a class of professional "wise men" is a vital one. But most of the references throughout the book to the "wisdom" of a later period refer to it only in very general terms as "late", or as coming from a time when wisdom was identified with the Law.

The writer believes that at the present time it is impossible to be more precise than this. Between the end of the monarchy and the time of Kohelet there still remains a gap in our knowledge stretching over several centuries. From that time onwards our knowledge becomes somewhat fuller; but in the interval between these two periods most of the material in our possession is still undateble and anonymous — anonymous in the sense not only that we cannot identify its authors, but that we cannot even say with any precision to what "circles", if any, they belonged. That there was an "intellectual tradition" in post-exilic Judaism, and that this was both a continuing and developing tradition, is certain; but at present we have no way of plotting its course. In as far as the history of this tradition is known, its study must go hand in hand with that of the identification of its literary deposit; but where it is not known, the latter study is an indispensable starting-point for the historical undertaking.

Index of Authors